In the World

Maksim Gorky

CONTENTS

CHAPTER I

CHAPTER II

CHAPTER III

CHAPTER IV

CHAPTER V

CHAPTER VI

CHAPTER VII

CHAPTER VIII

CHAPTER IX

CHAPTER X

CHAPTER XI

CHAPTER XII

CHAPTER XIII

CHAPTER XIV

CHAPTER XV

CHAPTER XVI

CHAPTER XVII

CHAPTER XVIII

CHAPTER XIX

CHAPTER XX

IN THE WORLD

CHAPTER I

I went out into the world as "shop-boy" at a fashionable boot-shop in the main street of the town. My master was a small, round man. He had a brown, rugged face, green teeth, and watery, mud-colored eyes. At first I thought he was blind, and to see if my supposition was correct, I made a grimace.

"Don't pull your face about!" he said to me gently, but sternly. The thought that those dull eyes could see me was unpleasant, and I did not want to believe that this was the case. Was it not more than probable that he had guessed I was making grimaces?

"I told you not to pull your face about," he said again, hardly moving his thick lips.

"Don't scratch your hands," his dry whisper came to me, as it were, stealthily. "You are serving in a first-class shop in the main street of the town, and you must not forget it. The door-boy ought to stand like a statue."

I did not know what a statue was, and I could n't help scratching my hands, which were covered with red pimples and sores, for they had been simply devoured by vermin.

"What did you do for a living when you were at home?" asked my master, looking at my hands.

I told him, and he shook his round head, which was closely covered with gray hair, and said in a shocked voice:

"Rag-picking! Why, that is worse than begging or stealing!"

I informed him, not without pride:

"But I stole as well."

At this he laid his hands on his desk, looking just like a cat with her paws up, and fixed his eyes on my face with a terrified expression as he whispered:

"Wha—a—t? How did you steal?"

I explained how and what I had stolen.

"Well, well, I look upon that as nothing but a prank. But if you rob me of boots or money, I will have you put in prison, and kept there for the rest of your life."

He said this quite calmly, and I was frightened, and did not like him any more.

Besides the master, there were serving in the shop my cousin, Sascha Jaakov, and the senior assistant, a competent, unctuous person with a red face. Sascha now wore a brown frock-coat, a false shirt-front, a cravat, and long trousers, and was too proud to take any notice of me.

When grandfather had brought me to my master, he had asked Sascha to help me and to teach me. Sascha had frowned with an air of importance as he said warning:

"He will have to do what I tell him, then."

Laying his hand on my head, grandfather had forced me to bend my neck.

"You are to obey him; he is older than you both in years and experience."

And Sascha said to me, with a nod:

"Don't forget what grandfather has said." He lost no time in profiting by his seniority.

"Kashirin, don't look so goggle-eyed," his master would advise him.

"I—I'm all right," Sascha would mutter, putting his head down. But the master would not leave him alone.

"Don't butt; the customers will think you are a goat."

The assistant smiled respectfully, the master stretched his lips in a hideous grin, and Sascha, his face flushing, retreated behind the counter. I did not like the tone of these conversations. Many of the words they used were unintelligible to me, and sometimes they seemed to be speaking in a strange language. When a lady customer came in, the master would take his hands out of his pockets, tug at his mustache, and fix a sweet smile upon his face—a smile which wrinkled his cheeks, but did not change the expression of his dull eyes. The assistant would draw himself up, with his elbows pressed closely against his sides, and his wrists respectfully dangling. Sascha would blink shyly, trying to hide his protruding eyes, while I would stand at the door, surreptitiously scratching my hands, and observing the ceremonial of selling.

Kneeling before the customer, the assistant would try on shoes with wonderfully deft fingers. He touched the foot of the woman so carefully that his hands trembled, as if he were afraid of breaking her leg. But the leg was stout enough. It looked like a bottle with sloping shoulders, turned neck downward.

One of these ladies pulled her foot away one day, shrieking:

"Oh, you are tickling me!"

"That is—because—you are so sensitive," the assistant explained hastily, with warmth.

It was comical to watch him fawning upon the customers, and I had to turn and look through the glass of the door to keep myself from laughing. But something used to draw me back to watch the sale. The proceedings of the assistant were very interesting, and while I looked at him I was thinking that I should never be able to make my fingers move so delicately, or so deftly put boots on other people's feet.

It often happened that the master went away from the shop into a little room behind it, and he would call Sascha to him, leaving the assistant alone with the customer. Once, lingering over the foot of a red-haired woman, he took it between his fingers and kissed it.

"Oh," breathed the woman, "what a bold man you are!"

He puffed out his cheeks and emitted a long-drawn-out sound:

"O—o—h!"

At this I laughed so much that, to keep my feet, I had to hang on to the handle of the door. It flew open, and my head knocked against one of the panes of glass and broke it. The assistant stamped his foot at me, my master hit me on the head with his heavy gold ring, and Sascha tried to pull my ears. In the evening, when we were on our way home, he said to me, sternly:

"You will lose your place for doing things like that. I'd like to know where the joke comes in." And then he explained: "If ladies take a fancy to the assistant, it is good for trade. A lady may not be in need of boots, but she comes in and buys what she does not want just to have a look at the assistant, who pleases her. But you—you can't understand! One puts oneself out for you, and—"

This incensed me. No one put himself out for me, and he least of all.

In the morning the cook, a sickly, disagreeable woman, used to call me before him. I had to clean the boots and brush the clothes of the master, the assistant, and Sascha, get the samovar ready, bring in wood for all the stoves, and wash up. When I got to the shop I had to sweep the floor, dust, get the tea ready, carry goods to the customers, and go home to fetch the dinner, my duty at the door being taken in the meantime by Sascha, who, finding it lowering to his dignity, rated me.

"Lazy young wretch! I have to do all your work for you."

This was a wearisome, dull life for me. I was accustomed to live independently in the sandy streets of Kunavin, on the banks of the turbid Oka, in the fields or woods, from morning to night. I was parted from grandmother and from my comrades. I had no one to speak to, and life was showing me her seamy, false side. There were occasions on which a customer went away without making a purchase, when all three would feel themselves affronted. The master would put his sweet smile away in his pocket as he said:

"Kashirin, put these things away." Then he would grumble:

"There's a pig of a woman The fool found it dull sitting at home, so she must come and turn our shop upside down! If you were my wife, I'd give you something!"

His wife, a dried-up woman with black eyes and a large nose, simply made a door-mat of him. She used to scold him as if he were a servant.

Often, after he had shown out a frequent customer with polite bows and pleasant words, they would all begin to talk about her in a vile and shameless manner, arousing in me a desire to run into the street after her and tell her what they said. I knew, of course, that people generally speak evil of one another behind one another's backs, but these spoke of every one in a particularly revolting manner, as if they were in the front rank of good people and had been appointed to judge the rest of the world. Envious of many of them, they were never known to praise any one, and knew something bad about everybody.

One day there came to the shop a young woman with bright, rosy cheeks and sparkling eyes, attired in a velvet cloak with a collar of black fur. Her face rose out of the fur like a wonderful flower. When she had thrown the cloak off her shoulders and handed it to Sascha, she looked still more beautiful. Her fine figure was fitted tightly with a blue-gray silk robe; diamonds sparkled in her ears. She reminded me of "Vassilissa the Beautiful," and I could have believed that she was in truth the governor's wife. They received her with particular respect, bending before her as if she were a bright light, and almost choking themselves in their hurry to get out polite words. All three rushed about the shop like wild things: their reflections bobbed up and down in the glass of the cupboard. But when she left, after having bought some expensive boots in a great hurry, the master, smacking his lips, whistled and said:

"Hussy!"

"An actress—that sums her up," said the assistant, contemptuously. They began to talk of the lovers of the lady and the luxury in which she lived.

After dinner the master went to sleep in the room behind the shop, and I, opening his gold watch, poured vinegar into the works. It was a moment of supreme joy to me when he awoke and came into the shop, with his watch in his hand, muttering wildly:

"What can have happened? My watch is all wet. I never remember such a thing happening before. It is all wet; it will be ruined."

In addition to the burden of my duties in the shop and the housework, I was weighed down by depression. I often thought it would be a good idea to behave so badly that I should get my dismissal. Snow-covered people passed the door of the shop without making a sound. They looked as if on their way to somebody's funeral. Having meant to accompany the body to the grave, they had been delayed, and, being late for the funeral procession, were hurrying to the grave-side. The horses quivered with the effort of making their way through the snow-drifts. From the belfry of the church behind the shop the bells rang out with a melancholy sound every day. It was Lent, and every stroke of the bell fell upon my brain as if it had been a pillow, not hurting, but stupefying and deafening, me. One day when I was in the yard unpacking a case of new goods just received, at the door of the shop, the watchman of the church, a crooked old man, as soft as if he were made of rags and as ragged as if he had been torn to pieces by dogs, approached me.

"Are you going to be kind and steal some goloshes for me?" he asked.

I was silent. He sat down on an empty case, yawned, made the sign of the cross over his mouth, and repeated:

"Will you steal them for me?"

"It is wrong to steal," I informed him.

"But people steal all the same. Old age must have its compensations."

He was pleasantly different from the people among whom I lived. I felt that he had a firm belief in my readiness to steal, and I agreed to hand him the goloshes through the window.

"That's right," he said calmly, without enthusiasm. "You are not deceiving me? No, I see that you are not."

He was silent for a moment, trampling the dirty, wet snow with the soles of his boots. Then he lit a long pipe, and suddenly startled me.

"But suppose it is I who deceive you? Suppose I take the goloshes to your master, and tell him that you have sold them to me for half a ruble? What then? Their price is two rubles, and you have sold them for half a ruble. As a present, eh?"

I gazed at him dumbly, as if he had already done what he said he would do; but he went on talking gently through his nose, looking at his boots, and blowing out blue smoke.

"Suppose, for example, that your master has said to me, 'Go and try that youngster, and see if he is a thief.' What then?"

"I shall not give you the goloshes," I said, angry and frightened.

"You must give them now that you have promised."

He took me by the arm and drew me to him, and, tapping my forehead with his cold fingers, drawled:

"What are you thinking of, with your 'take this' and 'take that'?"

"You asked me for them yourself."

"I might ask you to do lots of things. I might ask you to come and rob the church. Would you do it? Do you think you can trust everybody? Ah, you young fool!" He pushed me away from him and stood up.

"I don't want stolen goloshes. I am not a gentleman, and I don't wear goloshes. I was only making fun of you. For your simplicity, when Easter comes, I will let you come up into the belfry and ring the bells and look at the town."

"I know the town."

"It looks better from the belfry."

Dragging his broken boots in the snow, he went slowly round the corner of the church, and I looked after him, wondering dejectedly and fearfully whether the old man had really been making fun of me, or had been sent by my master to try me. I did not want to go back to the shop.

Sascha came hurriedly into the yard and shouted: "What the devil has become of you?"

I shook my pincers at him in a sudden access of rage. I knew that both he and the assistant robbed the master. They would hide a pair of boots or slippers in the stovepipe, and when they left the shop, would slip them into the sleeves of their overcoats. I did not like this, and felt alarmed about it, for I remembered the threats of the master.

"Are you stealing?" I had asked Sascha.

"Not I, but the assistant," he would explain crossly. "I am only helping him. He says, 'Do as I tell you,' and I have to obey. If I did not, he would do me some mischief. As for master, he was an assistant himself once, and he understands. But you hold your tongue."

As he spoke, he looked in the glass and set his tie straight with just such a movement of his naturally spreading fingers as the senior assistant employed. He was unwearying in his demonstrations of his seniority and power over me, scolding me in a bass voice, and ordering me about with threatening gestures. I was taller than he, but bony and clumsy, while he was compact, flexible, and fleshy. In his frock-coat and long trousers he seemed an important and substantial figure in my eyes, and yet there was something ludicrous and unpleasing about him. He hated the cook, a curious woman, of whom it was impossible to decide whether she was good or bad.

"What I love most in the world is a fight," she said, opening wide her burning black eyes. "I don't care what sort of fight it is, cock-fights, dog-fights, or fights between men. It is all the same to me."

And if she saw cocks or pigeons fighting in the yard, she would throw aside her work and watch the fight to the end, standing dumb and motionless at the window. In the evenings she would say to me and Sascha:

"Why do you sit there doing nothing, children? You had far better be fighting."

This used to make Sascha angry.

"I am not a child, you fool; I am junior assistant."

"That does not concern me. In my eyes, while you remain unmarried, you are a child."

"Fool! Blockhead!"

"The devil is clever, but God does not love him."

Her talk was a special source of irritation to Sascha, and he used to tease her; but she would look at him contemptuously, askance, and say:

"Ugh, you beetle! One of God's mistakes!"

Sometimes he would tell me to rub blacking or soot on her face when she was asleep, stick pins into her pillow, or play other practical jokes on her; but I was afraid of her. Besides, she slept very lightly and used to wake up frequently. Lighting the lamp, she would sit on the side of her bed, gazing fixedly at something in the corner. Sometimes she came over to me, where I slept behind the stove, and woke me up, saying hoarsely:

"I can't sleep, Leksyeka. I am not very well. Talk to me a little."

Half asleep, I used to tell her some story, and she would sit without speaking, swaying from side to side. I had an idea that her hot body smelt of wax and incense, and that she would soon die. Every moment I expected to see her fall face downward on the floor and die. In terror I would begin to speak loudly, but she would check me.

"'S-sh! You will wake the whole place up, and they will think that you are my lover."

She always sat near me in the same attitude, doubled up, with her wrists between her knees, squeezing them against the sharp bones of her legs. She had no chest, and even through the thick linen night-dress her ribs were visible, just like the ribs of a broken cask. After sitting a long time in silence, she would suddenly whisper:

"What if I do die, it is a calamity which happens to all." Or she would ask some invisible person, "Well, I have lived my life, have n't I?"

"Sleep!" she would say, cutting me short in the middle of a word, and, straightening herself, would creep noiselessly across the dark kitchen.

"Witch!" Sascha used to call her behind her back.

I put the question to him:

"Why don't you call her that to her face?"

"Do you think that I am afraid to?" But a second later he said, with a frown: "No, I can't say it to her face. She may really be a witch."

Treating every one with the same scornful lack of consideration, she showed no indulgence to me, but would drag me out of bed at six o'clock every morning, crying:

"Are you going to sleep forever? Bring the wood in! Get the samovar ready! Clean the doorplate!"

Sascha would wake up and complain:

"What are you bawling like that for? I will tell the master. You don't give any one a chance to, sleep."

Moving quickly about the kitchen with her lean, withered body, she would flash her blazing, sleepless eyes upon him.

"Oh, it's you, God's mistake? If you were my son, I would give you something!"

Sascha would abuse her, calling her "accursed one," and when we were going to the shop he said to me: "We shall have to do something to get her sent away. We'll put salt in everything when she's not looking. If everything is cooked with too much salt, they will get rid of her. Or paraffin would do. What are you gaping about?"

"Why don't you do it yourself?"

He snorted angrily:

"Coward!"

The cook died under our very eyes. She bent down to pick up the samovar, and suddenly sank to the floor without uttering a word, just as if some one had given her a blow on the chest. She moved over on her side, stretched out her arms, and blood trickled from her mouth.

We both understood in a flash that she was dead, but, stupefied by terror, we gazed at her a long time without strength to say a word. At last Sascha rushed headlong out of the kitchen, and I, not knowing what to do, pressed close to the window in the light. The master came in, fussily squatted down beside her, and touched her face with his finger.

"She is dead; that's certain," he said. "What can have caused it?" He went into the corner where hung a small image of Nikolai Chudovortz and crossed himself; and when he had prayed he went to the door and commanded:

"Kashirin, run quickly and fetch the police!"

The police came, stamped about, received money for drinks, and went. They returned later, accompanied by a man with a cart, lifted the cook by the legs and the head, and carried her into the street. The mistress stood in the doorway and watched them. Then she said to me:

"Wash the floor!"

And the master said:

"It is a good thing that she died in the evening."

I could not understand why it was a good thing. When we went to bed Sascha said to me with unusual gentleness:

"Don't put out the lamp!"

"Are you afraid?"

He covered his head with the blanket, and lay silent a long time. The night was very quiet, as if it were listening for something, waiting for something. It seemed to me that the next minute a bell rang out, and suddenly the whole town was running and shouting in a great terrified uproar.

Sascha put his nose out of the blanket and suggested softly:

"Let's go and lie on the stove together."

"It is hot there."

After a silence he said:

"How suddenly she went off, did n't she? I am sure she was a witch. I can't get to sleep."

"Nor I, either."

He began to tell tales about dead people—how they came out of their graves and wandered till midnight about the town, seeking the place where they had lived and looking for their relations.

"Dead people can only remember the town," he said softly; "but they forget the streets and houses at once."

It became quieter and quieter and seemed to be getting darker. Sascha raised his head and asked:

"Would you like to see what I have got in my trunk?"

I had long wanted to know what he hid in his trunk. He kept it locked with a padlock, and always opened it with peculiar caution. If I tried to peep he would ask harshly:

"What do you want, eh?"

When I agreed, he sat up in bed without putting his feet to the floor, and ordered me in a tone of authority to bring the trunk to the bed, and place it at his feet. The key hung round his neck with his baptismal cross. Glancing round at the dark corners of the kitchen, he frowned importantly, unfastened the lock, blew on the lid of the trunk as if it had been hot, and at length, raising it, took out several linen garments.

The trunk was half-full of chemist's boxes, packets of variously colored tea-paper, and tins which had contained blacking or sardines.

"What is it?"

"You shall see."

He put a foot on each side of the trunk and bent over it, singing softly:

"Czaru nebesnui———"

I expected to see toys. I had never possessed any myself, and pretended to despise them, but not without a feeling of envy for those who did possess them. I was very pleased to think that Sascha, such a serious character, had toys, although he hid them shamefacedly; but I quite understood his shame.

Opening the first box, he drew from it the frame of a pair of spectacles, put them on his nose, and, looking at me sternly, said:

"It does not matter about there not being any glasses. This is a special kind of spectacle."

"Let me look through them."

"They would not suit your eyes. They are for dark eyes, and yours are light," he explained, and began to imitate the mistress scolding; but suddenly he stopped, and looked about the kitchen with an expression of fear.

In a blacking tin lay many different kinds of buttons, and he explained to me with pride:

"I picked up all these in the street. All by myself! I already have thirty-seven."

In the third box was a large brass pin, also found in the street; hobnails, worn-out, broken, and whole; buckles off shoes and slippers; brass door-handles, broken bone cane-heads; girls' fancy combs, 'The Dream Book and Oracle;' and many other things of similar value.

When I used to collect rags I could have picked up ten times as many such useless trifles in one month. Sascha's things aroused in me a feeling of disillusion, of agitation, and painful pity for him. But he gazed at every single article with great attention, lovingly stroked them with his fingers, and stuck out his thick lips importantly. His protruding eyes rested on them affectionately and solicitously; but the spectacles made his childish face look comical.

"Why have you kept these things?"

He flashed a glance at me through the frame of the spectacles, and asked:

"Would you like me to give you something?"

"No; I don't want anything."

He was obviously offended at the refusal and the poor impression his riches had made. He was silent a moment; then he suggested quietly:

"Get a towel and wipe them all; they are covered with dust."

When the things were all dusted and replaced, he turned over in the bed, with his face to the wall. The rain was pouring down. It dripped from the roof, and the wind beat against the window. Without turning toward me, Sascha said:

"You wait! When it is dry in the garden I will show you a thing—something to make you gasp."

I did not answer, as I was just dropping off to sleep.

After a few seconds he started up, and began to scrape the wall with his hands. With quivering earnestness, he said:

"I am afraid—Lord, I am afraid! Lord, have mercy upon me! What is it?"

I was numbed by fear at this. I seemed to see the cook standing at the window which looked on the yard, with her back to me, her head bent, and her forehead pressed against the glass, just as she used to stand when she was alive, looking at a cock-fight. Sascha sobbed, and scraped on the wall. I made a great effort and crossed the kitchen, as if I were walking on hot coals, without daring to look around, and lay down beside him. At length, overcome by weariness, we both fell asleep.

A few days after this there was a holiday. We were in the shop till midday, had dinner at home, and when the master had gone to sleep after dinner, Sascha said to me secretly:

"Come along!"

I guessed that I was about to see the thing which was to make me gasp. We went into the garden. On a narrow strip of ground between two houses stood ten old lime-trees, their stout trunks covered with green lichen, their black, naked branches sticking up lifelessly, and not one rook's nest between them. They looked like monuments in a graveyard. There was nothing besides these trees in the garden; neither bushes nor grass. The earth on the pathway was trampled and black, and as hard as iron, and where the bare ground was visible under last year's leaves it was also flattened, and as smooth as stagnant water.

Sascha went to a corner of the fence which hid us from the street, stood under a lime-tree, and, rolling his eyes, glanced at the dirty windows of the neighboring house. Squatting on his haunches, he turned over a heap of leaves with his hands, disclosing a thick root, close to which were placed two bricks deeply embedded in the ground. He lifted these up, and beneath them appeared a piece of roof iron, and under this a square board. At length a large hole opened before my eyes, running under the root of the tree.

Sascha lit a match and applied it to a small piece of wax candle, which he held over the hole as he said to me:

"Look in, only don't be frightened."

He seemed to be frightened himself. The piece of candle in his hand shook, and he had turned pale. His lips drooped unpleasantly, his eyes were moist, and he stealthily put his free hand behind his back. He infected me with his terror, and I glanced very cautiously into the depths under the root, which he had made into a vault, in the back of which he had lit three little tapers that filled the cave with a blue light. It was fairly broad, though in depth no more than the inside of a pail. But it was broad, and the sides were closely covered with pieces of broken glass and broken earthenware. In the center, on an elevation, covered with a piece of red cloth, stood a little coffin ornamented with silver paper, half covered with a fragment of material which looked like a brocaded pall. From beneath this was thrust out a little gray bird's claw and the sharp-billed head of a sparrow. Behind the coffin rose a reading-stand, upon which lay a brass baptismal cross, and around which burned three wax tapers, fixed in candlesticks made out of gold and silver paper which had been wrapped round sweets.

The thin flames bowed toward the entrance to the cave. The interior was faintly bright with many colored gleams and patches of light. The odor of wax, the warm smell of decay and soil, beat against my face, made my eyes smart, and conjured up a broken rainbow, which made a great display of color. All this aroused in me such an overwhelming astonishment that it dispelled my terror.

"Is it good?"

"What is it for?"

"It is a chapel," he explained. "Is it like one?"

"I don't know."

"And the sparrow is a dead person. Perhaps there will be relics of him, because he suffered undeservedly."

"Did you find him dead?"

"No. He flew into the shed and I put my cap over him and smothered him."

"But why?"

"Because I chose to."

He looked into my eyes and asked again:

"Is it good?"

"No."

Then he bent over the hole, quickly covered it with the board, pressed the bricks into the earth with the iron, stood up, and, brushing the dirt from his knees, asked sternly:

"Why don't you like it?"

"I am sorry for the sparrow."

He stared at me with eyes which were perfectly stationary, like those of a blind person, and, striking my chest, cried:

"Fool, it is because you are envious that you say that you do not like it! I suppose you think that the one in your garden in Kanatnoe Street was better done."

I remembered my summer-house, and said with conviction:

"Certainly it was better."

Sascha pulled off his coat and threw it on the ground, and, turning up his sleeves, spat on his hands and said:

"If that is so, we will fight about it."

I did not want to fight. My courage was undermined by depression; I felt uneasy as I looked at the wrathful face of my cousin. He made a rush at me, struck my chest with his head, and knocked me over. Then he sat astride of me and cried:

"Is it to be life or death?"

But I was stronger than he and very angry. In a few minutes he was lying face downward with his hands behind his head and a rattling in his throat. Alarmed, I tried to help him up, but he thrust me away with his hands and feet. I grew still more alarmed. I went away to one side, not knowing what else to do, and he raised his head and said:

"Do you know what you have brought on yourself? I will work things so that when the master and mistress are not looking I shall have to complain of you, and then they will dismiss you."

He went on scolding and threatening me, and his words infuriated me. I rushed to the cave, took away the stones, and threw the coffin containing the sparrow over the fence into the street. I dug Out all the inside of the cave and trampled it under my feet.

Sascha took my violence strangely. Sitting on the ground, with his mouth partly covered and his eyebrows drawn together, he watched me, saying nothing. When I had finished, he stood up without any hurry, shook out his clothes, threw on his coat, and then said calmly and ominously:

"Now you will see what will happen; just wait a little! I arranged all this for you purposely; it is witchcraft. Aha!"

I sank down as if his words had physically hurt me, and I felt quite cold inside. But he went away without glancing back at me, which accentuated his calmness still more. I made up my mind to run away from the town the next day, to run away from my master, from Sascha with his witchcraft, from the whole of that worthless, foolish life.

The next morning the new cook cried out when she called me:

"Good gracious! what have you been doing to your face?"

"The witchcraft is beginning to take effect," I thought, with a sinking heart.

But the cook laughed so heartily that I also smiled involuntarily, and peeped into her glass. My face was thickly smeared with soot.

"Sascha did this?" I asked.

"Or I," laughed the cook.

When I began to clean the boots, the first boot into which I put my hand had a pin in the lining, which ran into my finger.

"This is his witchcraft!"

There were pins or needles in all the boots, put in so skilfully that they always pricked my palm. Then I took a bowl of cold water, and with great pleasure poured it over the head of the wizard, who was either not awake or was pretending to sleep.

But all the same I was miserable. I was always thinking of the coffin containing the sparrow, with its gray crooked claws and its waxen bill pathetically sticking upward, and all around the colored gleams which seemed to be trying unsuccessfully to form themselves into a rainbow. In my imagination the coffin was enlarged, the claws of the bird grew, stretched upward quivering, were alive.

I made up my mind to run away that evening, but in warming up some food on an oil-stove before dinner I absent-mindedly let it catch fire. When I was trying to put the flames out, I upset the contents of the vessel over my hand, and had to be taken to the hospital. I remember well that oppressive nightmare of the hospital. In what seemed to be a yellow-gray wilderness there were huddled together, grumbling and groaning, gray and white figures in shrouds, while a tall man on crutches, with eyebrows like whiskers, pulled his black beard and roared:

"I will report it to his Eminence!"

The pallet beds reminded me of the coffin, and the patients, lying with their noses upward, were like dead sparrows. The yellow walls rocked, the ceiling curved outward like a sail, the floor rose and fell beside my cot. Everything about the place was hopeless and miserable, and the twigs of trees tapped against the window like rods in some one's hand.

At the door there danced a red-haired, thin dead person, drawing his shroud round him with his thin hands and squeaking:

"I don't want mad people."

The man on crutches shouted in his ear:

"I shall report it to his Eminence!"

Grandfather, grandmother, and every one had told me that they always starved people in hospitals, so I looked upon my life as finished. A woman with glasses, also in a shroud, came to me, and wrote something on a slate hanging at the head of the bed. The chalk broke and fell all over me.

"What is your name?"

"I have no name."

"But you must have one."

"No."

"Now, don't be silly, or you will be whipped."

I could well believe that they would whip me; that was why I would not answer her. She made a hissing sound like a cat, and went out noiselessly, also like a cat.

Two lamps were lit. The yellow globes hung down from the ceiling like two eyes, hanging and winking, dazzled, and trying to get closer together.

Some one in the corner said:

"How can I play without a hand?"

"Ah, of course; they have cut off your hand."

I came to the conclusion at once that they cut off a man's hand because he played at cards! What would they do with me before they starved me?

My hands burned and smarted just as if some one were pulling the bones out of them. I cried softly from fright and pain, and shut my eyes so that the tears should not be seen; but they forced their way through my eyelids, and, trickling over my temples, fell into my ears.

The night came. All the inmates threw themselves upon their pallet beds, and hid themselves under gray blankets. Every minute it became quieter. Only some one could be heard muttering in a corner, "It is no use; both he and she are rotters."

I would have written a letter to grandmother, telling her to come and steal me from the hospital while I was still alive, but I could not write; my hands could not be used at all. I would try to find a way of getting out of the place.

The silence of the night became more intense every moment, as if it were going to last forever. Softly putting my feet to the floor, I went to the double door, half of which was open. In the corridor, under the lamp, on a wooden bench with a back to it, appeared a gray, bristling head surrounded by smoke, looking at me with dark, hollow eyes. I had no time to hide myself.

"Who is that wandering about? Come here!"

The voice was not formidable; it was soft. I went to him. I saw a round face with short hair sticking out round it. On the head the hair was long and stuck out in all directions like a silver halo, and at the belt of this person hung a bunch of keys. If his beard and hair had been longer, he would have looked like the Apostle Peter.

"You are the one with the burned hands? Why are you wandering about at night? By whose authority?"

He blew a lot of smoke at my chest and face, and, putting his warm hands on my neck, drew me to him.

"Are you frightened?"

"Yes."

"Every one is frightened when they come here first, but that is nothing. And you need not be afraid of me, of all people. I never hurt any one. Would you like to smoke? No, don't! It is too soon; wait a year or two. And where are your parents? You have none? Ah, well, you don't need them; you will be able to get along without them. Only you must not be afraid, do you see?"

It was a long time since I had come across any one who spoke to me simply and kindly in language that I could understand, and it was inexpressibly pleasant to me to listen to him. When he took me back to my cot I asked him:

"Come and sit beside me."

"All right," he agreed.

"Who are you?"

"I? I am a soldier, a real soldier, a Cossack. And I have been in the wars—well, of course I have! Soldiers live for war. I have fought with the Hungarians, with the Circassians, and the Poles, as many as you like. War, my boy, is a great profession."

I closed my eyes for a minute, and when I opened them, there, in the place of the soldier, sat grandmother, in a dark frock, and he was standing by her. She was saying:

"Dear me! So they are all dead?"

The sun was playing in the room, now gilding every object, then hiding, and then looking radiantly upon us all again, just like a child frolicking.

Babushka bent over me and asked:

"What is it, my darling? They have been mutilating you? I told that old red devil—"

"I will make all the necessary arrangements," said the soldier, going away, and grandmother, wiping the tears from her face, said:

"Our soldier, it seems, comes from Balakhna."

I still thought that I must be dreaming, and kept silence. The doctor came, bandaged my burns, and, behold! I was sitting with grandmother in a cab, and driving through the streets of the town. She told me:

"That grandfather of ours he is going quite out of his mind, and he is so greedy that it is sickening to look at him. Not long ago he took a hundred rubles out of the office-book of Xlist the furrier, a new friend of his. What a set-out there was! E-h-h-h!"

The sun shone brightly, and clouds floated in the sky like white birds. We went by the bridge across the Volga. The ice groaned under us, water was visible under the planks of the bridge, and the golden cross gleamed over the red dome of the cathedral in the market-place.

We met a woman with a broad face. She was carrying an armful of willow-branches. The spring was coming; soon it would be Easter.

"I love you very much, Grandmother!"

This did not seem to surprise her. She answered in a calm voice:

"That is because we are of the same family. But—and I do not say it boastfully—there are others who love me, too, thanks to thee, O Blessed Lady!" She added, smiling:

"She will soon be rejoicing; her Son will rise again! Ah, Variusha, my daughter!"

Then she was silent.

CHAPTER II

Grandfather met me in the yard; he was on his knees, chopping a wedge with a hatchet. He raised the ax as if he were going to throw it at my head, and then took off his cap, saying mockingly: "How do you do, your Holiness? Your Highness? Have you finished your term of serviced Well, now you can live as you like, yes. U-ugh! *you*—"

"We know all about it, we know all about it!" said grandmother, hastily waving him away, and when she went into her room to get the samovar ready she told me:

"Grandfather is fairly ruined now. What money there was he lent at interest to his godson Nikolai, but he never got a receipt for it. I don't quite know yet how they stand, but he is ruined; the money is lost. And all this because we have not helped the poor or had compassion on the unfortunate. God has said to Himself, 'Why should I do good to the Kashirins?' and so He has taken everything from us." Looking round, she went on:

"I have been trying to soften the heart of the Lord toward us a little, so that He may not press too hardly on the old man, and I have begun to give a little in charity, secretly and at night, from what I have earned. You can come with me to-day if you like. I have some money—"

Grandfather came in blinking and asked:

"Are you going to have a snack?"

"It is not yours," said grandmother. "However, you can sit down with us if you like; there's enough for you."

He sat down at the table, murmuring:

"Pour out—"

Everything in the room was in its old place. Only my mother's corner was sadly empty, and on the wall over grandfather's bed hung a sheet of paper on which was inscribed in large, printed letters:

"Jesus save, Life of the world! May Thy holy name be with me all the days and hours of my life!"

"Who wrote that?"

Grandfather did not reply, and grandmother, waiting a little, said with a smile:

"The price of that paper is—a hundred rubles!"

"That is not your business!" cried grandfather. "I give away everything to others."

"It is all right to give now, but time was when you did not give," said grandmother, calmly.

"Hold your tongue!" he shrieked.

This was all as it should be, just like old times.

In the corner, on a box, in a wicker basket, Kolia woke up and looked out, his blue, washed-out eyes hardly visible under their lids. He was grayer, more faded and fragile-looking, than ever. He did not recognize me, and, turning away in silence, closed his eyes. Sad news awaited me in the street. Viakhir was dead. He had breathed his last in Passion Week. Khabi had gone away to live in town. Yaz's feet had been taken off, and he would walk no more.

As he was giving me this information, black-eyed Kostrom said angrily:

"Boys soon die!"

"Well, but only Viakhir is dead."

"It is the same thing. Whoever leaves the streets is as good as dead. No sooner do we make friends, get used to our comrades, than they either are sent into the town to work or they die. There are new people living in your yard at Chesnokov's; Evsyenki is their name. The boy, Niushka, is nothing out of the ordinary. He has two sisters, one still small, and the other lame. She goes about on crutches; she is beautiful!"

After thinking a moment he added:

"Tchurka and I are both in love with her, and quarrel."

"With her?"

"Why with her? Between ourselves. With her—very seldom."

Of course I knew that big lads and even men fell in love. I was familiar also with coarse ideas on this subject. I felt uncomfortable, sorry for Kostrom, and reluctant to look at his angular figure and angry, black eyes.

I saw the lame girl on the evening of the same day. Coming down the steps into the yard, she let her crutch fall, and stood helplessly on the step, holding on to the balustrade with her transparent, thin, fragile hands. I tried to pick up the crutch, but my bandaged hands were not much use, and I had a lot of trouble and vexation in doing it. Meanwhile she, standing above me, and laughing gently, watched me.

"What have you done to your hands?" she said.

"Scalded them."

"And I—am a cripple. Do you belong to this yard? Were you long in the hospital? I was there a lo-o-ong time." She added, with a sigh, "A very long time."

She had a white dress and light blue overshoes, old, but clean; her smoothly brushed hair fell across her breast in a thick, short plait. Her eyes were large and serious; in their quiet depths burned a blue light which lit up the pale, sharp-nosed face. She smiled pleasantly, but I did not care about her. Her sickly figure seemed to say, "Please don't touch me!" How could my friends be in love with her?

"I have been lame a long time," she told me, willingly and almost boastfully. "A neighbor bewitched me; she had a quarrel with mother, and then bewitched me out of spite. Were you frightened in the hospital?"

"Yes."

I felt awkward with her, and went indoors.

About midnight grandmother tenderly awoke me.

"Are you coming? If you do something for other people, your hand will soon be well."

She took my arm and led me in the dark, as if I had been blind. It was a black, damp night; the wind blew continuously, making the river flow more swiftly and blowing the cold sand against my legs. Grandmother cautiously approached the darkened windows of the poor little houses, crossed herself three times, laid a five-copeck piece and three cracknel biscuits on the window-sills, and crossed herself again. Glancing up into the starless sky, she whispered:

"Holy Queen of Heaven, help these people! We are all sinners in thy sight, Mother dear."

Now, the farther we went from home, the denser and more intense the darkness and silence became. The night sky was pitch black, unfathomable, as if the moon and stars had disappeared forever. A dog sprang out from somewhere and growled at us. His eyes gleamed in the darkness, and I cravenly pressed close to grandmother.

"It is all right," she said; "it is only a dog. It is too late for the devil; the cocks have already begun to crow."

Enticing the dog to her, she stroked it and admonished it:

"Look here, doggie, you must not frighten my grandson."

The dog rubbed itself against my legs, and the three of us went on. Twelve times did grandmother place "secret alms" on a window-sill. It began to grow light: gray houses appeared out of the darkness; the belfry of Napolni Church rose up white like a piece of sugar; the brick wall of the cemetery seemed to become transparent.

"The old woman is tired," said grandmother; "it is time we went home. When the women wake up they will find that Our Lady has provided a little for their children. When there is never enough, a very little comes in useful. O Olesha, our people live so poorly and no one troubles about them!

> "The rich man about God never thinks;
> Of the terrible judgment he does not dream;
> The poor man is to him neither friend nor brother;
> All he cares about is getting gold together.
> But that gold will be coal in hell!

"That's how it is. But we ought to live for one another, while God is for us all. I am glad to have you with me again."

And I, too, was calmly happy, feeling in a confused way that I had taken part in something which I should never forget. Close to me shivered the brown dog, with its bare muzzle and kind eyes which seemed to be begging forgiveness.

"Will it live with us?"

"What? It can, if it likes. Here, I will give it a cracknel biscuit. I have two left. Let us sit down on this bench. I am so tired."

We sat down on a bench by a gate, and the dog lay at our feet, eating the dry cracknel, while grandmother informed me:

"There's a Jewess living here; she has about ten servants, more or less. I asked her, 'Do you live by the law of Moses?' But she answered, 'I live as if God were with me and mine; how else should I live?'"

I leaned against the warm body of grandmother and fell asleep.

*

Once more my life flowed on swiftly and full of interest, with a broad stream of impressions bringing something new to my soul every day, stirring it to enthusiasm, disturbing it, or causing me pain, but at any rate forcing me to think. Before long I also was using every means in my power to meet the lame girl, and I would sit with her on the bench by the gate, either talking or in silence. It was pleasant to be silent in her company. She was very neat, and had a voice like a singing bird. She used to tell me prettily of the way the Cossacks lived on the Don, where she had lived with her uncle, who was employed in some oil-works. Then her father, a locksmith, had gone to live at Nijni. "And I have another uncle who serves the czar himself."

In the evenings of Sundays and festivals all the inhabitants of the street used to stand "at the gate." The boys and girls went to the cemetery, the men to the taverns, and the women and children remained in the street. The women sat at the gate on the sand or on a small bench.

The children used to play at a sort of tennis, at skittles, and at *sharmazl*. The mothers watched the games, encouraging the skilful ones and laughing at the bad players. It was deafeningly noisy and gay. The presence and attention of the "grown-ups" stimulated us; the merest trifles brought into our games extra animation and passionate rivalry. But it seemed that we three, Kostrom, Tchurka, and I, were not so taken up with the game that we had not time, one or the other of us, to run and show off before the lame girl.

"Ludmilla, did you see that I knocked down five of the ninepins in that game of skittles?"

She would smile sweetly, tossing her head.

In old times our little company had always tried to be on the same side in games, but now I saw that Kostrom and Tchurka used to take opposite sides, trying to rival each other in all kinds of trials of skill and strength, often aggravating each other to tears and fights. One day they fought so fiercely that the adults had to interfere, and they had to pour water over the combatants, as if they were dogs. Ludmilla, sitting on a bench, stamped her sound foot on the ground, and when the fighters rolled toward her, pushed them away with her crutch, crying in a voice of fear:

"Leave off!"

Her face was white, almost livid; her eyes blazed and rolled like a person possessed with a devil.

Another time Kostrom, shamefully beaten by Tchurka in a game of skittles, hid himself behind a chest of oats in the grocer's shop, and crouched there, weeping silently. It was terrible to see him. His teeth were tightly clenched, his cheek-bones stood out, his bony face looked as if it had been turned to stone, and from his black, surly eyes flowed large, round tears. When I tried to console him he whispered, choking back his tears:

"You wait! I'll throw a brick at his head. You'll see."

Tchurka had become conceited; he walked in the middle of the street, as marriageable youths walk, with his cap on one side and his hands in his pocket. He had taught himself to spit through his teeth like a fine bold fellow, and he promised:

"I shall learn to smoke soon. I have already tried twice, but I was sick."

All this was displeasing to me. I saw that I was losing my friends, and it seemed to me that the person to blame was Ludmilla. One evening when I was in the yard going over the collection of bones and rags and all kinds of rubbish, she came to me, swaying from side to side and waving her right hand.

"How do you do?" she said, bowing her head three times. "Has Kostrom been with you? And Tchurka?"

"Tchurka is not friends with us now. It is all your fault. They are both in love with you and they have quarreled."

She blushed, but answered mockingly:

"What next! How is it my fault?"

"Why do you make them fall in love with you?"

"I did not ask them to," she said crossly, and as she went away she added: "It is all nonsense. I am older than they are; I am fourteen. People do not fall in love with big girls."

"A lot you know!" I cried, wishing to hurt her. "What about the shopkeeper, Xlistov's sister? She is quite old, and still she has the boys after her."

Ludmilla turned on me, sticking her crutch deep into the sand of the yard.

"You don't know anything yourself," she said quickly, with tears in her voice and her pretty eyes flashing finely. "That shopkeeper is a bad woman, and I—what am I? I am still a little girl; and—but you ought to read that novel, 'Kamchadalka,' the second part, and then you would have something to talk about."

She went away sobbing. I felt sorry for her. In her words was the ring of a truth of which I was ignorant. Why had she embroiled my comrades? But they were in love; what else was there to say?

The next day, wishing to smooth over my difference with Ludmilla, I bought some barley sugar, her favorite sweet, as I knew well.

"Would you like some?"

She said fiercely:

"Go away! I am not friends with you!" But presently she took the barley sugar, observing: "You might have had it wrapped up in paper. Your hands are so dirty!"

"I have washed them, but it won't come off."

She took my hand in her dry, hot hand and looked at it.

"How you have spoiled it!"

"Well, but yours are roughened."

"That is done by my needle. I do a lot of sewing." After a few minutes she suggested, looking round: "I say, let's hide ourselves somewhere and read 'Kamchadalka.' Would you like it?"

We were a long time finding a place to hide in, for every place seemed uncomfortable. At length we decided that the best place was the wash-house. It was dark there, but we could sit at the window, which overlooked a dirty corner between the shed and the neighboring slaughter-house. People hardly ever looked that way. There she used to sit sidewise to the window, with her bad foot on a stool and the sound one resting on the floor, and, hiding her face with the torn book, nervously pronounced many unintelligible and dull words. But I was stirred. Sitting on the floor, I could see how the grave eyes with the two pale-blue flames moved across the pages of the book. Sometimes they were filled with tears, and the girl's voice trembled as she quickly uttered the unfamiliar words, running them into one another unintelligibly. However, I grasped some of these words, and tried to make them into verse, turning them about in all sorts of ways, which effectually prevented me from understanding what the book said.

On my knees slumbered the dog, which I had named "Wind," because he was rough and long, swift in running, and howled like the autumn wind down the chimney.

"Are you listening?" the girl would ask. I nodded my head.

The mixing up of the words excited me more and more, and my desire to arrange them as they would sound in a song, in which each word lives and shines like a star in the sky, became more insistent. When it grew dark Ludmilla would let her pale hand fall on the book and ask:

"Isn't it good? You will see."

After the first evening we often sat in the washhouse. Ludmilla, to my joy, soon gave up reading "Kamchadalka." I could not answer her questions about what she had read from that endless book—endless, for there was a third book after the second part which we had begun to read, and the girl said there was a fourth. What we liked best was a rainy day, unless it fell on a Saturday, when the bath was heated. The rain drenched the yard. No one came out or looked at us in our dark comer. Ludmilla was in great fear that they would discover us.

I also was afraid that we should be discovered. We used to sit for hours at a time, talking about one thing and another. Sometimes I told her some of grandmother's tales, and Ludmilla told me about the lives of the Kazsakas, on the River Medvyedietz.

"How lovely it was there!" she would sigh. "Here, what is it? Only beggars live here."

Soon we had no need to go to the wash-house. Ludmilla's mother found work with a fur-dresser, and left the house the first thing in the morning. Her sister was at school, and her brother worked at a tile factory. On wet days I went to the girl and helped her to cook, and to clean the sitting-room and kitchen. She said laughingly:

"We live together—just like a husband and wife. In fact, we live better; a husband does not help his wife."

If I had money, I bought some cakes, and we had tea, afterward cooling the samovar with cold water, lest the scolding mother of Ludmilla should guess that it had been heated.

Sometimes grandmother came to see us, and sat down, making lace, sewing, or telling us wonderful stories, and when grandfather went to the town, Ludmilla used to come to us, and we feasted without a care in the world.

Grandmother said:

"Oh, how happily we live! With our own money we can do what we like."

She encouraged our friendship.

"It is a good thing when a boy and girl are friends. Only there must be no tricks," and she explained in the simplest words what she meant by "tricks." She spoke beautifully, as one inspired, and made me understand thoroughly that it is wrong to pluck the flower before it opens, for then it will have neither fragrance nor fruit.

We had no inclination for "tricks," but that did not hinder Ludmilla and me from speaking of that subject, on which one is supposed to be silent. Such subjects of conversation were in a way forced upon us because the relationship of the sexes was so often and tiresomely brought to our notice in their coarsest form, and was very offensive to us.

Ludmilla's father was a handsome man of forty, curly-headed and whiskered, and had an extremely masterful way of moving his eyebrows. He was strangely silent; I do not remember one word uttered by him. When he caressed his children he uttered unintelligible sounds, like a dumb person, and even when he beat his wife he did it in silence.

On the evenings of Sundays and festivals, attired in a light-blue shirt, with wide plush trousers and highly polished boots, he would go out to the gate with a harmonica slung with straps behind his back, and stand there exactly like a soldier doing sentry duty. Presently a sort of "promenade" would begin past our gate. One after the other girls and women would pass, glancing at Evsyenko furtively from under their eyelashes, or quite openly, while he stood sticking out his lower lip, and also looking with discriminating glances from, his dark eyes. There was something repugnantly dog-like in this silent conversation with the eyes alone, and from the slow, rapt movement of the women as they passed it seemed as if the chosen one, at an imperious flicker of the man's eyelid, would humbly sink to the dirty ground as if she were killed.

"Tipsy brute! Brazen face!" grumbled Ludmilla's mother. She was a tall, thin woman, with a long face and a bad-complexion, and hair which had been cut short after typhus. She was like a worn-out broom.

Ludmilla sat beside her, unsuccessfully trying to turn her attention from the street by asking questions about one thing and another.

"Stop it, you monster!" muttered the mother, blinking restlessly. Her narrow Mongol eyes were strangely bright and immovable, always fixed on something and always stationary.

"Don't be angry, Mamochka; it doesn't matter," Ludmilla would say. "Just look how the mat-maker's widow is dressed up!"

"I should be able to dress better if it were not for you three. You have eaten me up, devoured me," said the mother, pitilessly through her tears, fixing her eyes on the large, broad figure of the mat-maker's widow.

She was like a small house. Her chest stuck out like the roof, and her red face, half hidden by the green handkerchief which was tied round it, was like a dormer-window when the sun is reflected on it. Evsyenko, drawing his harmonica to his chest, began to play. The harmonica played many tunes; the sounds traveled a long way, and the children came from all the street around, and fell in the sand at the feet of the performer, trembling with ecstasy.

"You wait; I'll give you something!" the woman promised her husband.

He looked at her askance, without speaking. And the mat-maker's widow sat not far off on the Xlistov's bench, listening intently.

In the field behind the cemetery the sunset was red. In the street, as on a river, floated brightly clothed, great pieces of flesh. The children rushed along like a whirlwind; the warm air was caressing and intoxicating. A pungent odor rose from the sand, which had been made hot by the sun during the day, and peculiarly noticeable was a fat, sweet smell from the slaughter-house—the smell of blood. From the yard where the fur-dresser lived came the salt and bitter odor of tanning. The women's chatter, the drunken roar of the men, the bell-like voices of the children, the bass melody of the harmonica—all mingled together in one deep rumble. The earth, which is ever, creating, gave a mighty sigh. All was coarse and naked, but it instilled a great, deep faith in that gloomy life, so shamelessly animal. At times above the noise certain painful, never-to-be-forgotten words went straight to one's heart:

"It is not right for you all together to set upon one. You must take turns." "Who pities us when we do not pity ourselves?" "Did God bring women into the world in order to deride them?"

The night drew near, the air became fresher, the sounds became more subdued. The wooden houses seemed to swell and grow taller, clothing themselves with shadows. The children were dragged away from the yard to bed. Some of them were already asleep by the fence or at the feet or on the knees of their mothers. Most of the children grew quieter and more docile with the night. Evsyenko disappeared unnoticed; he seemed to have melted away. The mat-maker's widow was also missing. The bass notes of the harmonica could be heard somewhere in the distance, beyond the cemetery. Ludmilla's mother sat on a bench doubled up, with her back stuck out like a cat. My grandmother had gone out to take tea with a neighbor, a midwife, a great fat woman with a nose like a duck's, and a gold medal "for saving lives" on her flat, masculine-looking chest. The whole street feared her, regarding her as a witch, and it was related of her that she had carried out of the flames, when a fire broke out, the three children and sick wife of a certain colonel. There was a friendship between grandmother and her. When they met in the street they used to smile at each other from a long way off, as if they had seen something specially pleasant.

Kostrom, Ludmilla, and I sat on the bench at the gate. Tchurka had called upon Ludmilla's brother to wrestle with him. Locked in each other's arms they trampled down the sand and became angry.

"Leave off!" cried Ludmilla, timorously.

Looking at her sidewise out of his black eyes, Kostrom told a story about the hunter Kalinin, a grayhaired old man with cunning eyes, a man of evil fame, known to all the village. He had not long been dead, but they had not buried him in the earth in the graveyard, but had placed his coffin above ground, away from the other graves. The coffin was black, on tall trestles; on the lid were drawn in white paint a cross, a spear, a reed, and two bones. Every night, as soon as it grew dark, the old man rose from his coffin and walked about the cemetery, looking for something, till the first cock crowed.

"Don't talk about such dreadful things!" begged Ludmilla.

"Nonsense!" cried Tchurka, breaking away from her brother. "What are you telling lies for? I saw them bury the coffin myself, and the one above ground is simply a monument. As to a dead man walking about, the drunken blacksmith set the idea afloat." Kostrom, without looking at him, suggested:

"Go and sleep in the cemetery; then you will see." They began to quarrel, and Ludmilla, shaking her head sadly, asked:

"Mamochka, do dead people walk about at night?" "They do," answered her mother, as if the question had called her back from a distance.

The son of the shopkeeper Valek, a tall, stout, red-faced youth of twenty, came to us, and, hearing what we were disputing about, said:

"I will give three *greven* and ten cigarettes to whichever of you three will sleep till daylight on the coffin, and I will pull the ears of the one who is afraid—as long as he likes. Well?"

We were all silent, confused, and Ludmilla's mother said:

"What nonsense! What do you mean by putting the children up to such nonsense?"

"You hand over a ruble, and I will go," announced Tchurka, gruffly.

Kostrom at once asked spitefully:

"But for two *greven*—you would be afraid?" Then he said to Valek: "Give him the ruble. But he won't go; he is only making believe."

"Well, take the ruble."

Tchurka rose, and, without saying a word and without hurrying, went away, keeping close to the fence. Kostrom, putting his fingers in his mouth, whistled piercingly after him.; but Ludmilla said uneasily:

"O Lord, what a braggart he is! I never!"

"Where are you going, coward?" jeered Valek. "And you call yourself the first fighter in the street!" It was offensive to listen to his jeers. We did not like this overfed youth; he was always putting up little boys to do wrong, told them obscene stories of girls and women, and taught them to tease them. The children did what he told them, and suffered dearly for it. For some reason or other he hated my dog, and used to throw stones at it, and one day gave it some bread with a needle in it. But it was still more offensive to see Tchurka going away, shrinking and ashamed.

I said to Valek:

"Give me the ruble, and I will go."

Mocking me and trying to frighten me, he held out the ruble to Ludmilla's mother, who would not take it, and said sternly:

"I don't want it, and I won't have it!" Then she went out angrily.

Ludmilla also could not make up her mind to take the money, and this made Valek jeer the more. I was going away without obtaining the money when grandmother came along" and, being told all about it, took the ruble, saying to me softly:

"Put on your overcoat and take a blanket with you, for it grows cold toward morning."

Her words raised my hopes that nothing terrible would happen to me.

Valek laid it down on a condition that I should either lie or sit on the coffin until it was light, not leaving it, whatever happened, even if the coffin shook when the old man Kalinin began to climb out of the tomb. If I jumped to the ground I had lost.

"And remember," said Valek, "that I shall be watching you all night."

When I set out for the cemetery grandmother made the sign of the cross over me and kissed me.

"If you should see a glimpse of anything, don't move, but just say, 'Hail, Mary.'"

I went along quickly, my one desire being to begin and finish the whole thing. Valek, Kostrom, and another youth escorted me thither. As I was getting over the brick wall I got mixed up in the blanket, and fell down, but was up in the same moment, as if the earth had ejected me. There was a chuckle from the other side of the wall. My heart contracted; a cold chill ran down my back.

I went stumblingly on to the black coffin, against one side of which the sand had drifted, while on the other side could be seen the short, thick legs. It looked as if some one had tried to lift it up, and had succeeded only in making it totter. I sat on the edge of the coffin and looked around. The hilly cemetery was simply packed with gray crosses; quivering shadows fell upon the graves.

Here and there, scattered among the graves, slender willows stood up, uniting adjoining graves with their branches. Through the lace-work of their shadows blades of grass stuck up.

The church rose up in the sky like a snow-drift, and in the motionless clouds shone the small setting moon.

The father of Yaz, "the good-for-nothing peasant," was lazily ringing his bell in his lodge. Each time, as he pulled the string, it caught in the iron plate of the roof and squeaked pitifully, after which could be heard the metallic clang of the little bell. It sounded sharp and sorrowful.

"God give us rest!" I remembered the saying of the watchman. It was very painful and somehow it was suffocating. I was perspiring freely although the night was cool. Should I have time to run into the watchman's lodge if old Kalinin really did try to creep out of his grave?

I was well acquainted with the cemetery. I had played among the graves many times with Yaz and other comrades. Over there by the church my mother was buried.

Every one was not asleep yet, for snatches of laughter and fragments of songs were borne to me from the village. Either on the railway embankment, to which they were carrying sand, or in the village of Katizovka a harmonica gave forth a strangled sound. Along the wall, as usual, went the drunken blacksmith Myachov, singing. I recognized him by his song:

> "To our mother's door
> One small sin we lay.
> The only one she loves
> Is our Papasha."

It was pleasant to listen to the last sighs of life, but at each stroke of the bell it became quieter, and the quietness overflowed like a river over a meadow, drowning and hiding everything. One's soul seemed to float in boundless and unfathomable space, to be extinguished like the light of a catch in the darkness, becoming dissolved without leaving a trace in that ocean of space in which live only the unattainable stars, shining brightly, while everything on earth disappears as being useless and dead. Wrapping myself in the blanket, I sat on the coffin, with my feet tucked under me and my face to the church. Whenever I moved, the coffin squeaked, and the sand under it crunched.

Something twice struck the ground close to me, and then a piece of brick fell near by. I was frightened, but then I guessed that Valek and his friends were throwing things at me from the other side of the wall, trying to scare me. But I felt all the better for the proximity of human creatures.

I began unwillingly to think of my mother. Once she had found me trying to smoke a cigarette. She began to beat me, but I said:

"Don't touch me; I feel bad enough without that. I feel very sick."

Afterward, when I was put behind the stove as a punishment, she said to grandmother:

"That boy has no feeling; he does n't love any one." It hurt me to hear that. When my mother punished me I was sorry for her. I felt uncomfortable for her sake, because she seldom punished me deservedly or justly. On the whole, I had received a great deal of ill treatment in my life. Those people on the other side of the fence, for example, must know that I was frightened of being alone in the cemetery, yet they wanted to frighten me more. Why?

I should like to have shouted to them, "Go to the devil!" but that might have been disastrous. Who knew what the devil would think of it, for no doubt he was somewhere near? There was a lot of mica in the sand, and it gleamed faintly in the moonlight, which reminded me how, lying one day on a raft on the Oka, gazing into the water, a bream suddenly swam almost in my face, turned on its side, looking like a human cheek, and, looking at me with its round, bird-like eyes, dived to the bottom, fluttering like a leaf falling from a maple-tree.

My memory worked with increasing effort, recalling different episodes of my life, as if it were striving to protect itself against the imaginations evoked by terror.

A hedgehog came rolling along, tapping on the sand with its strong paws. It reminded me of a hobgoblin; it was just as little and as disheveled-looking.

I remembered how grandmother, squatting down beside the stove, said, "Kind master of the house, take away the beetles."

Far away over the town, which I could not see, it grew lighter. The cold morning air blew against my cheeks and into my eyes. I wrapped myself in my blanket. Let come what would!

Grandmother awoke me. Standing beside me and pulling off the blanket, she said:

"Get up! Aren't you chilled? Well, were you frightened?"

"I was frightened, but don't tell any one; don't tell the other boys."

"But why not?" she asked in amazement. "If you were not afraid, you have nothing to be proud about."

As he went home she said to me gently:

"You have to experience things for yourself in this world, dear heart. If you can't teach yourself, no one else can teach you."

By the evening I was the "hero" of the street, and every one asked me, "Is it possible that you were not afraid?" And when I answered, "I was afraid," they shook their heads and exclaimed, "Aha! you see!"

The shopkeeper went about saying loudly:

"It may be that they talked nonsense when they said that Kalinin walked. But if he did, do you think he would have frightened that boy? No, he would have driven him out of the cemetery, and no one would know where he went."

Ludmilla looked at me with tender astonishment. Even grandfather was obviously pleased with me. They all made much of me. Only Tchurka said gruffly:

"It was easy enough for him; his grandmother is a witch!"

CHAPTER III

Imperceptibly, like a little star at dawn, my brother Kolia faded away. Grandmother, he, and I slept in a small shed on planks covered with various rags. On the other side of the chinky wall of the outhouse was the family poultry-house. We could hear the sleepy, overfed fowls fluttering and clucking in the evening, and the golden, shrill-voiced cock awoke us in the morning.

"Oh, I should like to tear you to pieces!" grandmother would grumble when they woke her.

I was already awake, watching the sunbeams falling through the chinks upon my bed, and the silver specks of dust which danced in them. These little specks seemed to me just like the words in a fairy-tale. Mice had gnawed the planks, and red beetles with black spots ran about there.

Sometimes, to escape from the stifling fumes which arose from the soil in the fowl-house, I crept out of the wooden hut, climbed to the roof, and watched the people of the house waking up, eyeless, large, and swollen with sleep. Here appeared the hairy noddle of the boatman Phermanov, a surly drunkard, who gazed at the sun with blear, running eyes and grunted like a bear. Then grandfather came hurrying out into the yard and hastened to the wash-house to wash himself in cold water. The garrulous cook of the landlord, a sharp-nosed woman, thickly covered with freckles, was like a cuckoo. The landlord himself was like an old fat dove. In fact, they were all like some bird, animal, or wild beast.

Although the morning was so pleasant and bright, it made me feel sad, and I wanted to get away into the fields where no one came, for I had already learned that human creatures always spoil a bright day.

One day when I was lying on the roof grandmother called me, and said in a low voice, shaking her head as she lay on her bed:

"Kolia is dead."

The little boy had slipped from the pillow, and lay livid, lanky on the felt cover. His night-shirt had worked itself up round his neck, leaving bare his swollen stomach and crooked legs. His hands were curiously folded behind his back, as if he had been trying to lift himself up. His head was bent on one side.

"Thank God he has gone!" said grandmother as she did her hair. "What would have become of the poor little wretch had he lived?"

Treading almost as if he were dancing, grandfather made his appearance, and cautiously touched the closed eyes of the child with his fingers.

Grandmother asked him angrily:

"What do you mean by touching him with unwashen hands?"

He muttered:

"There you are! He gets born, lives, and eats, and all for nothing."

"You are half asleep," grandmother cut him short.

He looked at her vacantly, and went out in the yard, saying:

"I am not going to give him a funeral; you can do what you like about it."

"Phoo! you miserable creature!"

I went out, and did not return until it was close upon evening. They buried Kolia on the morning of the following day, and during the mass I sat by the reopened grave with my dog and Yaz's father. He had dug the grave cheaply, and kept praising himself for it before my face.

"I have only done this out of friendship; for any one else I should have charged so many rubles."

Looking into the yellow pit, from which arose a heavy odor, I saw some moist black planks at one side. At my slightest movement the heaps of sand around the grave fell to the bottom in a thin stream, leaving wrinkles in the sides. I moved on purpose, so that the sand would hide those boards.

"No larks now!" said Yaz's father, as he smoked.

Grandmother carried out the little coffin. The "trashy peasant" sprang into the hole, took the coffin from her, placed it beside the black boards, and, jumping out of the grave, began to hurl the earth into it with his feet and his spade. Grandfather and grandmother also helped him in silence. There were neither priests nor beggars there; only we four amid a dense crowd of crosses. As she gave the sexton his money, grandmother said reproachfully:

"But you have disturbed Varina's coffin."

"What else could I do? If I had not done that, I should have had to take some one else's piece of ground. But there's nothing to worry about."

Grandmother prostrated herself on the grave, sobbed and groaned, and went away, followed by grandfather, his eyes hidden by the peak of his cap, clutching at his worn coat.

"They have sown the seed in unplowed ground," he said suddenly, running along in front, just like a crow on the plowed field.

"What does he mean?" I asked grandmother. "God bless him! He has his thoughts," she answered.

It was hot. Grandmother went heavily; her feet sank in the warm sand. She halted frequently, mopping her perspiring face with her handkerchief.

"That black thing in the grave," I asked her, "was it mother's coffin?"

"Yes," she said angrily. "Ignorant dog! It is not a year yet, and our Varia is already decayed! It is the sand that has done it; it lets the water through. If that had to happen, it would have been better to—" "Shall we all decay?"

"All. Only the saints escape it."

"You—you will not decay!"

She halted, set my cap straight, and said to me seriously:

"Don't think about it; it is better not. Do you hear?"

But I did think of it. How offensive and revolting death was! How odious! I felt very badly about it.

When we reached home grandfather had already prepared the samovar and laid the table.

"Come and have some tea. I expect you are hot," he said. "I have put in my own tea as well. This is for us all."

He went to grandmother and patted her on the shoulder.

"Well, Mother, well?"

Grandmother held up her hands.

"Whatever does it all mean?"

"This is what it means: God is angry with us; He is tearing everything away from us bit by bit. If families lived together in unity, like fingers on a hand—"

It was long since he had spoken so gently and peaceably. I listened, hoping that the old man would extinguish my sense of injury, and help me to forget the yellow pit and the black moist boards in protuberance in its side. But grandmother cut him short harshly:

"Leave off, Father! You have been uttering words like that all your life, and I should like to know who is the better for them? All your life you have eaten into every one as rust corrodes iron."

Grandfather muttered, looked at her, and held his tongue.

In the evening, at the gate, I told Ludmilla sorrowfully about what I had seen in the morning, but it did not seem to make much impression on her.

"Orphans are better off. If my father and mother were to die, I should leave my sister to look after my brother, and I myself would go into a convent for the rest of my life. Where else should I go? I don't expect to get married, being lame and unable to work. Besides, I might bring crippled children into the world."

She spoke wisely, like all the women of our street, and it must have been from that evening that I lost interest in her. In fact, my life took a turn which caused me to see her very seldom.

A few days after the death of my brother, grandfather said to me:

"Go to bed early this evening, while it is still light, and I will call you. We will go into the forest and get some logs."

"And I will come and gather herbs," declared grandmother.

The forest of fir- and birch-trees stood on a marsh about three versts distant from the village. Abounding in withered and fallen trees, it stretched in one direction to the Oka, and in the other to the high road to Moscow. Beyond it, with its soft, black bristles looking like a black tent, rose the fir-thicket on the "Ridge of Savelov."

All this property belonged to Count Shuvalov, and was badly guarded. The inhabitants of Kunavin regarded it as their own, carried away the fallen trees and cut off the dried wood, and on occasion were not squeamish about cutting down living trees. In the autumn, when they were laying in a stock of wood for the winter, people used to steal out here by the dozen, with hatchets and ropes on their backs.

And so we three went out at dawn over the silver-green, dewy fields. On our left, beyond the Oka, above the ruddy sides of the Hill of Dyatlov, above white Nijni-Novgorod, on the hillocks in the gardens, on the golden domes of churches, rose the lazy Russian sun in its leisurely manner. A gentle wind blew sleepily from the turbid Oka; the golden buttercups, bowed down by the dew, sway to and fro; lilac-colored bells bowed dumbly to the earth; everlasting flowers of different colors stuck up dryly in the barren turf; the blood-red blossoms of the flower called "night beauty" opened like stars. The woods came to meet us like a dark army; the fir-trees spread out their wings like large birds; the birches looked like maidens. The acrid smell of the marshes flowed over the fields. My dog ran beside me with his pink tongue hanging out, often halting and snuffing the air, and shaking his foxlike head, as if in perplexity. Grandfather, in grandmother's short coat and an old peakless cap, blinking and smiling at something or other, walked as cautiously as if he were bent on stealing. Grandmother, wearing a blue blouse, a black skirt, and a white handkerchief about her head, waddled comfortably. It was difficult to hurry when walking behind her.

The nearer we came to the forest, the more animated grandfather became. Walking with his nose in the air and muttering, he began to speak, at first disjointedly and inarticulately, and afterward happily and beautifully, almost as if he had been drinking.

"The forests are the Lord's gardens. No one planted them save the wind of God and the holy breath of His mouth. When I was working on the boats in my youth I went to Jegoulya. Oh, Lexei, you will never have the experiences I have had! There are forests along the Oka, from Kasimov to Mouron, and there are forests on the Volga, too, stretching as far as the Urals. Yes; it is all so boundless and wonderful."

Grandmother looked at him askance, and winked at me, and he, stumbling over the hillocks, let fall some disjointed, dry words that have remained forever fixed in my memory.

"We were taking some empty oil-casks from Saratov to Makara on the Yamarka, and we had with us as skipper Kyril of Poreshka. The mate was a Tatar—Asaph, or some such name. When we reached Jegulia the wind was right in our faces, blowing with all its force; and as it remained in the same quarter and tossed us about, we went on shore to cook some food for ourselves. It was Maytime. The sea lay smooth around the land, and the waves just floated on her? like a flock of birds—like thousands of swans which sport on the Caspian Sea. The hills of Jegulia are green in the springtime; the sun floods the earth with gold. We rested; we became friendly; we seemed to be drawn to one another. It was gray and cold on the river, but on shore it was warm and fragrant. At eventide our Kyril—he was a harsh man and well on in years—stood up, took off his cap, and said: 'Well, children, I am no longer either chief or servant. Go away by yourselves, and I will go to the forest.' We were all startled. What was it that he was saying? We ought not to be left without some one responsible to be master. You see, people can't get on without a head, although it is only on the Volga, which is like a straight road. It is possible to lose one's way, for people alone are only like a senseless beast, and who cares what becomes of them? We were frightened; but he—he had made up his mind. I have no desire to go on living as your shepherd; I am going into the forest.' Some of us had half a mind to seize and keep him by force, but the others said, 'Wait!' Then the Tatar mate set up a cry: I shall go, too!' It was very bad luck. The Tatar had not been paid by the proprietors for the last two journeys; in fact, he had done half of a third one without pay, and that was a lot of money to lose in those days. We wrangled over the matter until night, and then seven of our company left us, leaving only sixteen or fourteen of us. That's what your forests do for people!"

"Did they go and join the brigands?"

"Maybe, or they may have become hermits. We did not inquire into the matter then."

Grandmother crossed herself.

"Holy Mother of God! When one thinks of people, one cannot help being sorry for them."

"We are all given the same powers of reason, you know, where the devil draws."

We entered the forest by a wet path between marshy hillocks and frail fir-trees. I thought that it must be lovely to go and live in the woods as Kyril of Poreshka had done. There are no chattering human creatures there, no fights or drunkenness. There I should be able to forget the repulsive greediness of grandfather and mother's sandy grave, all of which things hurt me, and weighed on my heart with an oppressive heaviness. When we came to a dry place grandmother said:

"We must have a snack now. Sit down."

In her basket there were rye bread, onions, cucumbers, salt, and curds wrapped in a cloth. Grandfather looked at all this in confusion and blinked.

"But I did not bring anything to eat, good Mother."

"There is enough for us all."

We sat down, leaning against the mast-like trunk of a fir-tree. The air was laden with a resinous odor; from the fields blew a gentle wind; the shave-grass waved to and fro. Grandmother plucked the herbs with her dark hands, and told me about the medicinal properties of St. John's-wort, betony, and rib-wort, and of the secret power of bracken. Grandfather hewed the fallen trees in pieces, and it was my part to carry the logs and put them all in one place; but I stole away unnoticed into the thicket after grandmother. She looked as if she were floating among the stout, hardy tree-trunks, and as if she were diving when she stooped to the earth, which was strewn with fir-cones. She talked to herself as she went along.

"We have come too early again. There will be hardly any mushrooms. Lord, how badly Thou lookest after the poor! Mushrooms are the treat of the poor."

I followed her silently and cautiously, not to attract her attention. I did not wish to interrupt her conversation with God, the herbs, and the frogs. But she saw me.

"Have you run away from grandfather?" And stooping to the black earth, splendidly decked in flowered vestments, she spoke of the time when God, enraged with mankind, flooded the earth with water and drowned all living creatures. "But the sweet Mother of God had beforehand collected the seeds of everything in a basket and hidden them, and when it was all over, she begged the sun: 'Dry the earth from end to end, and then will all the people sing thy praises.' The sun dried the earth, and she sowed the seed. God looked. Once more the earth was covered with living creatures, herbs, cattle, and people. 'Who has done this against My will?' He asked. And here she confessed, and as God had been sorry Himself to see the earth bare, He said to her, 'You have done well.'"

I liked this story, but it surprised me, and I said very gravely:

"But was that really so? The Mother of God was born long after the flood."

It was now grandmother's turn to be surprised.

"Who told you that?"

"It was written in the books at school."

This reassured her, and she gave me the advice:

"Put all that aside; forget it. It is only out of books; they are lies, those books." And laughing softly, gayly, "Think for a moment, silly! God was; and His Mother was not? Then of whom was He born?"

"I don't know."

"Good! You have learned enough to be able to say 'I don't know.'"

"The priest said that the Mother of God was born of Joachim and Anna."

Then grandmother was angry. She faced about, and looked sternly into my eyes.

"If that is what you think, I will slap you." But in the course of a few minutes she explained to me. "The Blessed Virgin always existed before any one and anything. Of Her was God born, and then—"

"And Christ, what about Him?"

Grandmother was silent, shutting her eyes in her confusion.

"And what about Christ? Eh? eh?"

I saw that I was victor, that I had caused the divine mysteries to be a snare to her, and it was not a pleasant thought.

We went farther and farther into the forest, into the dark-blue haze pierced by the golden rays of the sun. There was a peculiar murmur, dreamy, and arousing dreams. The crossbill chirped, the titmouses uttered their bell-like notes, the goldfinch piped, the cuckoo laughed, the jealous song of the chaffinch was heard unceasingly, and that strange bird, the hawfinch, sang pensively. Emerald-green frogs hopped around our feet; among the roots, guarding them, lay an adder, with his golden head raised; the squirrel cracked nuts, his furry tail peeping out among the fir-trees. The deeper one went into the forest, the more one saw.

Among the trunks of the fir-trees appeared transparent, aërial figures of gigantic people, which disappeared into the green mass through which the blue and silver sky shone. Under one's feet there was a splendid carpet of moss, sown with red bilberries, and moor-berries shone in the grass like drops of blood. Mushrooms tantalized one with their strong smell.

"Holy Virgin, bright earthly light," prayed grandmother, drawing a deep breath.

In the forest she was like the mistress of a house with all her family round her. She ambled along like a bear, seeing and praising everything and giving thanks. It seemed as if a certain warmth flowed from her through the forest, and when the moss, crushed by her feet, raised itself and stood up in her wake, it was peculiarly pleasing to me to see it.

As I walked along I thought how nice it would be to be a brigand; to rob the greedy and give the spoil to the poor; to make them all happy and satisfied, neither envying nor scolding one another, like bad-tempered curs. It was good to go thus to grandmother's God, to her Holy Virgin, and tell them all the truth about the bad lives people led, and how clumsily and offensively they buried one another in rubbishy sand. And there was so much that was unnecessarily repulsive and torturing on earth! If the Holy Virgin believed what I said, let her give me such an intelligence as would enable me to construct everything differently and improve the condition of things. It did not matter about my not being grown-up. Christ had been only a year older than I was when the wise men listened to Him.

Once in my preoccupation I fell into a deep pit, hurting my side and grazing the back of my neck. Sitting at the bottom of this pit in the cold mud, which was as sticky as resin, I realized with a feeling of intense humiliation that I should not be able to get out by myself, and I did not like the idea of frightening grandmother by calling out. However, I had to call her in the end. She soon dragged me out, and, crossing herself, said:

"The Lord be praised! It is a lucky thing that the bear's pit was empty. What would have happened to you if the master of the house had been lying there?" And she cried through her laughter.

Then she took me to the brook, washed my wounds and tied them up with strips of her chemise, after laying some healing leaves upon them, and took me into the railway signal-box, for I had not the strength to get all the way home.

And so it happened that almost every day I said to grandmother:

"Let us go into the forest."

She used to agree willingly, and thus we lived all the summer and far into the autumn, gathering herbs, berries, mushrooms, and nuts. Grandmother sold what we gathered, and by this means we were able to keep ourselves.

"Lazy beggars!" shrieked grandfather, though we never had food from him.

The forest called up a feeling of peace and solace in my heart, and in that feeling all my griefs were swallowed up, and all that was unpleasant was obliterated. During that time also my senses acquired a peculiar keenness, my hearing and sight became more acute, my memory more retentive, my storehouse of impressions widened.

And the more I saw of grandmother, the more she amazed me. I had been accustomed to regard her as a higher being, as the very best and the wisest creature upon the earth, and she was continually strengthening this conviction. For instance, one evening we had been gathering white mushrooms, and when we arrived at the edge of the forest on our way home grandmother sat down to rest while I went behind the tree to see if there were any more mushrooms. Suddenly I heard her voice, and this is what I saw: she was seated by the footpath calmly putting away the root of a mushroom, while near her, with his tongue hanging out, stood a gray, emaciated dog.

"You go away now! Go away!" said grandmother. "Go, and God be with you!"

Not long before that Valek had poisoned my dog, and I wanted very much to have this one. I ran to the path. The dog hunched himself strangely without moving his neck, and, looking at me with his green, hungry eyes, leaped into the forest, with his tail between his legs. His movements were not those of a dog, and when I whistled, he hurled himself wildly into the bushes.

"You saw?" said grandmother, smiling. "At first I was deceived. I thought it was a dog. I looked again and saw that I was mistaken. He had the fangs of a wolf, and the neck, too. I was quite frightened. 'Well,' I said, 'if you are a wolf, take yourself off!' It is a good thing that wolves are not dangerous in the summer."

She was never afraid in the forest, and always found her way home unerringly. By the smell of the grass she knew what kind of mushrooms ought to be found in such and such a place, what sort in another, and often examined me in the subject.

"What sort of trees do this and that fungus love? How do you distinguish the edible from the poisonous?"

By hardly visible scratches on the bark of a tree she showed me where the squirrel had made his home in a hollow, and I would climb up and ravage the nest of the animal, robbing him of his winter store of nuts. Sometimes there were as many as ten pounds in one nest. And one day, when I was thus engaged, a hunter planted twenty-seven shot in the right side of my body. Grandmother got eleven of them out with a needle, but the rest remained under my skin for many years, coming out by degrees.

Grandmother was pleased with me for bearing pain patiently.

"Brave boy!" she praised me. "He who is most patient will be the cleverest."

Whenever she had saved a little money from the sale of mushrooms and nuts, she used to lay it on window-sills as "secret alms," and she herself went about in rags and patches even on Sundays.

"You go about worse than a beggar. You put me to shame," grumbled grandfather.

"What does it matter to you? I am not your daughter. I am not looking for a husband."

Their quarrels had become more frequent.

"I am not more sinful than others," cried grandfather in injured tones, "but my punishment is greater."

Grandmother used to tease him.

"The devils know what every one is worth." And she would say to me privately: "My old man is frightened of devils. See how quickly he is aging! It is all from fear; eh, poor man!"

I had become very hardy during the summer, and quite savage through living in the forest, and I had lost all interest in the life of my contemporaries, such as Ludmilla. She seemed to me to be tiresomely sensible.

One day grandfather returned from the town very wet. It was autumn, and the rains were falling. Shaking himself on the threshold like a sparrow, he said triumphantly:

"Well, young rascal, you are going to a new situation to-morrow."

"Where now?" asked grandmother, angrily.

"To your sister Matrena, to her son."

"O Father, you have done very wrong."

"Hold your tongue, fool! They will make a man of him."

Grandmother let her head droop and said nothing more.

In the evening I told Ludmilla that I was going to live in the town.

"They are going to take me there soon," she informed me, thoughtfully. "Papa wants my leg to be taken off altogether. Without it I should get well."

She had grown very thin during the summer; the skin of her face had assumed a bluish tint, and her eyes had grown larger.

"Are you afraid?" I asked her.

"Yes," she replied, and wept silently.

I had no means of consoling her, for I was frightened myself at the prospect of life in town. We sat for a long time in painful silence, pressed close against each other. If it had been summer, I should have asked grandmother to come begging with me, as she had done when she was a girl. We might have taken Ludmilla with us; I could have drawn her along in a little cart. But it was autumn. A damp wind blew up the streets, the sky was heavy with rain-clouds, the earth frowned. It had begun to look dirty and unhappy.

CHAPTER IV

Once more I was in the town, in a two-storied white house which reminded me of a coffin meant to hold a lot of people. It was a new house, but it looked as if were in ill health, and was bloated like a beggar who has suddenly become rich and has overeaten. It stood sidewise to the street, and had eight windows to each floor, but where the face of the house ought to have been there were only four windows. The lower windows looked on a narrow passage and on the yard, and the upper windows on the laundress's little house and the causeway.

No street, as I understood the term, existed. In front of the house a dirty causeway ran in two directions, cut in two by a narrow dike. To the left, it extended to the House of Detention, and was heaped with rubbish and logs, and at the bottom stood a thick pool of dark-green filth. On the right, at the end of the causeway, the slimy Xvyexdin Pond stagnated. The middle of the causeway was exactly opposite the house, and half of it was strewn with filth and overgrown with nettles and horse sorrel, while in the other half the priest Doriedont Pokrovski had planted a garden in which was a summer-house of thin lathes painted red. If one threw stones at it, the lathes split with a crackling sound.

The place was intolerably depressing and shamelessly dirty. The autumn had ruthlessly broken up the filthy, rotten earth, changing it into a sort of red resin which clung to one's feet tenaciously. I had never seen so much dirt in so small a space before, and after being accustomed to the cleanliness of the fields and forests, this corner of the town aroused my disgust.

Beyond the causeway stretched gray, broken-down fences, and in the distance I recognized the little house in which I had lived when I was shop-boy. The nearness of that house depressed me still more. I had known my master before; he and his brother used to be among mother's visitors. His brother it was who had sung so comically:

"Andrei—papa, Andrei—papa—"

They were not changed. The elder, with a hook nose and long hair, was pleasant in manner and seemed to be kind; the younger, Victor, had the same horse-like face and the same freckles. Their mother, grandmother's sister, was very cross and fault-finding. The elder son was married. His wife was a splendid creature, white like bread made from Indian corn, with very large, dark eyes. She said to me twice during the first day:

"I gave your mother a silk cloak trimmed with jet."

Somehow I did not want to believe that she had given, and that my mother had accepted, a present. When she reminded me of it again, I said:

"You gave it to her, and that is the end of the matter; there is nothing to boast about."

She started away from me.

"Wh-a-at? To whom are you speaking?"

Her face came out in red blotches, her eyes rolled, and she called her husband.

He came into the kitchen, with his compasses in his hand and a pencil behind his ear, listened to what his wife had to say, and then said to me:

"You must speak properly to her and to us all. There must be no insolence." Then he said to his wife, impatiently, "Don't disturb me with your nonsense!"

"What do you mean—nonsense? If your relatives—"

"The devil take my relatives!" cried the master, rushing away.

I myself was not pleased to think that they were relatives of grandmother. Experience had taught me that relatives behave worse to one another than do strangers. Their gossip is more spiteful, since they know more of the bad and ridiculous sides of one another than strangers, and they fall out and fight more often.

I liked my master. He used to shake back his hair with a graceful movement, and tuck it behind his ears, and he reminded me somehow of "Good Business." He often laughed merrily; his gray eyes looked kindly upon me, and funny wrinkles played divertingly about his aquiline nose.

"You have abused each other long enough, wild fowl," he would say to his mother and his wife, showing his small, closely set teeth in a gentle smile.

The mother-in-law and the daughter-in-law abused each other all day. I was surprised to see how swiftly and easily they plunged into a quarrel. The first thing in the morning, with their hair unbrushed and their clothes unfastened, they would rush about the rooms as if the house were on fire, and they fussed about all day, only pausing to take breath in the dining-room at dinner, tea, or supper. They ate and drank till they could eat and drink no more, and at dinner they talked about the food and disputed lethargically, preparing for a big quarrel. No matter what it was that the mother-in-law had prepared, the daughter-in-law was sure to say:

"My mother did not cook it this way."

"Well, if that is so, she did it badly, that's all." "On the contrary, she did it better."

"Well, you had better go back to your mother."

"I am mistress here."

"And who am I?"

Here the master would intervene.

"That will do, wild fowl! What is the matter with you? Are you mad?"

For some inexplicable reason everything about that house was peculiar and mirth-provoking. The way from the kitchen to the dining-room lay through a small closet, the only one in the house, through which they carried the samovar and the food into the dining-room. It was the cause of merry witticisms and often of laughable misunderstandings. I slept in the kitchen, between that door and the one leading to the stairs. My head was hot from the heat of the cooking-stove, but the draft from the stairs blew on my feet. When I retired to bed, I used to take all the mats off the floor and wrap them round my feet.

The large reception-room, with its two pier-glasses, its pictures in gilt frames, its pair of card-tables, and its dozen Vienna chairs, was a dreary, depressing place. The small drawing-room was simply packed with a medley of soft furniture, with wedding presents, silver articles, and a tea-service. It was adorned with three lamps, one larger than the other two.

In the dark, windowless bedroom, in addition to the wide bed, there were trunks and cupboards from which came the odors of leaf tobacco and Persian camomile. These three rooms were always unoccupied, while the entire household squeezed itself into the little dining-room. Directly after breakfast, at eight o'clock, the master and his brother moved the table, and, laying sheets of white paper upon it, with cases, pencils, and saucers containing Indian ink, set to work, one at each end of the table. The table was shaky, and took up nearly the whole of the room, and when the mistress and the nurse came out of the nursery they had to brush past the corners.

"Don't come fussing about here!" Victor would cry.

"Vassia, please tell him not to shout at me," the mistress would say to her husband in an offended tone.

"All right; but don't come and shake the table," her husband would reply peaceably.

"I am stout, and the room is so small."

"Well, we will go and work in the large drawingroom."

But at that she cried indignantly:

"Lord! why on earth should you work in the large drawing-room?"

At the door of the closet appeared the angry face of Matrena Ivanovna, flushed with the heat of the stove. She called out:

"You see how it is, Vassia? She knows that you are working, and yet she can't be satisfied with the other four rooms."

Victor laughed maliciously, but the master said: "That will do!"

And the daughter-in-law, with a venomously eloquent gesture, sank into a chair and groaned:

"I am dying! I am dying!"

"Don't hinder my work, the devil take you!" roared the master, turning pale with the exertion. "This is nothing better than a mad-house. Here am I breaking my back to feed you. Oh, you wild fowl!"

At first these quarrels used to alarm me, especially when the mistress, seizing a table knife, rushed into the closet, and, shutting both the doors, began to shriek like a mad thing. For a minute the house was quiet, then the master, having tried to force the door, stooped down, and called out to me:

"Climb up on my back and unfasten the hook."

I swiftly jumped on his back, and broke the pane of glass over the door; but when I bent down, the mistress hit me over the head with the blade of the knife. However, I succeeded in opening the door, and the master, dragging his wife into the dining-room after a struggle, took the knife away from her. As I sat in the kitchen rubbing my bruised head, I soon came to the conclusion that I had suffered for nothing. The knife was so blunt that it would hardly cut a piece of bread, and it would certainly never have made an incision in any one's skin. Besides, there had been no need for me to climb on the master's back. I could have broken the glass by standing on a chair, and in any case it would have been easier for a grown person to have unfastened the hook, since his arms would have been longer. After that episode the quarrels in the house ceased to alarm me.

The brothers used to sing in the church choir; sometimes they used to sing softly over their work. The elder would begin in a baritone:

> "The ring, which was the maiden's heart,
> I cast from me into the sea."

And the younger would join with his tenor:

> "And I with that very ring
> Her earthly joy did ruin."

The mistress would murmur from the nursery:

"Have you gone out of your minds? Baby is asleep," or: "How can you, Vassia, a married man, be singing about girls? Besides, the bell will ring for vespers in a minute."

"What's the matter now? We are only singing a church tune."

But the mistress intimated that it was out of place to sing church tunes here, there, and everywhere. Besides, and she pointed eloquently to the little door.

"We shall have to change our quarters, or the devil knows what will become of us," said the master.

He said just as often that he must get another table, and he said it for three years in succession.

When I listened to my employers talking about people, I was always reminded of the boot-shop. They used to talk in the same way there. It was evident to me that my present masters also thought themselves better than any one in the town. They knew the rules of correct conduct to the minutest detail, and, guided by these rules, which were not at all clear to me, they judged others pitilessly and unsparingly. This sitting in judgment aroused in me a ferocious resentment and anger against the laws of my employers, and the breaking of those laws became a source of pleasure to me.

I had a lot of work to do. I fulfilled all the duties of a housemaid, washed the kitchen over on Wednesday, cleaning the samovar and all the copper vessels, and on Saturday cleaned the floor of the rest of the house and both staircases. I had to chop and bring in the wood for the stoves, wash up, prepare vegetables for cooking, and go marketing with the mistress, carrying her basket of purchases after her, besides running errands to the shops and to the chemist.

My real mistress, grandmother's sister, a noisy, indomitable, implacably fierce old woman, rose early at six o'clock, and after washing herself in a hurry, knelt before the icon with only her chemise on, and complained long to God about her life, her children, and her daughter-in-law.

"Lord," she would exclaim, with tears in her voice, pressing her two first fingers and her thumbs against her forehead—"Lord, I ask nothing, I want nothing; only give me rest and peace, Lord, by Thy power!"

Her sobs used to wake me up, and, half asleep, I used to peep from under the blanket, and listen with terror to her passionate prayers. The autumn morning looked dimly in at the kitchen window through panes washed by the rain. On the floor in the cold twilight her gray figure swayed from side to side; she waved her arms alarmingly. Her thin, light hair fell from her small head upon her neck and shoulders from under the swathing handkerchief, which kept slipping off. She would replace it angrily with her left hand, muttering "Oh, bother you!"

Striking her forehead with force, beating her breast and her shoulders, she would wail:

"And my daughter-in-law—punish her, O Lord, on my account! Make her pay for all that she has made me suffer! And open the eyes of my son—open his eyes and Victor's! Lord, help Victor; be merciful to him!"

Victorushka also slept in the kitchen, and, hearing the groans of his mother, would cry in a sleepy voice:

"Mamasha, you are funning down the young wife again. It is really dreadful."

"All right; go to sleep," the old woman would whisper guiltily. She would be silent for a minute perhaps, and then she would begin to murmur vindictively, "May their bones be broken, and may there be no shelter for them on earth, Lord!"

Even grandfather had never prayed so terribly.

When she had said her prayers she used to wake me up.

"Wake up! You will never get on if you do not get up early. Get the samovar ready! Bring the wood in! Did n't you get the sticks ready over night?"

I tried to be quick in order to escape hearing the frothy whisper of the old woman, but it was impossible to please her. She went about the kitchen like a winter snow-storm, hissing:

"Not so much noise, you little devil! Wake Victorushka up, and I will give you something! Now run along to the shop!"

On week-days I used to buy two pounds of wheaten bread and two copecks' worth of rolls for the young mistress. When I brought it in, the women would look at it suspiciously, and, weighing it in the palms of their hands, would ask;

"Was n't there a make-weight? No? Open your mouth!" And then they would cry triumphantly: "He has gobbled up the make-weight; here are the crumbs in his teeth! You see, Vassia?"

I worked willingly enough. It pleased me to abolish dirt from the house, to wash the floors, to clean the copper vessels, the warm-holes, and the door-handles. More than once I heard the women remark about me in their peaceful moments:

"He is zealous."

"And clean."

"Only he is very impudent."

"Well, Mother, who has educated him?"

They both tried to educate me to respect them, but I regarded them as half witted. I did not like them; I would not obey them, and I used to answer them back. The young mistress must have noticed what a bad effect their speeches had upon me, for she said with increasing frequency:

"You ought to remember from what a poor family you have been taken. I gave your mother a silk cloak trimmed with jet."

One day I said to her:

"Do you want me to skin myself to pay for the cloak?"

"Good gracious!" she cried in a tone of alarm, "this boy is capable of setting fire to the place!"

I was extremely surprised. Why did she say that? They both complained to the master about me on this occasion, and he said to me sternly:

"Now, my boy, you had better look out." But one day he said coolly to his wife and his mother: "You are a nice pair! You ride the boy as if he were a gelding! Any other boy would have run away long ago if you had not worked him to death first."

This made the women so angry that they wept, and his wife stamped her foot, crying:

"How can you speak like that before him, you longhaired fool? What can I do with him after this? And in my state of health, too!"

The mother cried sadly:

"May God forgive you, Vassia Vassilich! Only, mark my words, you are spoiling that boy."

When they had gone away raging, the master said to me sternly:

"You see, you little devil, what row's you cause! I shall take you back to your grandfather, and you can be a rag-picker again."

This insult was more than I could bear, and I said: "I had a better life as a rag-picker than I have with you. You took me as a pupil, and what have you taught me? To empty the dish-water!"

He took me by the hair, but not roughly, and looked into my eyes, saying in a tone of astonishment:

"I see you are rebellious. That, my lad, won't suit me. N-o-o."

I thought that I should be sent away for this, but a few days later he came into the kitchen with a roll of thick paper, a pencil, a square, and a ruler in his hands.

"When you have finished cleaning the knives, draw this."

On one sheet of paper was outlined the façade of a two-storied house, with many windows and absurd decorations.

"Here are compasses for you. Place dots on the paper where the ends of the lines come, and then draw from point to point with a ruler, lengthwise first—that will be horizontal—and then across—that will be vertical. Now get on with it."

I was delighted to have some clean work to do, but I gazed at the paper and the instruments with reverent fear, for I understood nothing about them. However, after washing my hands, I sat down to learn. I drew all the horizontal lines on the sheet and compared them. They were quite good, although three seemed superfluous. I drew the vertical lines, and observed with astonishment that the face of the house was absurdly disfigured. The windows had crossed over to the partition wall, and one came out behind the wall and hung in mid-air. The front steps were raised in the air to the height of the second floor; a cornice appeared in the middle of the roof; and a dormer-window on the chimney.

For a long time, hardly able to restrain my tears, I gazed at those miracles of inaccuracy, trying to make out how they had occurred; and not being able to arrive at any conclusion, I decided to rectify the mistakes by the aid of fancy. I drew upon the façade of the house, upon the cornices, and the edge of the roof, crows, doves, and sparrows, and on the ground in front of the windows, people with crooked legs, under umbrellas which did not quite hide their deformities. Then I drew slanting lines across the whole, and took my work to my master.

He raised his eyebrows, ruffled his hair, and gruffly inquired:

"What is all this about?"

"That is rain coming down," I explained. "When it rains, the house looks crooked, because the rain itself is always crooked. The birds—you see, these are all birds—are taking shelter. They always do that when it rains. And these people are running home. There—that is a lady who has fallen down, and that is a peddler with lemons to sell."

"I am much obliged to you," said my master, and bending over the table till his hair swept the paper, he burst out laughing as he cried:

"Och! you deserve to be torn up and thrown away yourself, you wild sparrow!"

The mistress came in, and having looked at my work, said to her husband:

"Beat him!"

But the master said peaceably:

"That's all right; I myself did not begin any better."

Obliterating the spoiled house with a red pencil, he gave me some paper.

"Try once more."

The second copy came out better, except that a window appeared in place of the front door. But I did not like to think that the house was empty, so I filled it with all sorts of inmates. At the windows sat ladies with fans in their hands, and cavaliers with cigarettes. One of these, a non-smoker, was making a "long nose" at all the others. A cabman stood on the steps, and near him lay a dog.

"Why, you have been scribbling over it again!" the master exclaimed angrily.

I explained to him that a house without inhabitants was a dull place, but he only scolded me.

"To the devil with all this foolery! If you want to learn, learn! But this is rubbish!"

When at length I learned to make a copy of the façade which resembled the original he was pleased.

"There, you see what you can do! Now, if you choose, we shall soon get on," and he gave me a lesson.

"Make a plan of this house, showing the arrangement of the rooms, the places of the doors and windows, and the rest. I shall not show you how. You must do it by yourself."

I went to the kitchen and debated. How was I to do it? But at this point my studies in the art of drawing came to a standstill.

The old mistress came to me and said spitefully:

"So you want to draw?"

Seizing me by the hair, she bumped my head on the table so hard that my nose and lips were bruised. Then she darted upon and tore up the paper, swept the instruments from the table, and with her hands on her hips said triumphantly:

"That was more than I could stand. Is an outsider to do the work while his only brother, his own flesh and blood, goes elsewhere?"

The master came running in, his wife rushed after him, and a wild scene began. All three flew at one another, spitting and howling, and it ended in the women weeping, and the master saying to me:

"You will have to give up the idea for a time, and not learn. You can see for yourself what comes of it!"

I pitied him. He was so crushed, so defenseless, and quite deafened by the shrieks of the women. I had realized before that the old woman did not like my studying, for she used to hinder me purposely, so I always asked her before I sat down to my drawing:

"There is nothing for me to do?"

She would answer frowningly:

"When there is I will tell you," and in a few minutes she would send me on some errand, or she would say: "How beautifully you cleaned the staircase to-day! The corners are full of dirt and dust. Go and sweep them!"

I would go and look, but there was never any dust. "Do you dare to argue with me?" she would cry. One day she upset *kvass* all over my drawings, and at another time she spilt oil from the image lamp over them. She played tricks on me like a young girl, with childish artfulness, and with childish ignorance trying to conceal her artfulness. Never before or since have I met a person who was so soon put into a temper and for such trivial reasons, nor any one so passionately fond of complaining about every one and everything. People, as a rule, are given to complaining, but she did it with a peculiar delight, as if she were singing a song.

Her love for her son was like an insanity. It amused me, but at the same time it frightened me by what I can only describe as its furious intensity. Sometimes, after her morning prayers, she would stand by the stove, with her elbows resting on the mantel-board, and would whisper hotly:

"My luck! My idol! My little drop of hot blood, like a jewel! Light as an angel! He sleeps. Sleep on, child! Clothe thy soul with happy dreams! Dream to thyself a bride, beautiful above all others, a princess and an heiress, the daughter of a merchant! As for your enemies, may they perish as soon as they are born! And your friends, may they live for a hundred years, and may the girls run after you like ducks after the drake!"

All this was inexpressibly ludicrous to me. Coarse, lazy Victor was like a woodpecker, with a woodpecker's large, mottled nose, and the same stubborn and dull nature. Sometimes his mother's whispers awoke him, and he muttered sleepily:

"Go to the devil, Mamasha! What do you mean by snorting right in my face? You make life unbearable."

Sometimes she stole away humbly, laughing:

"Well, go to sleep! Go to sleep, saucy fellow!"

But sometimes her legs seemed to give way, her feet came down heavily on the edge of the stove, and she opened her mouth and panted loudly, as if her tongue were on fire, gurgling out caustic words.

"So-o? It's your mother you are sending to the devil. Ach! you! My shame! Accursed heart-sore! The devil must have set himself in my heart to ruin you from birth!"

She uttered obscene words, words of the drunken streets. It was painful to listen to her. She slept little, fitfully jumping down from the stove sometimes several times in the night, and coming over to the couch to wake me.

"What is it?"

"Be quiet!" she would whisper, crossing herself and looking at something in the darkness. "O Lord, Elias the prophet, great martyr Varvara, save me from sudden death!"

She lighted the candle with a trembling hand. Her round, nosy face was swollen tensely; her gray eyes, blinking alarmingly, gazed fixedly at the surroundings, which looked different in the twilight. The kitchen, which was large, but encumbered with cupboards and trunks, looked small by night. There the moonbeams lived quietly; the flame of the lamp burning before the icon quivered; the knives gleamed like icicles on the walls; on the floor the black frying-pans looked like faces without eyes.

The old woman would clamber down cautiously from the stove, as if she were stepping into the water from a river-bank, and, slithering along with her bare feet, went into the corner, where over the wash-stand hung a ewer that reminded me of a severed head. There was also a pitcher of water standing there. Choking and panting, she drank the water, and then looked out of the window through the pale-blue pattern of hoar-frost on the panes.

"Have mercy on me, O God! have mercy on me!" she prayed in a whisper. Then putting out the candle, she fell on her knees, and whispered in an aggrieved tone: "Who loves me, Lord? To whom am I necessary?"

Climbing back on the stove, and opening the little door of the chimney, she tried to feel if the flue-plate lay straight, soiling her hands with soot, and fell asleep at that precise moment, just as if she had been struck by an invisible hand. When I felt resentful toward her I used to think what a pity it was that she had not married grandfather. She would have led him a life!

She often made me very miserable, but there were days when her puffy face became sad, her eyes were suffused with tears, and she said very touchingly:

"Do you think that I have an easy time? I brought children into the world, reared them, set them on their feet, and for what? To live with them and be their general servant. Do you think that is sweet to me? My son has brought a strange woman and new blood into the family. Is it nice for me? Well?"

"No, it is not," I said frankly.

"Aha! there you are, you see!" And she began to talk shamelessly about her daughter-in-law. "Once I went with her to the bath and saw her. Do you think she has anything to flatter herself about? Can she be called beautiful?"

She always spoke objectionably about the relations of husband and wife. At first her speeches aroused my disgust, but I soon accustomed myself to listen to them with attention and with great interest, feeling that there was something painfully true about them.

"Woman is strength; she deceived God Himself. That is so," she hissed, striking her hand on the table. "Through Eve are we all condemned to hell. What do you think of that?"

On the subject of woman's power she could talk endlessly, and it always seemed as if she were trying to frighten some one in these conversations. I particularly remembered that "Eve deceived God."

Overlooking our yard was the wing of a large building, and of the eight flats comprised in it, four were occupied by officers, and the fifth by the regimental chaplain. The yard was always full of officers' servants and orderlies, after whom ran laundresses, housemaids, and cooks. Dramas and romances were being carried on in all the kitchens, accompanied by tears, quarrels, and fights. The soldiers quarreled among themselves and with the landlord's workmen; they used to beat the women.

The yard was a seething pot of what is called vice, immorality, the wild, untamable appetites of healthy lads. This life, which brought out all the cruel sensuality, the thoughtless tyranny, the obscene boastfulness of the conqueror, was criticized in every detail by my employers at dinner, tea, and supper. The old woman knew all the stories of the yard, and told them with gusto, rejoicing in the misfortunes of others. The younger woman listened to these tales in silence, smiling with her swollen lips. Victor used to burst out laughing, but the master would frown and say:

"That will do, Mamasha!"

"Good Lord! I mustn't speak now, I suppose!" the story-teller complained; but Victor encouraged her.

"Go on, Mother! What is there to hinder you? We are all your own people, after all."

I could never understand why one should talk shamelessly before one's own people.

The elder son bore himself toward his mother with contemptuous pity, and avoided being alone with her, for if that happened, she would surely overwhelm him with complaints against his wife, and would never fail to ask him for money. He would hastily press into her hand a ruble or so or several pieces of small silver.

"It is not right, Mother; take the money. I do not grudge it to you, but it is unjust."

"But I want it for beggars, for candles when I go to church."

"Now, where will you find beggars there? You will end by spoiling Victor."

"You don't love your brother. It is a great sin on your part."

He would go out, waving her away.

Victor's manner to his mother was coarse and derisive. He was very greedy, and he was always hungry. On Sundays his mother used to bake custards, and she always hid a few of them in a vessel under the couch on which I slept. When Victor left the dinner-table he would get them out and grumble:

"Couldn't you have saved a few more, you old' fool?"

"Make haste and eat them before any one sees you."

"I will tell how you steal cakes for me behind their backs."

Once I took out the vessel and ate two custards, for which Victor nearly killed me. He disliked me as heartily as I disliked him. He used to jeer at me and make me clean his boots about three times a day, and when I slept in the loft, he used to push up the trapdoor and spit in the crevice, trying to aim at my head.

It may be that in imitation of his brother, who often said "wild fowl," Victor also needed to use some catchwords, but his were all senseless and particularly absurd.

"Mamasha! Left wheel! where are my socks?"

And he used to follow me about with stupid questions.

"Alesha, answer me. Why do we write 'sinenki' and pronounce it 'phiniki'? Why do we say 'Kolokola' and not 'Okolokola'? Why do we say 'K'derevou' and not 'gdye plachou'?"

I did not like the way any of them spoke, and having been educated in the beautiful tongue which grandmother and grandfather spoke, I could not understand at first how words that had no sort of connection came to be coupled together, such as "terribly funny," "I am dying to eat," "awfully happy." It seemed to me that what was funny could not be terrible, that to be happy could not be awful, and that people did not die for something to eat.

"Can one say that?" I used to ask them; but they jeered at me:

"I say, what a teacher! Do you want your ears plucked?"

But to talk of "plucking" ears also appeared incorrect to me. One could "pluck" grass and flowers and nuts, but not ears. They tried to prove to me that ears could be plucked, but they did not convince me, and I said triumphantly:

"Anyhow, you have not plucked my ears."

All around me I saw much cruel insolence, filthy shamelessness. It was far worse here than in the Kunavin streets, which were full of "houses of resort" and "street-walkers." Beneath the filth and brutality in Kunavin there was a something which made itself felt, and which seemed to explain it all—a strenuous, half-starved existence and hard work. But here they were overfed and led easy lives, and the work went on its way without fuss or worry. A corrosive, fretting weariness brooded over all.

My life was hard enough, anyhow, but I felt it still harder when grandmother came to see me. She would appear from the black flight of steps, enter the kitchen, cross herself before the icon, and then bow low to her younger sister. That bow bent me down like a heavy weight, and seemed to smother me.

"Ah, Akulina, is it you?" was my mistress's cold and negligent greeting to grandmother.

I should not have recognized grandmother. Her lips modestly compressed, her face changed out of knowledge, she set herself quietly on a bench near the door, keeping silence like a guilty creature, except when she answered her sister softly and submissively. This was torture to me, and I used to say angrily: "What are you sitting there for?"

Winking at me kindly, she replied:

"You be quiet. You are not master here.".

"He is always meddling in matters which do not concern him, however we beat him or scold him," and the mistress was launched on her complaints.

She often asked her sister spitefully:

"Well, Akulina, so you are living like a beggar?"

"That is a misfortune."

"It is no misfortune where there is no shame."

"They say that Christ also lived on charity."

"Blockheads say so, and heretics, and you, old fool, listen to them! Christ was no beggar, but the Son of God. He will come, it is said, in glory, to judge the quick and dead—and dead, mind you. You will not be able to hide yourself from Him, Matushka, although you may be burned to ashes. He is punishing you and Vassili now for your pride, and on my account, because I asked help from you when you were rich."

"And I helped you as much as it was in my power to do," answered grandmother, calmly, "and God will pay us back, you know."

"It was little enough you did, little enough."

Grandmother was bored and worried by her sister's untiring tongue. I listened to her squeaky voice and wondered how grandmother could put up with it. In that moment I did not love her.

The young mistress came out of her room and nodded affably to grandmother.

"Come into the dining-room. It is all right; come along!"

The master would receive grandmother joyfully.

"Ah, Akulina, wisest of all, how are you? Is old man Kashirin still alive?"

And grandmother would give him her most cordial smile.

"Are you still working your hardest?"

"Yes; always working, like a convict."

Grandmother conversed with him affectionately and well, but in the tone of a senior. Sometimes he called my mother to mind.

"Ye-es, Varvara Vassilievna. What a woman! A heroine, eh?"

His wife turned to grandmother and put in:

"Do you remember my giving her that cloak—black silk trimmed with jet?"

"Of course I do."

"It was quite a good one."

"Ye-es," muttered the master, "a cloak, a palm; and life is a trickster."[1]

[1] A play on the words "*tal'ma,* cloak; *pal'ma,* palm; *shelma,* trickster.

"What are you talking about?" asked his wife, suspiciously.

"I? Oh, nothing in particular. Happy days and good people soon pass away."

"I don't know what is the matter with you," said my mistress, uneasily.

Then grandmother was taken to see the new baby, and while I was clearing away the dirty cups and saucers from the table the master said to me:

"She is a good old woman, that grandmother of yours."

I was deeply grateful to him for those words, and when I was alone with grandmother, I said to her, with a pain in my heart:

"Why do you come here? Why? Can't you see how they—".

"Ach, Olesha, I see everything," she replied, looking at me with a kind smile on her wonderful face, and I felt conscience-stricken. Why, of course she saw everything and knew everything, even what was going on in my soul at that moment. Looking round carefully to see that no one was coming, she embraced me, saying feelingly:

"I would not come here if it were not for you. What are they to me? As a matter of fact, grandfather is ill, and I am tired with looking after him. I have not been able to do any work, so I have no money, and my son Mikhail has turned Sascha out. I have him now to give food and drink, too. They promised to give you six rubles a month, and I don't suppose you have had a ruble from them, and you have been here nearly half a year." Then she whispered in my ear: "They say they have to lecture you, scold you, they say that you do not obey; but, dear heart, stay with them. Be patient for two short years while you grow strong. You will be patient, yes?"

I promised. It was very difficult. That life oppressed me; it was a threadbare, depressing existence. The only excitement was about food, and I lived as in a dream. Sometimes I thought that I would have to run away, but the accursed winter had set in. Snow-storms raged by night, the wind rushed over the top of the house, and the stanchions cracked with the pressure of the frost. Whither could I run away?

*

They would not let me go out, and in truth it was no weather for walking. The short winter day, full of the bustle of housework, passed with elusive swiftness. But they made me go to church, on Saturday to vespers and on Sunday to high mass.

I liked being in church. Standing somewhere in a corner where there was more room and where it was darker, I loved to gaze from a distance at the iconastasis, which looked as if it were swimming in the candlelight flowing in rich, broad streams over the floor of the reading-desk. The dark figures of the icons moved gently, the gold embroidery on the vestments of the priests quivered joyfully, the candle flames burned in the dark-blue atmosphere like golden bees, and the heads of the women and children looked like flowers. All the surroundings seemed to blend harmoniously with the singing the choir. Everything seemed to be imbued with the weird spirit of legends. The church seemed to oscillate like a cradle, rocking in pitch-black space.

Sometimes I imagined that the church was sunk deep in a lake in which it lived, concealed, a life peculiar to itself, quite different from any other form of life. I have no doubt now that this idea had its source in grandmother's stories of the town of Kitej, and I often found myself dreamily swaying, keeping time, as it were, with the movement around me. Lulled into somnolence by the singing of the choir, the murmur of prayers, the breath of the congregation, I concentrated myself upon the melodious, melancholy story:

> "They are closing upon us, the accursed Tatars.
> Yes, these unclean beasts are closing in upon Kite;
> The glorious; yea, at the holy hour of matins.
> O Lord, our God!
> Holy Mother of God!
> Save Thy servants
> To sing their morning praises,
> To listen to the holy chants!
> *Oi*, let not the Tatars
> Jeer at holy church;
> Let them not put to shame
> Our women and maidens;
> Seize the little maids to be their toys,
> And the old men to be put to a cruel death!
> And the God of Sabaoth heard,
> The Holy Mother heard,
> These human sighs,
> These Christians' plaints.
> And He said, the Lord of Sabaoth,
> To the Holy Angel Michael,
> 'Go thou, Michael,
> Make the earth shake under Kitej;

> Let Kite; sink into the lake!'
> And there to this day
> The people do pray,
> Never resting, and never weary
> From matins to vespers,
> Through all the holy offices,
> Forever and evermore!"

At that time my head was full of grandmother's poetry, as full as a beehive of honey. I used even to think in verse.

I did not pray in church. I felt ashamed to utter the angry prayers and psalms of lamentation of grandfather's God in the presence of grandmother's God, Who, I felt sure, could take no more pleasure in them than I did myself, for the simple reason that they were all printed in books, and of course He knew them all by heart, as did all people of education. And this is why, when my heart was oppressed by a gentle grief or irritated by the petty grievances of every day, I tried to make up prayers for myself. And when I began to think about my uncongenial work, the words seemed to form themselves into a complaint without any effort on my part:

> "Lord, Lord! I am very miserable!
> Oh, let me grow up quickly,
> For this life I can't endure.
> O Lord, forgive!
> From my studies I get no benefit,
> For that devil's puppet, Granny Matrena,
> Howls at me like a wolf,
> And my life is very bitter!"

To this day I can remember some of these prayers. The workings of the brain in childhood leave a very deep impression; often they influence one's whole life.

I liked being in church; I could rest there as I rested in the forests and fields. My small heart, which was already familiar with grief and soiled by the mire of a coarse life, laved itself in hazy, ardent dreams. But I went to church only during the hard frosts, or when a snow-storm swept wildly up the streets, when it seemed as if the very sky were frozen, and the wind swept across it with a cloud of snow, and the earth lay frozen under the snow-drifts as if it would never live again.

When the nights were milder I used to like to wander through the streets of the town, creeping along by all the darkest corners. Sometimes I seemed to walk as if I had wings, flying along like the moon in the sky. My shadow crept in front of me, extinguishing the sparkles of light in the snow, bobbing up and down comically. The night watchman patrolled the streets, rattle in hand, clothed in a heavy sheepskin, his dog at his side. Vague outlines of people came out of yards and flitted along the streets, and the dog gave chase. Sometimes I met gay young ladies with their escorts. I had an idea that they also were playing truant from vespers.

Sometimes through a lighted *fortochka*[1] there came a peculiar smell, faint, unfamiliar, suggestive of a kind of life of which I was ignorant. I used to stand under the windows and inhale it, trying to guess what it was to live like the people in such a house lived. It was the hour of vespers, and yet they were singing merrily, laughing, and playing on a sort of guitar. The deep, stringy sound flowed through the *fortochka*.

[1] A small square of glass in the double window which is set on hinges and serves as a ventilator.

Of special interest to me were the one-storied, dwarfed houses at the corners of the deserted streets, Tikhonovski and Martinovski. I stood there on a moonlight night in mid-Lent and listened to the weird sounds—it sounded as if some one were singing loudly with his mouth closed—which floated out through the *fortochka* together with a warm steam. The words were indistinguishable, but the song seemed to be familiar and intelligible to me; but when I listened to that, I could not hear the stringy sound which languidly interrupted the flow of song. I sat on the curbstone thinking what a wonderful melody was being played on some sort of insupportable violin—insupportable because it hurt me to listen to it. Sometimes they sang so loudly that the whole house seemed to shake, and the panes of the windows rattled. Like tears, drops fell from the roof, and from my eyes also.

The night watchman had come close to me without my being aware of it, and, pushing me off the curbstone, said:

"What are you stuck here for?"

"The music," I explained.

"A likely tale! Be off now!"

I ran quickly round the houses and returned to my place under the window, but they were not playing now. From the *fortochka* proceeded sounds of revelry, and it was so unlike the sad music that I thought I must be dreaming. I got into the habit of running to this house every Saturday, but only once, and that was in the spring, did I hear the violoncello again, and then it played without a break till midnight. When I reached home I got a thrashing.

These walks at night beneath the winter sky through the deserted streets of the town enriched me greatly. I purposely chose streets far removed from the center, where there were many lamps, and friends of my master who might have recognized me. Then he would find out how I played truant from vespers. No "drunkards," "street-walkers," or policemen interfered with me in the more remote streets, and I could see into the rooms of the lower floors if the windows were not frozen over or curtained.

Many and diverse were the pictures which I saw through those windows. I saw people praying, kissing, quarreling, playing cards, talking busily and soundlessly the while. It was a cheap panoramic show representing a dumb, fish-like life.

I saw in one basement room two women, a young one and another who was her senior, seated at a table; opposite them sat a school-boy reading to them. The younger woman listened with puckered brows, leaning back in her chair; but the elder, who was thin, with luxuriant hair, suddenly covered her face with her hands, and her shoulders heaved. The school-boy threw down the book, and when the younger woman had sprung to her feet and gone away, he fell on his knees before the woman with the lovely hair and began to kiss her hands.

Through another window I saw a large, bearded man with a woman in a red blouse sitting on his knee. He was rocking her as if she had been a baby, and was evidently singing something, opening his mouth wide and rolling his eyes. The woman was shaking with laughter, throwing herself backward and swinging her feet. He made her sit up straight again, and again began to sing, and again she burst out laughing. I gazed at them for a long time, and went away only when I realized that they meant to keep up their merriment all night.

There were many pictures of this kind which will always remain in my memory, and often I was so attracted by them that I was late in returning home. This aroused the suspicions of my employers, who asked me:

"What church did you go to? Who was the officiating priest?"

They knew all the priests of the town; they knew what gospel would be read, in fact, they knew everything. It was easy for them to catch me in a lie.

Both women worshiped the wrathful God of my grandfather—the God Who demanded that we should approach Him in fear. His name was ever on their lips; even in their quarrels they threatened one another:

"Wait! God will punish you! He will plague you for this! Just wait!"

On the Sunday in the first week of Lent, the old woman cooked some butters and burned them all. Flushed with the heat of the stove, she cried angrily:

"The devil take you!" And suddenly, sniffing at the frying-pan, her face grew dark, and she threw the utensil on the floor and moaned: "Bless me, the pan has been used for flesh food! It is unclean! It did not catch when I used it clean on Monday."

Falling on her knees, she entreated with tears: "Lord God, Father, forgive me, accursed that I am! For the sake of Thy sufferings and passion forgive me! Do not punish an old fool, Lord!"

The burned fritters were given to the dog, the pan was destroyed, but the young wife began to reproach her mother-in-law in their quarrels.

"You actually cooked fritters in Lent in a pan which had been used for flesh-meat."

They dragged their God into all the household affairs, into every corner of their petty, insipid lives, and thus their wretched life acquired outward significance and importance, as if every hour was devoted to the service of a Higher Power. The dragging of God into all this dull emptiness oppressed me, and I used to look involuntarily into the corners, aware of being observed by invisible beings, and at night I was wrapped in a cloud of fear. It came from the corner where the ever-burning lamp flickered before the icon.

On a level with this shelf was a large window with two sashes joined by a stanchion. Fathomless, deep-blue space looked into the window, and if one made a quick movement, everything became merged in this deep-blue gulf, and floated out to the stars, into the deathly stillness, without a sound, just as a stone sinks when it is thrown into the water.

I do not remember how I cured myself of this terror, but I did cure myself, and that soon. Grandmother's good God helped me, and I think it was then that I realized the simple truth, namely, that no harm could come to me; that I should not be punished without fault of my own; that it was not the law of life that the innocent should suffer; and that I was not responsible for the faults of others.

I played truant from mass too, especially in the spring, the irresistible force of which would not let me go to church. If I had a seven-copeck piece given me for the collection, it was my destruction. I bought hucklebones, played all the time mass was going on, and was inevitably late home. And one day I was clever enough to lose all the coins which had been given me for prayers for the dead and the blessed bread, so that I had to take some one else's portion when the priest came from the altar and handed it round.

I was terribly fond of gambling, and it became a craze with me. I was skilful enough, and strong, and I swiftly gained renown in games of hucklebones, billiards, and skittles in the neighboring streets.

During Lent I was ordered to prepare for communion, and I went to confession to our neighbor Father Dorimedont Pokrovski. I regarded him as a hard man, and had committed many sins against him personally. I had thrown stones at the summer-house in his garden, and had quarreled with his children. In fact he might call to mind, if he chose, many similar acts annoying to him. This made me feel very uneasy, and when I stood in the poor little church awaiting my turn to go to confession my heart throbbed tremulously.

But Father Dorimedont greeted me with a good-natured, grumbling exclamation.

"Ah, it is my neighbor! Well, kneel down! What sins have you committed?"

He covered my head with a heavy velvet cloth. I inhaled the odor of wax and incense. It was difficult to speak, and I felt reluctant to do so.

"Have you been obedient to your elders?"

"No."

"Say, 'I have sinned.'"

To my own surprise I let fall:

"I have stolen."

"How was that? Where?" asked the priest, thoughtfully and without haste.

"At the church of the three bishops, at Pokrov, and at Nikoli."

"Well, that is in all the churches. That was wrong, my child; it was a sin. Do you understand?"

"I understand."

"Say, 'I have sinned.' What did you steal for? Was it for something to eat?"

"Sometimes and sometimes it was because I had lost money at play, and, as I had to take home some blessed bread, I stole it."

Father Dorimedont whispered something indistinctly and wearily, and then, after a few more questions, suddenly inquired sternly:

"Have you been reading forbidden books?"

Naturally I did not understand this question, and I asked:

"What books do you mean?"

"Forbidden books. Have you been reading any?"

"No; not one."

"Your sins are remitted. Stand up!"

I glanced at his face in amazement. He looked thoughtful and kind. I felt uneasy, conscience-stricken. In sending me to confession, my employers had spoken about its terrors, impressing on me to confess honestly even my slightest sins.

"I have thrown stones at your summer-house," I deposed.

The priest raised his head and, looking past me, said:

"That was very wrong. Now go!"

"And at your dog."

"Next!" called out Father Dorimedont, still looking past me.

I came away feeling deceived and offended. To be put to all that anxiety about the terrors of confession, and to find, after all, that it was not only far from terrible, but also uninteresting! The only interesting thing about it was the question about the forbidden books, of which I knew nothing. I remembered the school-boy reading to the women in that basement room, and "Good Business," who also had many black, thick books, with unintelligible illustrations.

The next day they gave me fifteen copecks and sent me to communion. Easter was late. The snow had been melted a long time, the streets were dry, the roadways sent up a cloud of dust, and the day was sunny and cheerful. Near the church was a group of workmen gambling with hucklebones. I decided that there was plenty of time to go to communion, and asked if I might join in.

"Let me play."

"The entrance-fee is one copeck," said a pock-marked, ruddy-faced man, proudly.

Not less proudly I replied:

"I put three on the second pair to the left."

"The stakes are on!" And the game began.

I changed the fifteen-copeck piece and placed my three copecks on the pair of hucklebones. Whoever hit that pair would receive that money, but if he failed to hit them, he had to give me three copecks. I was in luck. Two of them took aim and lost. I had won six copecks from grown-up men. My spirits rose greatly. But one of the players remarked:

"You had better look out for that youngster or he will be running away with his winnings."

This I regarded as an insult, and I said hotly: "Nine copecks on the pair at the extreme left." However, this did not make much impression on the players. Only one lad of my own age cried:

"See how lucky he is, that little devil from the Zvezdrinki; I know him."

A thin workman who smelt like a furrier said maliciously:

"He is a little devil, is he? Goo-oo-ood!"

Taking a sudden aim, he coolly knocked over my stake, and, bending down to me, said:

"Will that make you howl?"

"Three copecks on the pair to the right!"

"I shall have another three," he said, but he lost.

One could not put money on the same "horse" more than three times running, so I chose other hucklebones and won four more copecks. I had a heap of hucklebones. But when my turn came again, I placed money three times, and lost it all. Simultaneously mass was finished, the bell rang, and the people came out of church.

"Are you married?" inquired the furrier, intending to seize me by the hair; but I eluded him, and overtaking a lad in his Sunday clothes I inquired politely:

"Have you been to communion?"

"Well, and suppose I have; what then?" he answered, looking at me contemptuously.

I asked him to tell me how people took communion, what words the priest said, and what I ought to have done.

The young fellow shook me roughly and roared out in a terrifying voice:

"You have played the truant from communion, you heretic! Well, I am not going to tell you anything. Let your father skin you for it!"

I ran home expecting to be questioned, and certain that they would discover that I had not been to communion; but after congratulating me, the old woman asked only one question:

"How much did you give to the clerk? Much?"

"Five copecks," I answered, without turning a hair.

"And three copecks for himself; that would leave you seven copecks, animal!"

It was springtime. Each succeeding spring was clothed differently, and seemed brighter and pleasanter than the preceding one. The young grass and the fresh green birch gave forth an intoxicating odor. I had an uncontrollable desire to loiter in the fields and listen to the lark, lying face downward on the warm earth; but I had to clean the winter coats and help to put them away in the trunks, to cut up leaf tobacco, and dust the furniture, and to occupy myself from morning till night with duties which were to me both unpleasant and needless.

In my free hours I had absolutely nothing to live for. In our wretched street there was nothing, and beyond that I was not allowed to go. The yard was full of cross, tired workmen, untidy cooks, and washerwomen, and every evening I saw disgusting sights so offensive to me that I wished that I was blind.

I went up into the attic, taking some scissors and some colored paper with me, and cut out some lacelike designs with which I ornamented the rafters. It was, at any rate, something on which my sorrow could feed. I longed with all my heart to go to some place where people slept less, quarreled less, and did not so wearisomely beset God with complaints, and did not so frequently offend people with their harsh judgments.

On the Saturday after Easter they brought the miraculous icon of Our Lady of Vlandimirski from the Oranski Monastery to the town. The image became the guest of the town for half of the month of June, and blessed all the dwellings of those who attended the church. It was brought to my employers' house on a week-day. I was cleaning the copper things in the kitchen when the young mistress cried out in a scared voice from her room:

"Open the front door. They are bringing the Oranski icon here."

I rushed down, very dirty, and with greasy hands as rough as a brick opened the door. A young man with a lamp in one hand and a thurible in the other grumbled gently:

"Are you all asleep? Give a hand here!"

Two of the inhabitants carried the heavy icon-case up the narrow staircase. I helped them by supporting the edge, of it with my dirty hands and my shoulder. The monk came heavily behind me, chanting unwillingly with his thick voice:

"Holy Mother of God, pray for us!"

I thought, with sorrowful conviction:

"She is angry with me because I have touched her with dirty hands, and she will cause my hands to wither."

They placed the icon in the corner of the antichamber on two chairs, which were covered with a clean sheet, and on each side of it stood two monks, young and beautiful like angels. They had bright eyes, joyful expressions, and lovely hair.

Prayers were said.

"O, Mother Renowned," the big priest chanted, and all the while he was feeling the swollen lobe of his ear, which was hidden in his luxuriant hair.

"Holy Mother of God, pray for u-u-us!" sang the monks, wearily.

I loved the Holy Virgin. According to grandmother's stories it was she who sowed on the earth, for the consolation of the poor, all the flowers, all the joys, every blessing and beauty. And when the time came to salute her, without observing how the adults conducted themselves toward her, I kissed the icon palpitatingly on the face, the lips. Some one with powerful hands hurled me to the door. I do not remember seeing the monks go away, carrying the icon, but I remember very well how my employers sat on the floor around me and debated with much fear and anxiety what would become of me.

"We shall have to speak to the priest about him and have him taught," said the master, who scolded me without rancor.

"Ignoramus! How is it that you did not know that you should not kiss the lips? You must have been taught that at school."

For several days I waited, resigned, wondering what actually would happen to me. I had touched the icon with dirty hands; I had saluted it in a forbidden manner; I should not be allowed to go unpunished.

But apparently the Mother of God forgave the involuntary sin which had been prompted by sheer love, or else her punishment was so light that I did not notice it among the frequent punishments meted out to me by these good people.

Sometimes, to annoy the old mistress, I said compunctiously:

"But the Holy Virgin has evidently forgotten to punish me."

"You wait," answered the old woman, maliciously. "We shall see."

While I decorated the rafters of the attic with pink tea-wrappers, silver paper, leaves from trees, and all kinds of things, I used to sing anything that came into my head, setting the words to church melodies, as the Kalmucks do on the roads.

> "I am sitting in the attic
> With scissors in my hand,
> Cutting paper—paper.
> A dunce am I, and dull.
> If I were a dog,
> I could run where'er I wished;
> But now they all cry out to me:
> 'Sit down! Be silent, rogue,
> While your skin is whole!'"

The old woman came to look at my work, and burst out laughing.

"You should decorate the kitchen like that."

One day the master came up to the attic, looked at my performance, and said, with a sigh:

"You are an amusing fellow, Pyeshkov; the devil you are? I wonder what you will become, a conjurer or what? One can't guess." And he gave me a large Nikolaivski five-copeck piece.

By means of a thin wire I fastened the coin in the most prominent position among my works of art. In the course of a few days it disappeared. I believe that the old woman took it.

CHAPTER V

However, I did run away in the spring. One morning when I went to the shop for bread the shopkeeper, continuing in my presence a quarrel with his wife, struck her on the forehead with a weight. She ran into the street, and there fell down. People began to gather round at once. The woman was laid on a stretcher and carried to the hospital, and I ran behind the cab which took her there without noticing where I was going till I found myself on the banks of the Volga, with two *grevens* in my hand.

The spring sun shone caressingly, the broad expanse of the Volga flowed before me, the earth was full of sound and spacious, and I had been living like a mouse in a trap. So I made up my mind that I would not return to my master, nor would I go to grandmother at Kunavin; for as I had not kept my word to her, I was ashamed to go and see her, and grandfather would only gloat over my misfortunes.

For two or three days I wandered by the river-side, being fed by kind-hearted porters, and sleeping with them in their shelters. At length one of them said to me:

"It is no use for you to hang about here, my boy. I can see that. Go over to the boat which is called *The Good.* They want a washer-up."

I went. The tall, bearded steward in a black silk skullcap looked at me through his glasses with his dim eyes, and said quietly:

"Two rubles a month. Your passport?"

I had no passport. The steward pondered and then said:

"Bring your mother to see me."

I rushed to grandmother. She approved the course I had taken, told grandfather to go to the workman's court and get me a passport, and she herself accompanied me to the boat.

"Good!" said the steward, looking at us. "Come along."

He then took me to the stern of the boat, where sat at a small table, drinking tea and smoking a fat cigar at the same time, an enormous cook in white overalls and a white cap. The steward pushed me toward him.

"The washer-up."

Then he went away, and the cook, snorting, and with his black mustache bristling, called after him:

"You engage any sort of devil as long as he is cheap."

Angrily tossing his head of closely cropped hair, he opened his dark eyes very wide, stretched himself, puffed, and cried shrilly:

"And who may you be?"

I did not like the appearance of this man at all. Although he was all in white, he looked dirty. There was a sort of wool growing on his fingers, and hairs stuck out of his great ears.

"I am hungry," was my reply to him.

He blinked, and suddenly his ferocious countenance was transformed by a broad smile. His fat, brick-red cheeks widened to his very ears; he displayed his large, equine teeth; his mustache drooped, and all at once he had assumed the appearance of a kind, fat woman.

Throwing the tea overboard out of his glass, he poured out a fresh lot for me, and pushed a French roll and a large piece of sausage toward me.

"Peg away! Are your parents living? Can you steal? You needn't be afraid; they are all thieves here. You will soon learn."

He talked as if he were barking. His enormous, blue, clean-shaven face was covered all round the nose with red veins closely set together, his swollen, purple nose hung over his mustache. His lower lip was disfiguringly pendulous. In the corner of his mouth was stuck a smoking cigarette. Apparently he had only just come from the bath. He smelt of birch twigs, and a profuse sweat glistened on his temples and neck.

After I had drunk my tea, he gave me a ruble-note.

"Run along and buy yourself two aprons with this. Wait! I will buy them for you myself."

He set his cap straight and came with me, swaying ponderously, his feet pattering on the deck like those of a bear.

At night the moon shone brightly as it glided away from the boat to the meadows on the left. The old red boat, with its streaked funnel, did not hurry, and her propeller splashed unevenly in the silvery water. The dark shore gently floated to meet her, casting its shadow on the water, and beyond, the windows of the peasant huts gleamed charmingly. They were singing in the village. The girls were merry-making and singing—and when they sang "Aie Ludi," it sounded like "Alleluia."

In the wake of the steamer a large barge, also red, was being towed by a long rope. The deck was railed in like an iron cage, and in this cage were convicts condemned to deportation or prison. On the prow of the barge the bayonet of a sentry shone like a candle. It was quiet on the barge itself. The moon bathed it in a rich light while behind the black iron grating could be seen dimly gray patches. These were the convicts looking out on the Volga. The water sobbed, now weeping, now laughing timidly. It was as quiet here as in church, and there was the same smell of oil.

As I looked at the barge I remembered my early childhood; the journey from Astrakhan to Nijni, the iron faces of mother and grandmother, the person who had introduced me to this interesting, though hard, life, in the world. And when I thought of grandmother, all that I found so bad and repulsive in life seemed to leave me; everything was transformed and became more interesting, pleasanter; people seemed to be better and nicer altogether.

The beauty of the nights moved me almost to tears, and especially the barge, which looked so like a coffin, and so solitary on the broad expanse of the flowing river in the pensive quietness of the warm night. The uneven lines of the shore, now rising, now falling, stirred the imagination pleasantly. I longed to be good, and to be of use to others.

The people on our steamboat had a peculiar stamp. They seemed to me to be all alike, young and old, men and women. The boat traveled slowly. The busy folk traveled by fast boat, and all the lazy rascals came on our boat. They sang and ate, and soiled any amount of cups and plates, knives and forks and spoons from morning to night. My work was to wash up and clean the knives and forks, and I was busy with this work from six in the morning till close on midnight. During the day, from two till six o'clock, and in the evening, from ten till midnight, I had less work to do; for at those times the passengers took a rest from eating, and only drank, tea, beer, and vodka. All the buffet attendants, my chiefs, were free at that time, too. The cook, Smouri, drank tea at a table near the hatchway with his assistant, Jaakov Ivanich; the kitchen-man, Maxim; and Sergei, the saloon steward, a humpback with high cheek-bones, a face pitted with smallpox, and oily eyes. Jaakov told all sorts of nasty stories, bursting out into sobbing laughs and showing his long, discolored teeth. Sergei stretched his frog-like mouth to his ears. Frowning Maxim was silent, gazing at them with stern, colorless eyes.

"Asiatic! Mordovan!" said the old cook now and again in his deep voice.

I did not like these people. Fat, bald Jaakov Ivanich spoke of nothing but women, and that always filthily. He had a vacant-looking face covered with bluish pimples. On one cheek he had a mole with a tuft of red hair growing from it. He used to pull out these hairs by twisting them round a needle. Whenever an amiable, sprightly passenger of the female sex appeared on the boat, he waited upon her in a peculiar, timid manner like a beggar. He spoke to her sweetly and plaintively, he licked her, as it were, with the swift movements of his tongue. For some reason I used to think that such great fat creatures ought to be hang-men.

"One should know how to get round women," he would teach Sergei and Maxim, who would listen to him much impressed, pouting their lips and turning red.

"Asiatics!" Smouri would roar in accents of disgust, and standing up heavily, he gave the order, "Pyeshkov, march!"

In his cabin he would hand me a little book bound in leather, and lie down in his hammock by the wall of the ice-house.

"Read!" he would say.

I sat on a box and read conscientiously:

"'The *umbra* projected by the stars means that one is on good terms with heaven and free from profanity and vice.'"

Smouri, smoking a cigarette, puffed out the smoke and growled:

"Camels! They wrote—"

"'Baring the left bosom means innocence of heart.'" "Whose bosom?"

"It does not say."

"A woman's, it means. Eh, and a loose woman."

He closed his eyes and lay with his arms behind his head. His cigarette, hardly alight, stuck in the corner of his mouth. He set it straight with his tongue, stretched so that something whistled in his chest, and his enormous face was enveloped in a cloud of smoke. Sometimes I thought he had fallen asleep and I left off reading to examine the accursed book, which bored me to nauseation. But he said hoarsely: "Go on reading!"

"'The venerable one answered, "Look! My dear brother Suvyerin—"'"

"Syevyeverin—"

"It is written Suvyerin."

"Well, that's witchcraft. There is some poetry at the end. Run on from there."

I ran on.

> "Profane ones, curious to know our business,
> Never will your weak eyes spy it out,
> Nor will you learn how the fairies sing."

"Wait!" said Smouri. "That is not poetry. Give me the book."

He angrily turned over the thick, blue leaves, and then put the book under the mattress.

"Get me another one."

To my grief there were many books in his black trunk clamped with iron. There were "Precepts of Peace," "Memories of the Artillery," "Letters of Lord Sydanhall," "Concerning Noxious Insects and their Extinction, with Advice against the Pest," books which seemed to have no beginning and no end. Sometimes the cook set me to turn over all his books and read out their titles to him, but as soon as I had begun he called out angrily:

"What is it all about? Why do you speak through your teeth? It is impossible to understand you. What the devil has Gerbvase to do with me? Gervase! *Umbra* indeed!"

Terrible words, incomprehensible names were wearily remembered, and they tickled my tongue. I had an incessant desire to repeat them, thinking that perhaps by pronouncing them I might discover their meaning. And outside the port-hole the water unweariedly sang and splashed. It would have been pleasant to go to the stern, where the sailors and stokers were gathered together among the chests, where the passengers played cards, sang songs, and told interesting stories. It would have been pleasant to sit among them and listen to simple, intelligible conversation, to gaze on the banks of the Kama, at the fir-trees drawn out like brass wires, at the meadows, wherein small lakes remained from the floods, looking like pieces of broken glass as they reflected the sun.

Our steamer was traveling at some distance from the shore, yet the sound of invisible bells came to us, reminding us of the villages and people. The barks of the fishermen floated on the waves like crusts of bread. There, on the bank a little village appeared, here a crowd of small boys bathed in the river, men in red blouses could be seen passing along a narrow strip of sand. Seen from a distance, from the river, it was a very pleasing sight; everything looked like tiny toys of many colors.

I felt a desire to call out some kind, tender words to the shore and the barge. The latter interested me greatly; I could look at it for an hour at a time as it dipped its blunt nose in the turbid water. The boat dragged it along as if it were a pig: the tow-rope, slackening, lashed the water, then once more drew taut and pulled the barge along by the nose. I wanted very much to see the faces of those people who were kept like wild animals in an iron cage. At Perm, where they were landed, I made my way to the gangway, and past me came, in batches of ten, gray people, trampling dully, rattling their fetters, bowed down by their heavy knapsacks. There were all sorts, young and old, handsome and ugly, all exactly like ordinary people except that they were differently dressed and were disfiguringly close-shaven. No doubt these were robbers, but grandmother had told me much that was good about robbers. Smouri looked much more like a fierce robber than they as he glanced loweringly at the barge and said loudly:

"Save me, God, from such a fate!"

Once I asked him:

"Why do you say that? You cook, while those others kill and steal."

"I don't cook; I only prepare. The women cook," he said, bursting out laughing; but after thinking a moment he added: "The difference between one person and another lies in stupidity. One man is clever, another not so clever, and a third may be quite a fool. To become clever one must read the right books—black magic and what not. One must read all kinds of books and then one will find the right ones."

He was continually impressing upon me:

"Read! When you don't understand a book, read it again and again, as many as seven times; and if you do not understand it then, read it a dozen times."

To every one on the boat, not excluding the taciturn steward, Smouri spoke roughly. Sticking out his lower lip as if he were disgusted, and, stroking his mustache, he pelted them with words as if they were stones. To me he always showed kindness and interest, but there was something about his interest which rather frightened me. Sometimes I thought he was crazy, like grandmother's sister. At times he said to me:

"Leave off reading."

And he would lie for a long time with closed eyes, breathing stertorously, his great stomach shaking. His hairy fingers, folded corpse-like on his chest, moved, knitting invisible socks with invisible needles. Suddenly he would begin growling:

"Here are you! You have your intelligence. Go and live! Rut intelligence is given sparingly, and not to all alike. If all were on the same level intellectually—but they are not. One understands, another does not, and there are some people who do not even wish to understand!"

Stumbling over his words, he related stories of his life as a soldier, the drift of which I could never manage to catch. They seemed very uninteresting to me. Besides, he did not tell them from the beginning, but as he recollected them.

"The commander of the regiment called this soldier to him and asked: 'What did the lieutenant say to you?' So he told everything just as it had happened—a soldier is bound to tell the truth—but the lieutenant looked at him as if he had been a wall, and then turned away, hanging his head. Yes—"

He became indignant, puffed out clouds of smoke, and growled:

"How was I to know what I could say and what I ought not to say? Then the lieutenant was condemned to be shut up in a fortress, and his mother said—ah, my God! I am not learned in anything."

It was hot. Everything seemed to be quivering and tinkling. The water splashed against the iron walls of the cabin, and the wheel of the boat rose and fell. The river flowed in a broad stream between the rows of lights. In the distance could be seen the line of the meadowed bank. The trees drooped. When one's hearing had become accustomed to all the sounds, it seemed as if all was quiet, although the soldiers in the stern of the boat howled dismally, "Se-e-even! Se-e-ven!"

I had no desire to take part in anything. I wanted neither to listen nor to work, but only to sit somewhere in the shadows, where there was no greasy, hot smell of cooking; to sit and gaze, half asleep, at the quiet, sluggish life as it slipped away on the water.

"Read!" the cook commanded harshly.

Even the head steward was afraid of him, and that mild man of few words, the dining-room steward, who looked like a *sandre*, was evidently afraid of Smouri too.

"*Ei!* You swine!" he would cry to this man. "Come here! Thief! Asiatic!"

The sailors and stokers were very respectful to him, and expectant of favors. He gave them the meat from which soup had been made, and inquired after their homes and their families. The oily and smoke-dried White Russian stokers were counted the lowest people on the boat. They were all called by one name, Yaks, and they were teased, "Like a Yak, I amble along the shore."

When Smouri heard this, he bristled up, his face became suffused with blood, and he roared at the stokers:

"Why do you allow them to laugh at you, you mugs? Throw some sauce in their faces."

Once the boatswain, a handsome, but ill-natured, man, said to him:

"They are the same as Little Russians; they hold the same faith."

The cook seized him by the collar and belt, lifted him up in the air, and said, shaking him:

"Shall I knock you to smithereens?"

They quarreled often, these two. Sometimes it even came to a fight, but Smouri was never beaten. He was possessed of superhuman strength, and besides this, the captain's wife, with a masculine face and smooth hair like a boy's, was on his side.

He drank a terrible amount of vodka, but never became drunk. He began to drink the first thing in the morning, consuming a whole bottle in four gulps, and after that he sipped beer till close on evening. His face gradually grew brown, his eyes widened.

Sometimes in the evening he sat for hours in the hatchway, looking large and white, without breaking his silence, and his eyes were fixed gloomily on the distant horizon. At those times they were all more afraid of him than ever, but I was sorry for him. Jaakov Ivanich would come out from the kitchen, perspiring and glowing with the heat. Scratching his bald skull and waving his arm, he would take cover or say from a distance:

"The fish has gone off."

"Well, there is the salted cabbage."

"But if they ask for fish-soup or boiled fish?"

"It is ready. They can begin gobbling."

Sometimes I plucked up courage to go to him. He looked at me heavily.

"What do you want?"

"Nothing."

"Good.".

On one of these occasions, however, I asked him:

"Why is every one afraid of you? For you are good."

Contrary to my expectations, he did not get angry.

"I am only good to you."

But he added distinctly, simply, and thoughtfully:

"Yes, it is true that I am good to every one, only I do not show it. It does not do to show that to people, or they will be all over you. They will crawl over those who are kind as if they were mounds in a morass, and trample on them. Go and get me some beer."

Having drunk the bottle, he sucked his mustache and said:

"If you were older, my bird, I could teach you a lot. I have something to say to a man. I am no fool. But you must read books. In them you will find all you need. They are not rubbish—books. Would you like some beer?"

"I don't care for it."

"Good boy! And you do well not to drink it. Drunkenness is a misfortune. Vodka is the devil's own business. If I were rich, I would spur you on to study. An uninstructed man is an ox, fit for nothing but the yoke or to serve as meat. All he can do is to wave his tail."

The captain's wife gave him a volume of Gogol. I read "The Terrible Vengeance" and was delighted with it, but Smouri cried angrily:

"Rubbish! A fairy-tale! I know. There are other books."

He took the book away from me, obtained another one from the captain's wife, and ordered me harshly:

"Read Tarass'—what do you call it? Find it! She says it is good; good for whom? It may be good for her, but not for me, eh? She cuts her hair short. It is a pity her ears were not cut off too."

When *Tarass* called upon *Ostap* to fight, the cook laughed loudly.

"That's the way! Of course! You have learning, but I have strength. What do they say about it? Camels!"

He listened with great attention, but often grumbled:

"Rubbish! You could n't cut a man in half from his shoulders to his haunches; it can't be done. And you can't thrust a pike upward; it would break it. I have been a soldier myself."

Andrei's treachery aroused his disgust.

'There's a mean creature, eh? Like women! *Tfoo!*

But when *Tarass* killed his son, the cook let his feet slip from the hammock, bent himself double, and wept. The tears trickled down his cheeks, splashed upon the deck as he breathed stertorously and muttered:

"Oh, my God! my God!"

And suddenly he shouted to me:

"Go on reading, you bone of the devil!"

Again he wept, with even more violence and bitterness, when I read how *Ostap* cried, out before his death, "Father, dost thou hear?"

"Ruined utterly!" exclaimed Smouri. "Utterly! Is that the end? *Ekh!* What an accursed business! He was a man, that *Tar ass*. What do you think? Yes, he was a man."

He took the book out of my hands and looked at it with attention, letting his tears fall on its binding.

"It is a fine book, a regular treat."

After this we read "Ivanhoe." Smouri was very pleased with Richard Plantagenet.

"That was a real king," he said impressively.

To me the book had appeared dry. In fact, our tastes did not agree at all. I had a great liking for "The Story of Thomas Jones," an old translation of "The History of Tom Jones, Foundling," but Smouri grumbled:

"Rubbish! What do I care about your Thomas? Of what use is he to me? There must be some other books."

One day I told him that I knew that there were other books, forbidden books. One could read them only at night, in underground rooms. He opened his eyes wide.

"Wha-a-t's that? Why do you tell me these lies?"

"I am not telling lies. The priest asked me about them when I went to confession, and, for that matter, I myself have seen people reading them and crying over them."

The cook looked sternly in my face and asked:

"Who was crying?"

"The lady who was listening, and the other actually ran away because she was frightened."

"You were asleep. You were dreaming," said Smouri, slowly covering his eyes, and after a silence he muttered: "But of course there must be something hidden from me somewhere. I am not so old as all that, and with my character—well, however that may be—"

He spoke to me eloquently for a whole hour.

Imperceptibly I acquired the habit of reading, and took up a book with pleasure. What I read therein was pleasantly different from life, which was becoming harder and harder for me.

Smouri also recreated himself by reading, and often took me from my work.

"Pyeshkov, come and read."

"I have a lot of washing up to do."

"Let Maxim wash up."

He coarsely ordered the senior kitchen-helper to do my work, and this man would break the glasses out of spite, while the chief steward told me quietly:

"I shall have you put off the boat."

One day Maxim on purpose placed several glasses in a bowl of dirty water and tea-leaves. I emptied the water overboard, and the glasses went flying with it.

"It is my fault," said Smouri to the head steward. "Put it down to my account."

The dining-room attendants began to look at me with lowering brows, and they used to say:

"*Ei!* you bookworm! What are you paid for?"

And they used to try and make as much work as they could for me, soiling plates needlessly. I was sure that this would end badly for me, and I was not mistaken.

One evening, in a little shelter on the boat, there sat a red-faced woman with a girl in a yellow coat and a new pink blouse. Both had been drinking. The woman smiled, bowed to every one, and said on the note O, like a church clerk:

"Forgive me, my friends; I have had a little too much to drink. I have been tried and acquitted, and I have been drinking for joy."

The girl laughed, too, gazing at the other passengers with glazed eyes. Pushing the woman away, she said:

"But you, you plaguy creature—we know you."

They had berths in the second-class cabin, opposite the cabin in which Jaakov Ivanich and Sergei slept.

The woman soon disappeared somewhere or other, and Sergei took her place near the girl, greedily stretching his frog-like mouth.

That night, when I had finished my work and had laid myself down to sleep on the table, Sergei came to me, and seizing me by the arm, said:

"Come along! We are going to marry you."

He was drunk. I tried to tear my arm away from him, but he struck me.

"Come along!"

Maxim came running in, also drunk, and the two dragged me along the deck to their cabin, past the sleeping passengers. But by the door of the cabin stood Smouri, and in the doorway, holding on to the jamb, Jaakov Ivanich. The girl stuck her elbow in his back, and cried in a drunken voice:

"Make way!"

Smouri got me out of the hands of Sergei and Maxim, seized them by the hair, and, knocking their heads together, moved away. They both fell down.

"Asiatic!" he said to Jaakov, slamming the door on him. Then he roared as he pushed me along:

"Get out of this!"

I ran to the stern. The night was cloudy, the river black. In the wake of the boat seethed two gray lines of water leading to the invisible shore; between these two lines the barge dragged on its way. Now on the right, now on the left appeared red patches of light, without illuminating anything. They disappeared, hidden by the sudden winding of the shore. After this it became still darker and more gruesome.

The cook came and sat beside me, sighed deeply, and pulled at his cigarette.

"So they were taking you to that creature? *Ekh!* Dirty beasts! I heard them trying."

"Did you take her away from them?"

"Her?" He abused the girl coarsely, and continued in a sad tone:

"It is all nastiness here. This boat is worse than a village. Have you ever lived in a village?"

"No."

"In a village there is nothing but misery, especially in the winter."

Throwing his cigarette overboard, he was silent. Then he spoke again.

"You have fallen among a herd of swine, and I am sorry for you, my little one. I am sorry for all of them, too. Another time I do not know what I should have done. Gone on my knees and prayed. What are you doing, sons of ——? What are you doing, blind creatures? Camels!"

The steamer gave a long-drawn-out hoot, the tow-rope splashed in the water, the lights of lanterns jumped up and down, showing where the harbor was. Out of the darkness more lights appeared.

"Pyani Bor [a certain pine forest]. Drunk," growled the cook. "And there is a river called Pyanaia, and there was a captain called Pyenkov, and a writer called Zapivokhin, and yet another captain called Nepei-pivo.[1] I am going on shore."

The coarse-grained women and girls of Kamska dragged logs of wood from the shore in long trucks. Bending under their load-straps, with pliable tread, they arrived in pairs at the stoker's hold, and, emptying their sooty loads into the black hole, cried ringingly:

"Logs!"

[1] Pyanaia means "drunk," and the other names mentioned come from the same root. Nepei-pivo means, "Do not drink beer."

When they brought the wood the sailors would take hold of them by the breasts or the legs. The women squealed, spat at the men, turned back, and defended themselves against pinches and blows with their trucks. I saw this a hundred times, on every voyage and at every land-stage where they took in wood, and it was always the same thing.

I felt as if I were old, as if I had lived on that boat for many years, and knew what would happen in a week's time, in the autumn, in a year.

It was daylight now. On a sandy promontory above the harbor stood out a forest of fir-trees. On the hills and through the forests women went laughing and singing. They looked like soldiers as they pushed their long trucks.

I wanted to weep. The tears seethed in my breast; my heart was overflowing with them. It was painful. But it would be shameful to cry, and I went to help the sailor Blyakhin wash the deck.

Blyakhin was an insignificant-looking man. He had a withered, faded look about him, and always stowed himself away in corners, whence his small, bright eyes shone.

"My proper surname is not Blyakhin, but——because, you see, my mother was a loose woman. I have a sister, and she also. That happened to be their destiny. Destiny, my brother, is an anchor for all of us. You want to go in one direction, but wait!"

And now, as he swabbed the deck, he said softly to me:

"You see what a lot of harm women do! There it is? Damp wood smolders for a long time and then bursts into flame. I don't care for that sort of thing myself; it does not interest me. And if I had been born a woman, I should have drowned myself in a black pool. I should have been safe then with Holy Christ, and could do no one any harm. But while one is here there is always the chance of kindling a fire. Eunuchs are no fools, I assure you. They are clever people, they are good at divination, they put aside all small things and serve God alone—cleanly."

The captain's wife passed us, holding her skirts high as she came through the pools of water. Tall and well built, she had a simple, bright face. I wanted to run after her and beg her from my heart:

"Say something to me! Say something!"

The boat drew slowly away from the pier. Blyakhin crossed himself and said:

"We are off!"

CHAPTER VI

At Sarapulia, Maxim left the boat. He went away in silence, saying farewell to no one, serious and calm. Behind him, laughing, came the gay woman, and, following her, the girl, looking disheveled, with swollen eyes. Sergei was on his knees a long time before the captain's cabin, kissing the panel of the door, knocking his forehead against it, and crying:

"Forgive me! It was not my fault, but Maxim's."

The sailors, the stewards, and even some of the passengers knew that he was lying, yet they advised:

"Come, forgive him!"

But the captain drove him away, and even kicked him with such force that he fell over. Notwithstanding, he forgave him, and Sergei at once rushed on deck, carrying a tray of tea-things, looking with inquiring, dog-like expression into the eyes of the passengers.

In Maxim's place came a soldier from Viatski, a bony man, with a small head and brownish red eyes. The assistant cook sent him first to kill some fowls. He killed a pair, but let the rest escape on deck. The passengers tried to catch them, but three hens flew overboard. Then the soldier sat on some wood near the fowl-house, and cried bitterly.

"What's the matter, you fool?" asked Smouri, angrily. "Fancy a soldier crying!"

"I belong to the Home Defense Corps," said the soldier in a low voice.

That was his ruin. In half an hour every one on the boat was laughing at him. They would come quite close to him, fix their eyes on his face, and ask:

"Is this the one?"

And then they would go off into harsh, insulting, absurd laughter.

At first the soldier did not see these people or hear their laughter; he was drying his tears with the sleeve of his old shirt, exactly as if he were hiding them up his sleeve. But soon his brown eyes flashed with rage, and he said in the quick speech of Viatski:

"What are you staring at me for? *Oi*, may you be torn to bits!"

But this only amused the passengers the more, and they began to snap their fingers at him, to pluck at his shirt, his apron, to play with him as if he had been a goat, baiting him cruelly until dinner-time. At dinner some one put a piece of squeezed lemon on the handle of a wooden spoon, and tied it behind his back by the strings of his apron. As he moved, the spoon waggled behind him, and every one laughed, but he was in a fluster, like an entrapped mouse, ignorant of what had aroused their laughter.

Smouri sat behind him in silence. His face had become like a woman's. I felt sorry for the soldier, and asked:

"May I tell him about the spoon?"

He nodded his head without speaking.

When I explained to the soldier what they were laughing at, he hastily seized the spoon, tore it off, threw it on the floor, crushed it with his foot, and took hold of my hair with both hands. We began to fight, to the great satisfaction of the passengers, who made a ring round us at once.

Smouri pushed the spectators aside, separated us, and, after boxing my ear, seized the soldier by the ear. When the passengers saw how the little man danced under the hand of the cook they roared with excitement, whistled, stamped their feet, split their sides with laughter.

"Hurrah! Garrison! Butt the cook in the stomach!"

This wild joy on the part of others made me feel that I wanted to throw myself upon them and hit their dirty heads with a lump of wood.

Smouri let the soldier go, and with his hands behind his back turned upon the passengers like a wild boar, bristling, and showing his teeth terrifyingly.

"To your places! March! March!"

The soldier threw himself upon me again, but Smouri seized him round the body with one hand and carried him to the hatchway, where he began to pump water on his head, turning his frail body about as if he were a rag-doll.

The sailors came running on the scene, with the boatswain and the captain's mate. The passengers crowded about again. A head above the others stood the head-steward, quiet, dumb, as always.

The soldier, sitting on some wood near the kitchen door, took off his boots and began to wring out his leggings, though they were not wet. But the water dripped from his greasy hair, which again amused the passengers.

"All the same," said the soldier, "I am going to kill that boy."

Taking me by the shoulder, Smouri said something to the captain's mate. The sailors sent the passengers away, and when they had all dispersed, he asked the soldier:

"What is to be done with you?"

The latter was silent, looking at me with wild eyes, and all the while putting a strange restraint upon himself.

"Be quiet, you devilskin!" said Smouri.

"As you are not the piper, you can't call the tune," answered the soldier.

I saw that the cook was confused. His blown-out cheeks became flabby; he spat, and went away, taking me with him. I walked after him, feeling foolish, with backward glances at the soldier. But Smouri muttered in a worried tone:

"There's a wild creature for you! What? What do you think of him?"

Sergei overtook us and said in a whisper:

"He is going to kill himself."

"Where is he?" cried Smouri, and he ran.

The soldier was standing at the door of the steward's cabin with a large knife in his hand. It was the knife which was used for cutting off the heads of fowls and for cutting up sticks for the stoves. It was blunt, and notched like a saw. In front of the cabin the passengers were assembled, looking at the funny little man with the wet head. His snub-nosed face shook like a jelly; his mouth hung wearily open; his lips twitched. He roared:

"Tormentors! Tormentors!"

Jumping up on something, I looked over the heads of people into their faces. They were smiling, giggling, and saying to one another:

"Look! Look!"

When he pushed his crumpled shirt down into his trousers with his skinny, childish hand, a good-looking man near me said:

"He is getting ready to die, and he takes the trouble to hitch up his trousers."

The passengers all laughed loudly. It was perfectly plain that they did not think it probable that the soldier would really kill himself, nor did I think so; but Smouri, after one glance at him, pushed the people aside with his stomach, saying:

"Get away, you fools!"

He called them fools over and over again, and approaching one little knot of people, said:

"To your place, fool!"

This was funny; but, however, it seemed to-be true, for they had all been acting like one big fool from the first thing in the morning. When he had driven the passengers-off, he approached the soldier, and, holding out his hand, said:

"Give me that knife."

"I don't care," said the soldier, holding out the handle of the knife.

The cook gave the knife to me, and pushed the soldier into the cabin.

"Lie down and go to sleep. What is the matter with you, eh?"

The soldier sat on a hammock in silence.

"He shall bring you something to eat and some vodka. Do you drink vodka?"

"A little sometimes."

"But, look you, don't you touch him. It was not he who made fun of you, do you hear? I tell you that it was not he."

"But why did they torment me?" asked the soldier, softly.

Smouri answered gruffly after a pause:

"How should I know?"

As he came with me to the kitchen he muttered:

"Well, they have fastened upon a poor wretch this time, and no mistake! You see what he is? There you are! My lad, people can be sent out of their minds; they can really. Stick to them like bugs, and the thing is done. In fact, there are some people here like bugs—worse than bugs!"

When I took bread, meat, and vodka to the soldier he was still sitting in the hammock, rocking himself and crying softly, sobbing like a woman.

I placed the plate on the table, saying:

"Eat."

"Shut the door."

"That will make it dark."

"Shut it, or they will come crawling in here."

I went away. The sight of the soldier was unpleasant to me. He aroused my commiseration and pity and made me feel uncomfortable. Times without number grandmother had told me:

"One must have pity on people. We are all unhappy. Life is hard for all of us."

"Did you take it to him?" asked the cook. "Well, how is he—the soldier?"

"I feel sorry for him."

"Well, what's the matter now, eh?"

"One can't help being sorry for people."

Smouri took me by the arm, drew me to him, and said:

"You do not pity in vain, but it is waste of time to chatter about it. When you are not accustomed to mix jellies, you must teach yourself the way."

And pushing me away from him, he added gruffly: "This is no place for you. Here, smoke."

I was deeply distressed, quite crushed by the behavior of the passengers. There was something inexpressibly insulting and oppressive in the way they had worried the soldier and had laughed with glee when Smouri had him by the ear. What pleasure could they find in such a disgusting, pitiful affair? What was there to cause them to laugh so joyfully?

There they were again, sitting or lying under the awning, drinking, making a buzz of talk, playing cards, conversing seriously and sensibly, looking at the river, just as if they had never whistled and hooted an hour ago. They were all as quiet and lazy as usual. From morning to night they sauntered about the boat like pieces of fluff or specks of dust in the sunbeams. In groups of ten they would stroll to the hatchway, cross themselves, and leave the boat at the landing-stage from which the same kind of people embarked as they landed, bending their backs under the same heavy wallets and trunks and dressed in the same fashion.

This continual change of passengers did not alter the life on the boat one bit. The new passengers spoke of the same things as those who had left: the land, labor, God, women, and in the same words. "It is ordained by the Lord God that we should suffer; all we can do is to be patient. There is nothing else to be done. It is fate."

It was depressing to hear such words, and they exasperated me. I could not endure dirt, and I did not wish to endure evil, unjust, and insulting behavior toward myself. I was sure that I did not deserve such treatment. And the soldier had not deserved it, either. Perhaps he had meant to be funny.

Maxim, a serious, good-hearted fellow, had been dismissed from the ship, and Sergei, a mean fellow, was left. And why did these people, capable of goading a man almost to madness, always submit humbly to the furious shouts of the sailors, and listen to their abuse without taking offense?

"What are you rolling about on the deck for?" cried the boatswain, blinking his handsome, though malevolent, eyes. "If the boat heeled, it would be the end of you, you devils."

The "devils" went peaceably enough to the other deck, but they chased them away from there, too, as if they had been sheep.

"Ah, accursed ones!"

On hot nights, under the iron awning, which had been made red-hot by the sun during the day, it was suffocating. The passengers crawled over the deck like beetles, and lay where they happened to fall. The sailors awoke them at the landing-stages by prodding them with marlinespikes.

"What are you sprawling in the way for? Go away to your proper place!"

They would stand up, and move sleepily in the direction whither they were pushed. The sailors were of the same class as themselves, only they were dressed differently; but they ordered them about as if they were policemen. The first thing which I noticed about these people was that they were so quiet, so timid, so sadly meek. It was terrible when through that crust of meekness burst the cruel, thoughtless spirit of mischief, which had very little fun in it. It seemed to me that they did not know where they were being taken; it was a matter of indifference to them where they were landed from the boat. Wherever they went on shore they stayed for a short time, and then they embarked again on our boat or another, starting on a fresh journey. They all seemed to have strayed, to have no relatives, as if all the earth were strange to them. And every single one of them was senselessly cowardly.

Once, shortly after midnight, something burst in the machinery and exploded like a report from a cannon. The deck was at once enveloped in a cloud of steam, which rose thickly from the engine-room and crept through every crevice. An invisible person shouted deafeningly:

"Gavrilov, some red lead—and some felt!"

I slept near the engine-room, on the table on which the dishes were washed up, and the explosion and shaking awoke me. It was quiet on deck. The engine uttered a hot, steamy whisper; a hammer sounded repeatedly. But in the course of a few minutes all the saloon passengers howled, roared with one voice, and suddenly a distressing scene was in progress.

In a white fog which swiftly rarefied, women with their hair loose, disheveled men with round eyes like fishes' eyes, rushed about, trampling one another, carrying bundles, bags, boxes, stumbling, falling, calling upon God and St. Nicholas, striking one another. It was very terrible, but at the same time it was interesting. I ran after them to see what they would do next.

This was my first experience of a night alarm, yet I understood at once that the passengers had made a mistake. The boat had not slowed down. On the right hand, quite near, gleamed the life-belts. The night was light, the full moon stood high. But the passengers rushed wildly about the deck, and now those traveling in the other classes had come up, too. Some one jumped overboard. He was followed by another, and yet a third. Two peasants and a monk with heavy pieces of wood broke off a bench which was screwed to the desk. A large cage of fowls was thrown into the water from the stern. In the center of the deck, near the steps leading to the captain's bridge, knelt a peasant who prostrated himself before the people as they rushed past him, and howled like a wolf:

"I am Orthodox and a sinner—"

"To the boats, you devils!" cried a fat gentleman who wore only trousers and no shirt, and he beat his breast with his fist.

The sailors came running, seized people by the collars, knocked their heads together, and threw them on the deck. Smouri approached heavily, wearing his overcoat over his nightclothes, addressed them all in a resounding voice:

"Yes, you ought to be ashamed of yourselves. What are you making all this fuss for? Has the steamer stopped, eh? Are we going slower? There is the shore. Those fools who jumped into the water have caught the life-belts, they have had to drag them out. There they are. Do you see? Two boats—"

He struck the third-class passengers on the head with his fist, and they sank like sacks to the deck.

The confusion was not yet hushed when a lady in a cloak flew to Smouri with a tablespoon in her hand, and, flourishing it in his face, cried:

"How dare you?"

A wet gentleman, restraining her, sucked his mustache and said irritably:

"Let him alone, you imbecile!"

Smouri, spreading out his hands, blinked with embarrassment, and asked me:

"What's the matter, eh? What does she want with me? This is nice, I must say! Why, I never saw her before in my life!"

And a peasant, with his nose bleeding, cried:

"Human beings, you call them? Robbers!"

Before the summer I had seen two panics on board the steamboat, and on both occasions they were caused not by real danger, but by the mere possibility of it. On a third occasion the passengers caught two thieves, one of them was dressed like a foreigner, beat them for almost an hour, unknown to the sailors, and when the latter took their victims away from them, the passengers abused them.

"Thieves shield thieves. That is plain. You are rogues yourselves, and you sympathize with rogues."

The thieves had been beaten into unconsciousness. They could not stand when they were handed over to the police at the next stopping-place.

There were many other occasions on which my feelings were aroused to a high pitch, and I could not make up my mind as to whether people were bad or good, peaceful or mischief-making, and why they were so peculiarly cruel, lusting to work malevolence, and ashamed of being kind.

I asked the cook about this, but he enveloped his face in a cloud of smoke, and said briefly in a tone of vexation:

"What are you chattering about now? Human creatures are human creatures. Some are clever, some are fools. Read, and don't talk so much. In books, if they are the right sort, you will find all you want to know."

I wanted to please him by giving him a present of some books.

In Kazan I bought, for five copecks, "The Story of how a Soldier Saved Peter the Great"; but at that time the cook was drinking and was very cross, so I began to read it myself. I was delighted with it, it was so simple, easy to understand, interesting, and short. I felt that this book would give great pleasure to my teacher; but when I took it to him he silently crushed it in his hand into a round ball and threw it overboard.

"That for your book, you fool!" he said harshly. "I teach you like a dog, and all you want to do is to gobble up idle tales, eh?" He stamped and roared. "What kind of book is that? Do I read nonsense? Is what is written there true? Well, speak!"

"I don't know."

"Well, I do know. If a man's head were cut off, his body would fall down the staircase, and the other man would not have climbed on the haystack. Soldiers are not fools. He would have set fire to the hay, and that would have been the end. Do you understand?"

"Yes."

"That's right. I know all about Czar Peter, and that never happened to him. Run along."

I realized that the cook was right, but nevertheless the book pleased me. I bought the "Story" again and read it a second time. To my amazement, I discovered that it was really a bad book. This puzzled me, and I began to regard the cook with even more respect, while he said to me more frequently and more crossly than ever:

"Oh, what a lot you need to be taught! This is no place for you."

I also felt that it was no place for me. Sergei behaved disgustingly to me, and several times I observed him stealing pieces of the tea-service, and giving them to the passengers on the sly. I knew that this was theft. Smouri had warned me more than once:

"Take care. Do not give the attendants any of the cups and plates from your table."

This made life still harder for me, and I often longed to run away from the boat into the forest; but Smouri held me back. He was more tender to me every day, and the incessant movement on the boat held a terrible fascination for me. I did not like it when we stayed in port, and I was always expecting something to happen, and that we should sail from Kama to Byela, as far as Viatka, and so up the Volga, and I should see new places, towns, and people. But this did not happen. My life on the steamer came to an abrupt end. One evening when we were going from Kazan to Nijni the steward called me to him. I went. He shut the door behind me, and said to Smouri, who sat grimly on a small stool:

"Here he is."

Smouri asked me roughly:

"Have you been giving Serejka any of the dinner- and tea-services?"

"He helps himself when I am not looking."

The steward said softly:

"He does not look, yet he knows."

Smouri struck his knee with his fist; then he scratched his knee as he said:

"Wait; take time."

I pondered. I looked at the steward. He looked at me, and there seemed to be no eyes behind his glasses.

He lived without making a noise. He went about softly, spoke in low tones. Sometimes his faded beard and vacant eyes peeped out from some corner and instantly vanished. Before going to bed he knelt for a long time in the buffet before the icon with the ever-burning lamp. I could see him through the chink of the door, looking like a black bundle; but I had never succeeded in learning how the steward prayed, for he simply knelt and looked at the icon, stroking his beard and sighing.

After a silence Smouri asked:

"Has Sergei ever given you any money?"

"No."

"Never?"

"Never."

"He does not tell lies," said Smouri to the steward, who answered at once in his low voice:

"It comes to the same thing, please—"

"Come!" cried the cook to me, and he came to my table, and rapped my crown lightly with his fingers.

"Fool! And I am a fool, too. I ought to have looked after you."

At Nijni the steward dismissed me. I received nearly eight rubles, the first large money earned by me. When Smouri took farewell of me he said roughly:

"Well, here you are. Now keep your eyes open,—do you understand? You mustn't go about with your mouth open."

He put a tobacco-pouch of colored beads into my hand.

"There you are! That is good handwork. My godchild made it for me. Well, good-by. Read books; that is the best thing you can do."

He took me under the arms, lifted me up, kissed me, and placed me firmly on the jetty. I was sorry for him and for myself. I could hardly keep from crying when I saw him returning to the steamer, pushing aside the porters, looking so large, heavy, solitary. So many times since then I have met people like him, kind, lonely, cut off from the lives of other people.

CHAPTER VII

Grandfather and grandmother had again gone into the town. I went to them, prepared to be angry and warlike; but my heart was heavy. Why had they accounted me a thief?

Grandmother greeted me tenderly, and at once went to prepare the samovar. Grandfather asked as mockingly as usual:

"Have you saved much money?"

"What there is belongs to me," I answered, taking a seat by the window. I triumphantly produced a box of cigarettes from my pocket and began to smoke importantly.

"So-o-o," said grandfather, looking at me fixedly—"so that sit! You smoke the devil's poison? Isn't it rather soon?"

"Why, I have even had a pouch given to me," I boasted.

"A pouch?" squeaked grandfather. "What! Are you saying this to annoy me?"

He rushed upon me, with his thin, strong hands outstretched, his green eyes flashing. I leaped up, and stuck my head into his stomach. The old man sat on the floor, and for several oppressive moments looked at me, amazedly blinking, his dark mouth open. Then he asked quietly:

"You knock me down, your grandfather? The father of your mother?"

"You have knocked me about enough in the past," I muttered, not understanding that I had acted abominably.

Withered and light, grandfather rose from the floor, sat beside me, deftly snatched the cigarette from me, threw it out of the window, and said in a tone of fear:

"You mad fool! Don't you understand that God will punish you for this for the rest of your life? Mother,"—he turned to grandmother,—"did you see that? He knocked me down—he! Knocked me down! Ask him!"

She did not wait to ask. She simply came over to me, seized me by the hair, and beat me, saying:

"And for that—take this—and this!"

I was not hurt, but I felt deeply insulted, especially by grandfather's laughter. He jumped on a chair, slapped his legs with his hands, and croaked through his laughter:

"Th-a-t's right! Tha-a-t's right!"

I tore myself away, and ran out to the shed, where I lay in a corner crushed, desolate, listening to the singing of the samovar.

Then grandmother came to me, bent over me, and whispered hardly audibly:

"You must forgive me, for I purposely did not hurt you. I could not do otherwise than I did, for grandfather is an old man. He has to be treated with care. He has fractured some of his small bones, and, besides, sorrow has eaten into his heart. You must never do him any harm. You are not a little boy now. You must remember that. You must, Olesha! He is like a child, and nothing more."

Her words laved me like warm water. That friendly whisper made me feel ashamed of myself, and, light-hearted, I embraced her warmly. We kissed.

"Go to him. Go along. It is all right, only don't smoke before him yet. Give him time to get used to the idea."

I went back to the room, glanced at grandfather, and could hardly keep from laughing. He really was as pleased as a child. He was radiant, twisting his feet, and running his paws through his red hair as he sat by the table.

"Well, goat, have you come to butt me again? Ach, you—brigand! Just like your father! Freemason! You come back home, never cross yourself; and start smoking at once. Ugh, you—Bonaparte! you copeck's worth of goods!"

I said nothing. He had exhausted his supply of words and was silent from fatigue. But at tea he began to lecture me.

"The fear of God is necessary to men; it is like a bridle to a horse. We have no friend except God. Man is a cruel enemy to man." That men were my enemies, I felt was the truth, but the rest did not interest me.

"Now you will go back to Aunt Matrena, and in the spring you can go on a steamboat again. Live with them during the winter. And you need not tell them that you are leaving in the spring."

"Now, why should he deceive people?" said grandmother, who had just deceived grandfather by pretending to give me a beating.

"It is impossible to live without deceit," declared grandfather. "Just tell me now. Who lives without deceiving others?"

In the evening, while grandfather was reading his office, grandmother and I went out through the gate into the fields. The little cottage with two windows in which grandfather lived was on the outskirts of the town, at the back of Kanatni Street, where grandfather had once had his own house.

"So here we are again!" said grandmother, laughing. "The old man cannot find a resting-place for his soul, but must be ever on the move. And he does not even like it here; but I do."

Before us stretched for about three versts fields of scanty herbage, intersected by ditches, bounded by woods and the line of birches on the Kazan highroad. From the ditches the twigs of bushes projected, the rays of a cold sunset reddened them like blood. A soft evening breeze shook the gray blades of grass. From a nearer pathway, also like blades of grass, showed the dark form of town lads and girls. On the right, in the distance, stood the red walls of the burial-ground of the Old Believers. They called it "The Bugrovski Hermitage." On the left, beyond the causeway, rose a dark group of trees; there was the Jewish cemetery. All the surroundings were poor, and seemed to lie close to the wounded earth. The little houses on the outskirts of the town looked timidly with their windows on the dusty road. Along the road wandered small, ill-fed fowl. Toward the Dyevichia Monastery went a herd of lowing cows, from the camp came the sound of martial music. The brass instruments brayed.

A drunken man came along, ferociously holding out a harmonica. He stumbled and muttered:

"I am coming to thee—without fail."

"Fool!" said grandmother, blinking in the red sunlight. "Where are you going? Soon you will fall down and go to sleep, and you will be robbed in your sleep. You will lose your harmonica, your consolation."

I told her all about the life on the boat as I looked about me. After what I had seen I found it dull here; I felt like a fish out of water. Grandmother listened in silence and with attention, just as I liked to listen to her. When I told her about Smouri she crossed herself and said:

"He is a good man, help him, Mother of God; he is good! Take care, you, that you do not forget him! You should always remember what is good, and what is bad simply forget."

It was very difficult for me to tell her why they had dismissed me, but I took courage and told her. It made no impression whatever on her. She merely said calmly:

"You are young yet; you don't know how to live."

"That is what they all say to one another, 'You don't know how to live'—peasants, sailors, Aunt Matrena to her son. But how does one learn?"

She compressed her lips and shook her head.

"I don't know myself."

"And yet you say the same as the others!"

"And why should I not say it?" replied grandmother, calmly. "You must not be offended. You are young; you are not expected to know. And who does know, after all? Only rogues. Look at your grandfather. Clever and well educated as he is, yet he does not know."

"And you—have you managed your life well?"

"I? Yes. And badly also; all ways."

People sauntered past us, with their long shadows following them. The dust rose like smoke under their feet, burying those shadows. Then the evening sadness became more oppressive. The sound of grandfather's grumbling voice flowed from the window:

"Lord, in Thy wrath do not condemn me, nor in Thy rage punish me!"

Grandmother said, smiling:

"He has made God tired of him. Every evening he has his tale of woe, and about what? He is old now, and he does not need anything; yet he is always complaining and working himself into a frenzy about something. I expect God laughs when He hears his voice in the evening. There's Vassili Kashirin grumbling again!' Come and go to bed now." . . . .

I made up my mind to take up the occupation of catching singing-birds. I thought it would be a good way of earning a living. I would catch them, and grandmother would sell them. I bought a net, a hoop, and a trap, and made a cage. At dawn I took my place in a hollow among the bushes, while grandmother went in the woods with a basket and a bag to find the last mushrooms, bulbs, and nuts.

The tired September sun had only just risen. Its pale rays were now extinguished by clouds, now fell like a silver veil upon me in the causeway. At the bottom of the hollow it was still dusk, and a white mist rose from it. Its clayey sides were dark and bare, and the other side, which was more sloping, was covered with grass, thick bushes, and yellow, brown, and scarlet leaves. A fresh wind raised them and swept them along the ditch.

On the ground, among the turnip-tops, the goldfinch uttered its cry. I saw, among the ragged, gray grass, birds with red caps on their lively heads. About me fluttered curious titmouses. They made a great noise and fuss, comically blowing out their white cheeks, just like the young men of Kunavin Street on a Sunday. Swift, clever, spiteful, they wanted to know all and to touch everything, and they fell into the trap one after the other. It was pitiful to see how they beat their wings, but my business was strictly commerce. I changed the birds over into the spare cage and hid them in a bag. In the dark they kept quiet.

A flock of siskins settled on a hawthorn-bush. The bush was suffused by sunlight. The siskins were glad of the sun and chirped more merrily than ever. Their antics were like those of schoolboys. The thirsty, tame, speckled magpie, late in setting out on his journey to a warmer country, sat on the bending bough of a sweetbriar, cleaning his wing feathers and insolently looking at his prey with his black eyes. The lark soared on high, caught a bee, and, carefully depositing it on a thorn, once more settled on the ground, with his thievish head alert. Noiselessly flew the talking-bird,—the hawfinch,—the object of my longing dreams, if only

I could catch him. A bullfinch, driven from the flock, was perched on an alder-tree. Red, important, like a general, he chirped angrily, shaking his black beak.

The higher the sun mounted, the more birds there were, and the more gayly they sang. The hollow was full of the music of autumn. The ceaseless rustle of the bushes in the wind, and the passionate songs of the birds, could not drown that soft, sweetly melancholy noise. I heard in it the farewell song of summer. It whispered to me words meant for my ears alone, and of their own accord they formed themselves into a song. At the same time my memory unconsciously recalled to my mind pictures of the past. From somewhere above grandmother cried:

"Where are you?"

She sat on the edge of the pathway. She had spread out a handkerchief on which she had laid bread, cucumber, turnips, and apples. In the midst of this display a small, very beautiful cut-glass decanter stood. It had a crystal stopper, the head of Napoleon, and in the goblet was a measure of vodka, distilled from herbs.

"How good it is, O Lord!" said grandmother, gratefully.

"I have composed a song."

"Yes? Well?"

I repeated to her something which I thought was like poetry.

> "That winter draws near the signs are many;
> Farewell to thee, my summer sun!"

But she interrupted without hearing me out.

"I know a song like that, only it is a better one."

And she repeated in a singsong voice:

> "*Oi*, the summer sun has gone
> To dark nights behind the distant woods!
> *Ekh!* I am left behind, a maiden,
> Alone, without the joys of spring.
> Every morn I wander round;
> I trace the walks I took in May.
> The bare fields unhappy look;
> There it was I lost my youth.
> *Oi*, my friends, my kind friends,
> Take my heart from my white breast,
> Bury my heart in the snow!"

My conceit as an author suffered not a little, but I was delighted with this song, and very sorry for the girl.

Grandmother said:

"That is how grief sings. That was made up by a young girl, you know. She went out walking all the springtime, and before the winter her dear love had thrown her over, perhaps for another girl. She wept because her heart was sore. You cannot speak well and truly on what you have not experienced for yourself. You see what a good song she made up."

When she sold a bird for the first time, for forty copecks, she was very surprised.

"Just look at that! I thought it was all nonsense, just a boy's amusement; and it has turned out like this!"

"You sold it too cheaply."

"Yes; well?"

On market-days she sold them for a ruble, and was more surprised than ever. What a lot one might earn by just playing about!

"And a woman spends whole days washing clothes or cleaning floors for a quarter of a ruble, and here you just catch them! But it is n't a nice thing to do, you know, to keep birds in a cage. Give it up, Olesha!"

But bird-catching amused me greatly; I liked it. It gave me my independence and inconvenienced no one but the birds. I provided myself with good implements. Conversations with old bird-catchers taught me a lot. I went alone nearly three versts to catch birds: to the forest of Kstocski, on the banks of the Volga, where in the tall fir-trees lived and bred crossbills, and most valuable to collectors, the Apollyon titmouse, a long-tailed, white bird of rare beauty.

Sometimes I started in the evening and stayed out all night, wandering about on the Kasanski high-road, and sometimes in the autumn rains and through deep mud. On my back I carried an oilskin bag in which were cages, with food to entice the birds. In my hand was a solid cane of walnut wood. It was cold and terrifying in the autumn darkness, very terrifying. There stood by the side of the road old lightning-riven birches; wet branches brushed across my head. On the left under the hill, over the black Volga, floated rare lights on the masts of the last boats and barges, looking as if they were in an unfathomable abyss. The wheels splashed in the water, the sirens shrieked.

From the hard ground rose the huts of the road-side villages. Angry, hungry dogs ran in circles round my legs. The watchman collided with me, and cried in terror:

"Who is that? He whom the devils carry does not come out till night, they say."

I was very frightened lest my tackle should be taken from me, and I used to take five-copeck pieces with me to give to the watchmen. The watchman of the village of Thokinoi made friends with me, and was always groaning over me.

"What, out again? O you fearless, restless night-bird, eh?"

His name was Niphront. He was small and gray, like a saint. He drew out from his breast a turnip, an apple, a handful of peas, and placed them in my hand, saying:

"There you are, friend. There is a little present for you. Eat and enjoy it." And conducting me to the bounds of the village, he said, "Go, and God be with you!"

I arrived at the forest before dawn, laid my traps, and spreading out my coat, lay on the edge of the forest and waited for the day to come. It was still. Everything was wrapped in the deep autumn sleep. Through the gray mist the broad meadows under the hill were hardly visible. They were cut in two by the Volga, across which they met and separated again, melting away in the fog. In the distance, behind the forest on the same side as the meadows, rose without hurry the bright sun. On the black mane of the forest lights flashed out, and my heart began to stir strangely, poignantly. Swifter and swifter the fog rose from the meadows, growing silver in the rays of the sun, and, following it, the bushes, trees, and hayricks rose from the ground. The meadows were simply flooded with the sun's rays and flowed on each side, red-gold. The sun just glanced at the still water by the bank, and it seemed as if the whole river moved toward the sun as it rose higher and higher, joyfully blessed and warmed the denuded, chilled earth, which gave forth the sweet smell of autumn. The transparent air made the earth look enormous, boundlessly wide. Everything seemed to be floating in the distance, and to be luring one to the farthest ends of the world. I saw the sunrise ten times during those months, and each time a new world was born before my eyes, with a new beauty.

I loved the sun so much that its very name delighted me. The sweet sound of it was like a bell hidden in it. I loved to close my eyes and place my face right in the way of its hot rays to catch it in my hands when it came, like a sword, through the chinks of the fence or through the branches. Grandfather had read over and over again "Prince Mikhail Chernigovski and the Lady Theodora who would not Worship the Sun," and my idea of these people was that they were black, like Gipsies, harsh, malignant, and always had bad eyes, like poor Mordovans. When the sun rose over the meadows I involuntarily smiled with joy.

Over me murmured the forest of firs, shaking off the drops of dew with its green paws. In the shadows and on the fern-leaves glistened, like silver brocade, the rime of the morning frost. The reddening grass was crushed by the rain; immovable stalks bowed their heads to the ground: but when the sun's rays fell on them a slight stir was noticeable among the herbs, as if, may be, it was the last effort of their lives.

The birds awoke. Like gray balls of down, they fell from bough to bough. Flaming crossbills pecked with their crooked beaks the knots on the tallest firs. On the end of the fir-branches sang a white Apollyon titmouse, waving its long, rudder-like tail, looking askance suspiciously with its black, beady eyes at the net which I had spread. And suddenly the whole forest, which a minute ago had been solemnly pensive, was filled with the sound of a thousand bird-voices, with the bustle of living beings, the purest on the earth. In their image, man, the father of earthly beauty, created for his own consolation, elves, cherubim, and seraphim, and all the ranks of angels.

I was rather sorry to catch the little songsters, and had scruples about squeezing them into cages. I would rather have merely looked at them; but the hunter's passion and the desire to earn money drove away my pity.

The birds mocked me with their artfulness. The blue titmouse, after a careful examination of the trap, understood her danger, and, approaching sidewise without running any risk, helped herself to some seed between the sticks of the trap. Titmouses are very clever, but they are very curious, and that is their undoing. The proud bullfinches are stupid, and flocks of them fall into the nets, like over-fed citizens into a church. When they find themselves shut up, they are very astonished, roll their eyes, and peck my fingers with their stout beaks. The crossbill entered the trap calmly and seriously. This grasping, ignorant bird, unlike all the others, used to sit for a long time before the net, stretching out his long beak, and leaning on his thick tail. He can run up the trunk of trees like the woodpecker, always escorting the titmouse. About this smoke-gray singing-bird there is something unpleasant. No one loves it. And it loves no one. Like the magpie, it likes to steal and hide bright things.

Before noon I had finished my catch, and went home through the forest. If I had gone by the high-road past the villages, the boys and young men would have taken my cages away from me and broken up my tackle. I had already experienced that once.

I arrived home in the evening tired and hungry, but I felt that I had grown older, had learned something new, and had gained strength during that day. This new strength gave me the power to listen calmly and without resentment to grandfather's jeers; seeing which, grandfather began to speak sensibly and seriously.

"Give up this useless business! Give it up! No one ever got on through birds. Such a thing has never happened that I know of. Go and find another place, and let your intelligence grow up there. Man has not been given life for nothing; he is God's grain, and he must produce an ear of corn. Man is like a ruble; put out at good interest it produces three rubles. You think life is easy to live? No, it is not all easy. The world of men is like a dark night, but every man must make his own light. To every person is given enough for his ten fingers to hold, but every one wants to grasp by handfuls. One should be strong, but if one is weak, one must be artful. He who has little strength is weak, and he is neither in heaven nor in hell. Live as if you are with others, but remember that you are alone. Whatever happens, never trust any one. If you believe your own eyes, you will measure crookedly. Hold your tongue. Neither town or house was built by the tongue, but rubles are made by the ax. You are neither a fool nor a Kalmuck, to whom all riches are like lice on sheep."

He could talk like this all the evening, and I knew his words by heart. The words pleased me, but I distrusted their meaning. From what he said it was plain that two forces hindered man from doing as he wished, God and other people.

Seated at the window, grandmother wound the cotton for her lace. The spindle hummed under her skilful hands. She listened for a long time to grandfather's speech in silence, then she suddenly spoke.

"It all depends upon whether the Mother of God smiles upon us."

"What's that?" cried grandfather. "God! I have not forgotten about God. I know all about God. You old fool, has God sown fools on the earth, eh?"

*

In my opinion the happiest people on earth were Cossacks and soldiers. Their lives were simple and gay. On fine mornings they appeared in the hollow near our house quite early. Scattering over the bare fields like white mushrooms, they began a complicated, interesting game. Agile and strong in their white blouses, they ran about the field with guns in their hands, disappeared in the hollow, and suddenly, at the sound of the bugle, again spread themselves over the field with shouts of "Hurrah!" accompanied by the ominous sounds of the drum. They ran straight at our house with fixed bayonets, and they looked as if they would knock it down and sweep it away, like a hayrick, in a minute. I cried "Hurrah!" too, and ran with them, quite carried away. The wicked rattle of the drum aroused in me a passionate desire to destroy something, to break down the fence, to hit other boys. When they were resting, the soldiers used to give me a treat by teaching me how to signal and by showing me their heavy guns. Sometimes one of them would stick his bayonet into my stomach and cry, with a pretense of anger:

"Stick the cockroach!"

The bayonet gleamed; it looked as if it were alive, and seemed to wind about like a snake about to coil itself up. It was rather terrifying, but more pleasant.

The Mordovan drummer taught me to strike the drum with my fingers. At first he used to take me by the wrist, and, moving them so that he hurt me, would thrust the sticks into my crushed fingers.

"Hit it—one, two-one-tw-o-o! Rum te—tum! Beat it—left—softly, right—loudly, rum te—!" he shouted threateningly, opening wide his bird-like eyes.

I used to run about the field with the soldiers, almost to the end of the drill, and after it was finished, I used to escort them across the town to the barracks, listening to their loud songs, looking into their kind faces, all as new as five-ruble pieces just coined. The close-packed mass of happy men passing up the streets in one united body aroused a feeling of friendliness in me, a desire to throw myself in among them as into a river, to enter into them as into a forest. These men were frightened of nothing; they could conquer anything; they were capable of anything; they could do anything they liked; and they were all simple and good.

But one day during the time they were resting a young non-commissioned officer gave me a fat cigarette.

"Smoke this! I would not give them to any one. In fact I hardly like to give you one, my dear boy, they are so good."

I smoked it. He moved away a few steps, and suddenly a red flame blinded me, burning my fingers, my nose, my eyebrows. A gray, acrid smoke made me splutter and cough. Blinded, terrified, I stamped on the ground, and the soldiers, who had formed a ring around me, laughed loudly and heartily. I ran away home. Whistles and laughter followed me; something cracked like a shepherd's whip. My burned fingers hurt me, my face smarted, tears flowed from my eyes; but it was not the pain which oppressed me, only a heavy, dull amazement. Why should this amuse these good fellows?

When I reached home I climbed up to the attic and sat there a long time brooding over this inexplicable cruelty which stood so repulsively in my path. I had a peculiarly clear and vivid memory of the little soldier from Sarapulia standing before me, as large as life, and saying:

"Well, do you understand?"

Soon I had to go through something still more depressing and disgusting.

I had begun to run about in the barracks of the Cossacks, which stood near the Pecherski Square. The Cossacks seemed different from the soldiers, not because they rode so skilfully oh horseback and were dressed more beautifully, but because they spoke in a different way, sang different songs, and danced beautifully. In the evening, after they had seen to their horses, they used to gather in a ring near the stables, and a little red-haired Cossack, shaking his tufts of hair, sang softly in a high-pitched voice, like a trumpet. The long-drawn-out, sad song flowed out upon the Don and the blue Dounia. His eyes were closed, like the eyes of a linnet, which often sings till it falls dead from the branch to the ground. The collar of his Cossack shirt was undone. His collar-bone was visible, looking like a copper band. In fact, he was altogether metallic, coppery. Swaying on his thin legs, as if the earth under him were rocking, spreading out his hands, he seemed sightless, but full of sound. He, as it were, ceased to be a man, and became a brass instrument. Sometimes it seemed to me that he was falling, that he would fall on his back to the ground, and die like the linnet, because he put into the song all his soul and all his strength.

With their hands in their pockets or behind their broad backs, his comrades stood round in a ring, sternly looking at his brassy face. Beating time with their hands, softly spitting into space, they joined in earnestly, softly, as if they were in the choir in church. All of them, bearded and shaven, looked like icons, stern and set apart from other people. The song was long, like a long street, and as level, as broad and as wide. When I listened to him I forgot everything else, whether it was day or night upon the earth, whether I was an old man or a little boy. Everything else was forgotten. The voice of the singer died away. The sighs of the horses were audible as they grieved for their native steppes, and gently, but surely, the autumn night crept up from the fields. My heart swelled and almost burst with a multitude of extraordinary feelings, and a great, speechless love for human creatures and the earth.

The little copper-colored Cossack seemed to me to be no man, but something much more significant—a legendary being, better and on a higher plane than ordinary people. I could not talk to him. When he asked me a question I smiled blissfully and remained shyly silent. I was ready to follow him anywhere, silently and humbly, like a dog. All I wanted was to see him often, and to hear him sing.

CHAPTER VIII

When the snows came, grandfather once more took me to grandmother's sister.

"It will do you no harm," he said to me.

I seemed to have had a wonderful lot of experience during the summer. I felt that I had grown older and cleverer, and the dullness of my master's house seemed worse than ever. They fell ill as often as ever, upsetting their stomachs with offensive poisons, and giving one another detailed accounts of the progress of their illnesses. The old woman prayed to God in the same terrible and malignant way. The young mistress had grown thin, but she moved about just as pompously and slowly as when she was expecting her child. When she stitched at the baby-clothes she always sang the same song softly to herself:

> "Spiria, Spiria, Spiridon,
> Spiria, my little brother,
> I will sit in the sledge myself
> And Spiria on the foot-board."

If any one went into the room she left off singing at once and cried angrily:

"What do you want?"

I fully believed that she knew no other song but that.

In the evenings they used to call me into the sitting-room, and the order was given:

"Now tell us how you lived on the boat."

I sat on a chair near the door and spoke. I liked to recall a different life from this which I was forced to lead against my will. I was so interested that I forgot my audience, but not for long.

The women, who had never been on a boat, asked me:

"But it was very alarming, was n't it?"

I did not understand. Why should it be alarming?

"Why, the boat might go down any moment, and every one would be drowned."

The master burst out laughing, and I, although I knew that boats did not sink just because there were deep places, could not convince the women. The old woman was certain that the boat did not float on the water, but went along on wheels on the bottom of the river, like a cart on dry land.

"If they are made of iron, how can they float? An ax will not float; no fear!"

"But a scoop does not sink in the water."

"There's a comparison to make! A scoop is a small thing, nothing to speak of."

When I spoke of Smouri and his books they regarded me with contempt. The old lady said that only fools and heretics wrote books.

"What about the Psalms and King David?"

"The Psalms are sacred writings, and King David prayed God to forgive him for writing the Psalms."

"Where does it say so?"

"In the palms of my hands; that's where! When I get hold of you by the neck you will learn where."

She knew everything; she spoke on all subjects with conviction and always savagely.

"A Tatar died on the Pechorka, and his soul came out of his mouth as black as tar."

"Soul? Spirit?" I said, but she cried contemptuously:

"Of a Tatar! Fool!"

The young mistress was afraid of books, too.

"It is very injurious to read books, and especially when you are young," she said. "At home, at Grebeshka, there was a young girl of good family who read and read, and the end of it was that she fell in love with the deacon, and the deacon's wife so shamed her that it was terrible to see. In the street, before everybody."

Sometimes I used words out of Smouri's books, in one of which, one without beginning or end, was written, "Strictly speaking, no one person really invented powder; as is always the case, it appeared at the end of a long series of minor observations and discoveries." I do not know why I remembered these words so well. What I liked best of all was the joining of two phrases, "strictly speaking, no one person really invented powder." I was aware of force underlying them; but they brought me sorrow, ludicrous sorrow. It happened thus.

One day when my employers proposed that I should tell them about something which had happened on the boat I answered:

"I have n't anything left to tell, strictly speaking." This amazed them. They cried:

"What? What's that you said?"

And all four began to laugh in a friendly fashion, repeating:

"'Strictly speaking,'—ah, Lord!"

Even the master said to me:

"You have thought that out badly, old fellow." And for a long time after that they used to call me:

"Hi, 'strictly speaking,' come here and wipe up the floor after the baby, strictly speaking."

This stupid banter did not offend, but it greatly surprised, me. I lived in a fog of stupefying grief, and I worked hard in order to fight against it. I did not feel my inefficiencies when I was at work. In the house were two young children. The nurses never pleased the mistresses, and were continually being changed. I had to wait upon the children, to wash baby-clothes every day, and every week I had to go to the Jandarmski Fountain to rinse the linen. Here I was derided by the washerwomen:

"Why are you doing women's work?"

Sometimes they worked me up to such a pitch that I slapped them with the wet, twisted linen. They paid me back generously for this, but I found them merry and interesting.

The Jandarmski Fountain ran along the bottom of a deep causeway and fell into the Oka. The causeway cut the town off from the field which was called, from the name of an ancient god, Yarilo. On that field, near Semika, the inhabitants of the town had made a promenade. Grandmother had told me that in the days of her youth people still believed in Yarilo and offered sacrifices to him. They took a wheel, covered it with tarred tow, and let it roll down the hill with cries and songs, watching to see if the burning wheel would roll as far as the Oka. If it did, the god Yarilo had accepted the sacrifice; the summer would be sunny and happy.

The washerwomen were for the most part from Yarilo, bold, headstrong women who had the life of the town at their finger-ends. It was very interesting to hear their tales of the merchants, *chinovniks*, and officers for whom they worked. To rinse the linen in winter in the icy water of the river was work for a galley-slave. All the women had their hands so frost-bitten that the skin was broken. Bending over the stream, inclosed in a wooden trough, under an old penthouse full of crevices, which was no protection against either wind or snow, the women rinsed the linen. Their faces were flushed, pinched by the frost. The frost burned their wet fingers; they could not bend them. Tears trickled from their eyes, but they chatted all the time, telling one another different stories, bearing themselves with a peculiar bravery toward every one and everything.

The best of all the stories were told by Natalia Kozlovski, a woman of about thirty, fresh-faced, strong, with laughing eyes and a peculiarly facile and sharp tongue. All her companions had a high regard for her; she was consulted on all sorts of affairs, and much admired for her skill in work, for the neatness of her attire, and because she had been able to send her daughter to the high school. When, bending under the weight of two baskets of wet linen, she came down the hill on the slippery footpath, they greeted her gladly, and asked solicitously:

"Well, and how is the daughter?"

"Very well, thank you; she is learning well, thank God!"

"Look at that now! She will be a lady."

"That's why I am having her taught. Where do the ladies with the painted faces come from? They all come from us, from the black earth. And where else should they come from? He who has the most knowledge has the longest arms and can take more, and the one who takes the most has the honor and glory. God sends us into the world as stupid children and expects to take us back as wise old people, which means that we must learn!"

When she spoke every one was silent, listening attentively to her fluent, self-confident speech. They praised her to her face and behind her back, amazed at her cleverness, her intellect; but no one tried to imitate her. She had sewn brown leather from the leg of a boot, over the sleeve of her bodice which saved her from the necessity of baring her arms to the elbow, and prevented her sleeves from getting wet. They all said what a good idea it was, but not one of them followed her example. When I did so they laughed at me.

"*Ekh*, you? Letting a woman teach you!"

With reference to her daughter she said:

"That is an important affair. There will be one more young lady in the world. Is that a small thing? But of course she may not be able to finish her studies; she may die. And it is not an easy life for those who are students, you see. There was that daughter of the Bakhilovs. She studied and studied, and even became a teacher herself. Once you become a teacher, you know, you are settled for life."

"Of course, if they marry, they can do without education; that is, if they have something else to recommend them."

"A woman's wit lies not in her head."

It was strange and embarrassing to hear them speak about themselves with such lack of reticence. I knew how sailors, soldiers, and tillers of the soil spoke about women. I heard men always boasting among themselves of their skill in deceiving women, of cunning in their relations with them. I felt that their attitude toward "females" was hostile, but generally there was a ring of something in these boastings which led me to suppose that these stories were merely brag, inventions, and not the truth.

The washerwomen did not tell one another about their love adventures, but in whatever they said about men I detected an undercurrent of derision, of malice, and I thought it might be true that woman was strength.

"Even when they don't go about among their fellows and make friends, they come to women, every one of them!" said Natalia one day, and an old woman cried to her in a rheumy voice:

"And to whom else should they go? Even from God monks and hermits come to us."

These conversations amid the weeping splash of the water, the slapping of wet clothes on the ground, or against the dirty chinks, which not even the snow could hide with its clean cover—these shameless, malicious conversations about secret things, about that from which all races and peoples have sprung, roused in me a timid disgust, forced my thoughts and feelings to fix themselves on "the romances" which surrounded and irritated me. For me the understanding of the "romances" was closely intertwined with representations of obscure, immoral stories.

However, whether I was with the washerwomen, or in the kitchen with the orderlies or in cellars where lived the field laborers, I found it much more interesting than to be at home, where the stilted conversations were always on the same lines, where the same things happened over and over again, arousing nothing but a feeling of constraint and embittered boredom. My employers dwelt within the magic circle of food, illness, sleep, and the anxieties attendant on preparing for eating and sleeping. They spoke of sin and of death, of which they were much afraid. They rubbed against one another as grains of corn are rubbed against the grindstone, which they expect every moment to crush them. In my free time I used to go into the shed to chop wood, desiring to be alone. But that rarely happened. The orderlies used to come and talk about the news of the yard.

Ermokhin and Sidorov came more often than the others. The former was a long, bow-backed Kalougan, with thick, strong veins all over him, a small head, and dull eyes. He was lazy and irritatingly stupid; he moved slowly and clumsily, and when he saw a woman he blinked and bent forward, just as if he were going to throw himself at her feet. All the yard was amazed by his swift conquest of the cooks and the maids, and envied him. They were all afraid of his bear-like strength. Sidorov, a lean, bony native of Tula, was always sad, spoke softly, and loved to gaze into dark corners. He would relate some incident in a low voice, or sit in silence, looking into the darkest corner.

"What are you looking at?"

"I thought I saw a mouse running about. I love mice; they run to and fro so quietly."

I used to write letters home for these orderlies—love-letters. I liked this, but it was pleasanter to write letters for Sidorov than for any of the others. Every Saturday regularly he sent a letter to his sister at Tula.

He invited me into his kitchen, sat down beside me at the table, and, rubbing his close-cropped hair hard, whispered in my ear:

"Well, go on. Begin it as it ought to be begun. 'My dearest sister, may you be in good health for many years'—you know how it ought to go. And now write, 'I received the ruble; only you need not have sent it. But I thank you. I want for nothing; we live well here.' As a matter of fact, we do not live at all well, but like dogs; but there is no need to write that. Write that we live well. She is little, only fourteen years old. Why should she know? Now write by yourself, as you have been taught."

He pressed upon me from the left side, breathing into my ear hotly and odorously, and whispered perseveringly:

"Write 'if any one speaks tenderly to you, you are not to believe him. He wants to deceive you, and ruin you.'"

His face was flushed by his effort to keep back a cough. Tears stood in his eyes. He leaned on the table and pushed against me.

"You are hindering me!"

"It is all right; go on! 'Above all, never believe gentlemen. They will lead a girl wrong the first time they see her. They know exactly what to say. And if you have saved any money, give it to the priest to keep for you, if he is a good man. But the best thing, is to bury it in the ground, and remember the spot.'"

It was miserable work trying to listen to this whisper, which was drowned by the squeaking of the tin ventilator in the *fortochka*. I looked at the blackened front of the stove, at the china cupboard covered with flies. The kitchen was certainly very dirty, overrun with bugs, redolent with an acrid smell of burnt fat, kerosene, and smoke. On the stove, among the sticks of wood, cockroaches crawled in and out. A sense of melancholy stole over my heart. I could have cried with pity for the soldier and his sister. Was it possible, was it right that people should live like this?

I wrote something, no longer listening to Sidorov's whisper. I wrote of the misery and repulsiveness of life, and he said to me, sighing:

"You have written a lot; thank you. Now she will know what she has to be afraid of."

"There is nothing for her to be afraid of," I said angrily, although I was afraid of many things myself.

The soldier laughed, and cleared his throat.

"What an oddity you are! How is there nothing to be afraid of? What about gentlemen, and God? Is n't that something?"

When he received a letter from his sister he said restlessly:

"Read it, please. Be quick!"

And he made me read the badly scrawled, insultingly short, and nonsensical letter three times.

He was good and kind, but he behaved toward women like all the others; that is, with the primitive coarseness of an animal. Willingly and unwillingly, as I observed these affairs, which often went on under my eyes, beginning and ending with striking and impure swiftness, I saw Sidorov arouse in the breast of a woman a kind feeling of pity for him in his soldier's life, then intoxicate her with tender lies, and then tell Ermokhin of his conquest, frowning and spitting his disgust, just as if he had been taking some bitter medicine. This made my heart ache, and I angrily asked the soldiers why they all deceived women, lied to them, and then, jeering among themselves at the woman they had treated so, gave her away and often beat her.

One of them laughed softly, and said:

"It is not necessary for you to know anything about such things. It is all very bad; it is sin. You are young; it is too early for you."

But one day I obtained a more definite answer, which I have always remembered.

"Do you think that she does not know that I am deceiving her?" he said, blinking and coughing. "She kno-o-ows. She wants to be deceived. Everybody lies in such affairs; they are a disgrace to all concerned. There is no love on either side; it is simply an amusement. It is a dreadful disgrace. Wait, and you will know for yourself. It was for that God drove them out of paradise, and from that all unhappiness has come."

He spoke so well, so sadly, and so penitently that he reconciled me a little to these "romances." I began to have a more friendly feeling toward him than towards Ermokhin, whom I hated, and seized every occasion of mocking and teasing. I succeeded in this, and he often pursued me across the yard with some evil design, which only his clumsiness prevented him from executing.

"It is forbidden," went on Sidorov, speaking of women.

That it was forbidden I knew, but that it was the cause of human unhappiness I did not believe. I saw that people were unhappy, but I did not believe what he said, because I sometimes saw an extraordinary expression in the eyes of people in love, and was aware of a peculiar tenderness in those who loved. To witness this festival of the heart was always pleasant to me.

However, I remember that life seemed to me to grow more and more tedious, cruel, fixed for ever in those forms of it which I saw from day to day. I did not dream of anything better than that which passed interminably before my eyes.

But one day the soldiers told me a story which stirred me deeply. In one of the flats lived a cutter-out, employed by the best tailor in the town, a quiet, meek foreigner. He had a little, childless wife who read books all day long. Over the noisy yard, amid houses full of drunken people, these two lived, invisible and silent. They had no visitors, and never went anywhere themselves except to the theater in holiday-time.

The husband was engaged from early morning until late at night. The wife, who looked like an undersized girl, went to the library twice a week. I often saw her walking with a limp, as if she were slightly lame, as far as the dike, carrying books in a strap, like a school-girl. She looked unaffected, pleasant, new, clean, with gloves on her small hands. She had a face like a bird, with little quick eyes, and everything about her was pretty, like a porcelain figure on a mantel-shelf. The soldiers said that she had some ribs missing in her left side, and that was what made her sway so curiously as she walked; but I thought this very nice, and at once set her above all the other ladies in the yard—the officers' wives. The latter, despite their loud voices, their variegated attire, and *haut tournure*, had a soiled look about them, as if they had been lying forgotten for a long time, in a dark closet among other unneeded things.

The little wife of the cutter-out was regarded in the yard as half witted. It was said that she had lost her senses over books, and had got into such a condition that she could not manage the housekeeping; that her husband had to go to the market himself in search of provisions, and order the dinner and supper of the cook, a great, huge foreign female. She had only one red eye, which was always moist, and a narrow pink crevice in place of the other. She was like her mistress, they said of her. She did not know how to cook a dish of fried veal and onions properly, and one day she ignominiously bought radishes, thinking she was buying parsley. Just think what a dreadful thing that was!

All three were aliens in the building, as if they had fallen by accident into one of the compartments of a large hen-house. They reminded me of a titmouse which, taking refuge from the frost, flies through the *fortochka* into a stifling and dirty habitation of man.

And then the orderlies told me how the officers had played an insulting and wicked trick on the tailor's little wife. They took turns to write her a letter every day, declaring their love for her, speaking of their sufferings and of her beauty. She answered them, begging them to leave her in peace, regretting that she had been the cause of unhappiness to any one, and praying God that He would help them to give up loving her. When any one of them received a letter like that, they used to read it all together, and then make up another letter to her, signed by a different person.

When they told me this story, the orderlies laughed too, and abused the lady.

"She is a wretched fool, the crookback," said Ermokhin in a bass voice, and Sidorov softly agreed with him.

"Whatever a woman is, she likes being deceived. She knows all about it."

I did not believe that the wife of the cutter-out knew that they were laughing at her, and I resolved at once to tell her about it. I watched for the cook to go down into the cellar, and I ran up the dark staircase to the flat of the little woman, and slipped into the kitchen. It was empty. I went on to the sitting-room. The tailor's wife was sitting at the table. In one hand she held a heavy gold cup, and in the other an open book. She was startled. Pressing the book to her bosom, she cried in a low voice:

"Who is that? Auguste! Who are you?"

I began to speak quickly and confusedly, expecting every minute that she would throw the book at me. She was sitting in a large, raspberry-colored armchair, dressed in a pale-blue wrap with a fringe at the hem and lace on the collar and sleeves over her shoulders was spread her flaxen, wavy hair. She looked like an angel from the gates of heaven. Leaning against the back of her chair, she looked at me with round eyes, at first angrily, then in smiling surprise.

When I had said what I wanted to say, and, losing my courage, turned to the door, she cried after me:

"Wait!"

Placing the cup on the tray, throwing the book on the table, and folding her hands, she said in a husky, grown-up voice:

"What a funny boy you are! Come closer!"

I approached very cautiously. She took me by the hand, and, stroking it with her cold, small fingers, said:

"Are you sure that no one sent you to tell me this? No? All right; I see that you thought of it yourself."

Letting my hand go, she closed her eyes, and said softly and drawingly:

"So that is how the soldiers speak of me?"

"Leave this place," I advised her earnestly.

"Why?"

"They will get the better of you."

She laughed pleasantly. Then she asked:

"Do you study? Are you fond of books?"

"I have no time for reading."

"If you were fond of it, you would find the time. Well, thank you."

She held out a piece of silver money to me, grasped between her first finger and her thumb. I felt ashamed to take that cold thing from her, but I did not dare to refuse. As I went out, I laid it on the pedestal of the stair-banisters.

I took away with me a deep, new impression from that woman. It was as if a new day had dawned for me. I lived for several days in a state of joy, thinking of the spacious room and the tailor's wife sitting in it, dressed in pale blue and looking like an angel. Everything around her was unfamiliarly beautiful. A dull-gold carpet lay under her feet; the winter day looked through the silver panes of the window, warming itself in her presence. I wanted very much to look at her again. How would it be if I went to her and asked her for a book?

I acted upon this idea. Once more I saw her in the same place, also with a book in her hand; but she had a red handkerchief tied round her face, and her eyes were swollen. As she gave me a book with a black binding, she indistinctly called out something. I went away feeling sad, carrying the book, which smelt of creosote and aniseed drops. I hid it in the attic, wrapping it up in a clean shirt and some paper; for I was afraid that my employers might find it and spoil it.

They used to take the "Neva" for the sake of the patterns and prizes, but they never read it. When they had looked at the pictures, they put it away in a cupboard in the bedroom, and at the end of the year they had been bound, placing them under the bed, where already lay three volumes of "The Review of Painting." When I washed the floor in the bedroom dirty water flowed under these books. The master subscribed to the "Russian Courier," but when he read it in the evening he grumbled at it.

"What the devil do they want to write all tins for? Such dull stuff!"

On Saturday, when I was putting away the linen in the attic, I remembered about the book. I undid it from its wrappings, and read the first lines: "Houses are like people; they all have physiognomies of their own." The truth of this surprised me, and I went on reading farther, standing at the dormer-window until I was too cold to stay longer. But in the evening, when they had gone to vespers, I carried the book into the kitchen and buried myself in the yellow, worn pages, which were like autumn leaves. Without effort, they carried me into another life, with new names and new standards, showed me noble heroes, gloomy villains, quite unlike the people with whom I had to do. This was a novel by Xavier de Montepaine. It was long, like all his novels, simply packed with people and incidents, describing an unfamiliar, vehement life. Everything in this novel was wonderfully clear and simple, as if a mellow light hidden between the lines illuminated the good and evil. It helped one to love and hate, compelling one to follow with intense interest the fates of the people, who seemed so inextricably entangled. I was seized with sudden desires to help this person, to hinder that, forgetting that this life, which had so unexpectedly opened before me, had its existence only on paper. I forgot everything else in the exciting struggles. I was swallowed up by a feeling of joy on one page, and by a feeling of grief on the next.

I read until I heard the bell ring in the front hall. I knew at once who it was that was ringing, and why.

The candle had almost burned out. The candlestick, which I had cleaned only that morning, was covered with grease; the wick of the lamp, which I ought to have looked after, had slipped out of its place, and the flame had gone out. I rushed about the kitchen trying to hide the traces of my crime. I slipped the book under the stove-hole, and began to put the lamp to rights. The nurse came running out of the sitting-room.

"Are you deaf? They have rung!"

I rushed to open the door.

"Were you asleep?" asked the master roughly. His wife, mounting the stairs heavily, complained that she had caught cold. The old lady scolded me. In the kitchen she noticed the burned-out candle at once, and began to ask me what I had been doing. I said nothing. I had only just come down from the heights, and I was all to pieces with fright lest they should find the book. She cried out that I would set the house on fire. When the master and his wife came down to supper she complained to them.

"There, you see, he has let the candle gutter, he will set the house on fire."

While they were at supper the whole four of them lashed me with their tongues, reminding me of all my crimes, wilful and involuntary, threatening me with perdition; but I knew quite well that they were all speaking not from ill-feeling, or for my good, but simply because they were bored. And it was curious to observe how empty and foolish they were compared with the people in books.

When they had finished eating, they grew heavy, and went wearily to bed. The old woman, after disturbing God with her angry complaints, settled herself on the stove and was silent. Then I got up, took the book from the stove-hole, and went to the window. It was a bright night, and the moon looked straight into the window; but my sight was not good enough to see the small print. My desire to read was tormenting me. I took a brass saucepan from the shelf and reflected the light of the moon from it on the book; but it became still more difficult and blurred. Then I betook myself to the bench in the corner where the icon was, and, standing upon it, began to read by the light of the small lamp. But I was very tired, and dozed, sinking down on the bench. I was awakened by the cries and blows of the old woman. She was hitting me painfully over the shoulders with the book, which she held in her hand. She was red with rage, furiously tossing her brown head, barefooted, and wearing only her night-dress. Victor roared from the loft:

"Mamasha, don't make such a noise! You make life unbearable."

"She has found the book. She will tear it up!" I thought.

My trial took place at breakfast-time. The master asked me, sternly:

"Where did you get that book?"

The women exclaimed, interrupting each other. Victor sniffed contemptuously at the pages and said:

"Good gracious! what does it smell of?"

Learning that the book belonged to the priest, they looked at it again, surprised and indignant that the priest should read novels. However, this seemed to calm them down a little, though the master gave me another long lecture to the effect that reading was both injurious and dangerous.

"It is the people who read books who rob trains and even commit murders."

The mistress cried out, angry and terrified:

"Have you gone out of your mind? What do you want to say such things to him for?"

I took Montepaine to the soldier and told him what had happened. Sidorov took the book, opened a small trunk, took out a clean towel, and, wrapping the novel in it, hid it in the trunk.

"Don't you take any notice of them. Come and read here. I shan't tell any one. And if you come when I am not here, you will find the key hanging behind the icon. Open the trunk and read."

The attitude my employers had taken with regard to the book raised it to the height of an important and terrible secret in my mind. That some "readers" had robbed a train or tried to murder some one did not interest me, but I remembered the question the priest had asked me in confession, the reading of the gymnasiast in the basement, the words of Smouri, the "proper books," and grandfather's stories of the black books of freemasonry. He had said:

"In the time of the Emperor Alexander Pavlovich of blessed memory the nobles took up the study of 'black books' and freemasonry. They planned to hand over the whole Russian people to the Pope of Rome, if you please! But General Arakcheev caught them in the act, and, without regard to their position, sent them all to Siberia, into prison. And there they were; exterminated like vermin."

I remembered the *"umbra"* of Smouri's book and "Gervase" and the solemn, comical words:

> Profane ones who are curious to know our business,
> Never shall your weak eyes spy it out!

I felt that I was on the threshold of the discovery of some great secret, and went about like a lunatic. I wanted to finish reading the book, and was afraid that the soldier might lose it or spoil it somehow. What should I say to the tailor's wife then?

The old woman watched me sharply to see that I did not run to the orderly's room, and taunted me:

"Bookworm! Books! They teach dissoluteness. Look at that woman, the bookish one. She can't even go to market herself. All she can do is to carry on with the officers. She receives them in the daytime. I kno-o-w."

I wanted to cry, "That's not true. She does not carry on," but I was afraid to defend the tailor's wife, for then the old woman might guess that the book was hers.

I had a desperately bad time of it for several days. I was distracted and worried, and could not sleep for fear that Montepaine had come to grief. Then one day the cook belonging to the tailor's household stopped me in the yard and said:

"You are to bring back that book."

I chose the time after dinner, when my employers lay down to rest, and appeared before the tailor's wife embarrassed and crushed. She looked now as she had the first time, only she was dressed differently. She wore a gray skirt and a black velvet blouse, with a turquoise cross upon her bare neck. She looked like a hen bullfinch. When I told her that I had not had time to read the book, and that I had been forbidden to read, tears filled my eyes. They were caused by mortification, and by joy at seeing this woman.

"Foo! what stupid people!" she said, drawing her fine brows together. "And your master has such an interesting face, too! Don't you fret about it. I will write to him."

"You must not! Don't write!" I begged her. "They will laugh at you and abuse you. Don't you know that no one in the yard likes you, that they all laugh at you, and say that you are a fool, and that some of your ribs are missing?"

As soon as I had blurted this out I knew that I had said something unnecessary and insulting to her. She bit her lower lip, and clapped her hands on her hips as if she were riding on horseback. I hung my head in confusion and wished that I could sink into the earth; but she sank into a chair and laughed merrily, saying over and over again:

"Oh, how stupid! how stupid! Well, what is to be done?" she asked, looking fixedly at me. Then she sighed and said, "You are a strange boy, very strange."

Glancing into the mirror beside her, I saw a face with high cheek-bones and a short nose, a large bruise on the forehead, and hair, which had not been cut for a long time, sticking out in all directions. That is what she called "a strange boy." The strange boy was not in the least like a fine porcelain figure.

"You never took the money that I gave you. Why?"

"I did not want it."

She sighed.

"Well, what is to be done? If they will allow you to read, come to me and I will give you some books."

On the mantel-shelf lay three books. The one which I had brought back was the thickest. I looked at it sadly. The tailor's wife held out her small, pink hand to me.

"Well, good-by!"

I touched her hand timidly, and went away quickly.

It was certainly true what they said about her not knowing anything. Fancy calling two *gravities* money! It was just like a child.

But it pleased me.

CHAPTER IX

I have sad and ludicrous reasons for remembering the burdensome humiliations, insults, and alarms which my swiftly developed passion for reading brought me.

The books of the tailor's wife looked as if they were terribly expensive, and as I was afraid that the old mistress might burn them in the stove, I tried not to think of them, and began to buy small colored books from the shop where I bought bread in the mornings.

The shopkeeper was an ill-favored fellow with thick lips. He was given to sweating, had a white, wizen face covered with scrofulous scars and pimples, and his eyes were white. He had short, clumsy fingers on puffy hands. His shop took the place of an evening club for grown-up people; also for the thoughtless young girls living in the street. My master's brother used to go there every evening to drink beer and play cards. I was often sent to call him to supper, and more than once I saw, in the small, stuffy room behind the shop, the capricious, rosy wife of the shopkeeper sitting on the knee of Victorushka or some other young fellow.

Apparently this did not offend the shopkeeper; nor was he offended when his sister, who helped him in the shop, warmly embraced the drunken men, or soldiers, or, in fact any one who took her fancy. The business done at the shop was small. He explained this by the fact that it was a new business, although the shop had been open since the autumn. He showed obscene pictures to his guests and customers, allowing those who wished to copy the disgraceful verses beneath them.

I read the foolish little books of Mischa Evstignev, paying so many copecks for the loan of them. This was dear, and the books afforded me no pleasure at all. "Guyak, or, the Unconquerable Truth," "Franzl, the Venitian," "The Battle of the Russians with the Kabardines," or "The Beautiful Mahomedan Girl, Who Died on the Grave of her Husband,"—all that kind of literature did not interest me either, and often aroused a bitter irritation. The books seemed to be laughing at me, as at a fool, when they told in dull words such improbable stories.

"The Marksmen," "Youri Miloslavski," "Monks' Secrets," "Yapacha, the Tatar Freebooter," and such books I like better. I was the richer for reading them; but what I liked better than all was the lives of the saints. Here was something serious in which I could believe, and which at times deeply stirred me. All the martyrs somehow reminded me of "Good Business," and the female martyrs of grandmother, and the holy men of grandfather in his best moments.

I used to read in the shed when I went there to chop wood, or in the attic, which was equally uncomfortable and cold. Sometimes, if a book interested me or I had to read it quickly, I used to get up in the night and light the candle; but the old mistress, noticing that my candle had grown smaller during the night, began to measure the candles with a piece of wood, which she hid away somewhere. In the morning, if my candle was not as long as the measure, or if I, having found the measure, had not broken it to the length of the burned candle, a wild cry arose from the kitchen. Sometimes Victorushka called out loudly from the loft:

"Leave off that howling, Mamasha! You make life unbearable. Of course he burns the candles, because he reads books. He gets them from the shop. I know. Just look among his things in the attic."

The old woman ran up to the attic, found a book, and burned it to ashes.

This made me very angry, as you may imagine, but my love of reading increased. I understood that if a saint had entered that household, my employers would have set to work to teach him, tried to set him to their own tune. They would have done this for something to do. If they had left off judging people, scolding them, jeering at them, they would have forgotten how to talk, would have been stricken with dumbness, and would not have been themselves at all. When a man is aware of himself, it must be through his relations with other people. My employers could not behave themselves toward those about them otherwise than as teachers, always ready to condemn; and if they had taught somebody to live exactly as they lived themselves, to think and feel in the same way, even then they would have condemned him for that very reason. They were that sort of people.

I continued to read on the sly. The old woman destroyed books several times, and I suddenly found myself in debt to the shopkeeper for the enormous amount of forty-seven copecks. He demanded the money, and threatened to take it from my employers' money when they sent me to make purchases.

"What would happen then?" he asked jeeringly.

To me he was unbearably repulsive. Apparently he felt this, and tortured me with various threats from which he derived a peculiar enjoyment. When I went into the shop his pimply face broadened, and he would ask gently:

"Have you brought your debt?"

"No."

This startled him. He frowned.

"How is that? Am I supposed to give you things out of charity? I shall have to get it from you by sending you to the reformatory."

I had no way of getting the money, my wages were paid to grandfather. I lost my presence of mind. What would happen to me? And in answer to my entreaty that he wait for settlement of the debt, the shopkeeper stretched out his oily, puffy hand, like a bladder, and said:

"Kiss my hand and I will wait."

But when I seized a weight from the counter and brandished it at him, he ducked and cried:

"What are you doing? What are you doing? I was only joking."

Knowing well that he was not joking, I resolved to steal the money to get rid of him. In the morning when I was brushing the master's clothes, money jingled in his trousers' pockets, and sometimes it fell out and rolled on the floor. Once some rolled into a crack in the boards under the staircase. I forgot to say anything about this, and remembered it only several days afterward when I found two *greven* between the boards. When I gave it back to the master his wife said to him:

"There, you see! You ought to count your money when you leave it in your pockets."

But my master, smiling at me, said:

"He would not steal, I know."

Now, having made up my mind to steal, I remembered these words and his trusting smile, and felt how hard it would be for me to rob him. Several times I took silver out of the pockets and counted it, but I could not take it. For three days I tormented myself about this, and suddenly the whole affair settled itself quickly and simply. The master asked me unexpectedly:

"What is the matter with you, Pyeshkov? You have become dull lately. Are n't you well, or what?"

I frankly told him all my troubles. He frowned.

"Now you see what books lead to! From them, in some way or another, trouble always comes."

He gave me half a ruble and admonished me sternly:

"Now look here; don't you go telling my wife or my mother, or there will be a row."

Then he smiled kindly and said:

"You are very persevering, devil take you! Never mind; it is a good thing. Anyhow, give up books. When the New Year comes, I will order a good paper, and you can read that."

And so in the evenings, from tea-time till supper-time, I read aloud to my employers "The Moscow Gazette," the novels of Bashkov, Rokshnin, Rudinskovski, and other literature, for the nourishment of people who suffered from deadly dullness.

I did not like reading aloud, for it hindered me from understanding what I read. But my employers listened attentively, with a sort of reverential eagerness, sighing, amazed at the villainy of the heroes, and saying proudly to one another:

"And we live so quietly, so peacefully; we know nothing of such things, thank God!"

They mixed up the incidents, ascribed the deeds of the famous brigand Churkin to the postboy Thoma Kruchin, and mixed the names. When I corrected their mistakes they were surprised.

"What a memory he has!"

Occasionally the poems of Leonide Grave appeared in "The Moscow Gazette." I was delighted with them. I copied several of them into a note-book, but my employers said of the poet:

"He is an old man, you know; so he writes poetry." "A drunkard or an imbecile, it is all the same."

I liked the poetry of Strujkin, and the Count Memento Mori, but both the women said the verses were clumsy.

"Only the Petrushki or actors talk in verse."

It was a hard life for me on winter evenings, under the eyes of my employers, in that close, small room. The dead night lay outside the window, now and again the ice cracked. The others sat at the table in silence, like frozen fish. A snow-storm would rattle the windows and beat against the walls, howl down the chimney, and shake the flue-plate. The children cried in the nursery. I wanted to sit by myself in a dark corner and howl like a wolf.

At one end of the table sat the women, knitting socks or sewing. At the other sat Victorushka, stooping, copying plans unwillingly, and from time to time calling out:

"Don't shake the table! Goats, dogs, mice!"

At the side, behind an enormous embroidery-frame, sat the master, sewing a tablecloth in cross-stitch. Under his fingers appeared red lobsters, blue fish, yellow butterflies, and red autumn leaves. He had made the design himself, and had sat at the work for three winters. He had grown very tired of it, and often said to me in the daytime, when I had some spare time:

"Come along, Pyeshkov; sit down to the tablecloth and do some of it!"

I sat down, and began to work with the thick needle. I was sorry for my master, and always did my best to help him. I had an idea that one day he would give up drawing plans, sewing, and playing at cards, and begin doing something quite different, something interesting, about which he often thought, throwing his work aside and gazing at it with fixed, amazed eyes, as at something unfamiliar to him. His hair fell over his forehead and cheeks; he looked like a laybrother in a monastery.

"What are you thinking of?" his wife would ask him.

"Nothing in particular," he would reply, returning to his work.

I listened in dumb amazement. Fancy asking a man what he was thinking of. It was a question which could not be answered. One's thoughts were always sudden and many, about all that passed before one's eyes, of what one saw yesterday or a year ago. It was all mixed up together, elusive, constantly moving and changing.

The serial in "The Moscow Gazette" was not enough to last the evening, and I went on to read the journals which were put away under the bed in the bedroom. The young mistress asked suspiciously:

"What do you find to read there? It is all pictures."

But under the bed, besides the "Painting Review," lay also "Flames," and so we read "Count Tyatin-Baltiski," by Saliass. The master took a great fancy to the eccentric hero of the story, and laughed mercilessly, till the tears ran down his cheeks, at the melancholy adventures of the hero, crying:

"Really, that is most amusing!"

"Piffle!" said the mistress to show her independence of mind.

The literature under the bed did me a great service. Through it, I had obtained the right to read the papers in the kitchen, and thus made it possible to read at night.

To my joy, the old woman went to sleep in the nursery for the nurse had a drunken fit. Victorushka did not interfere with me. As soon as the household was asleep, he dressed himself quietly, and disappeared somewhere till morning. I was not allowed to have a light, for they took the candles into the bedrooms, and I had no money to buy them for myself; so I began to collect the tallow from the candlesticks on the quiet, and put it in a sardine tin, into which I also poured lamp oil, and, making a wick with some thread, was able to make a smoky light. This I put on the stove for the night.

When I turned the pages of the great volumes, the bright red tongue of flame quivered agitatedly, the wick was drowned in the burning, evil-smelling fat, and the smoke made my eyes smart. But all this unpleasantness was swallowed up in the enjoyment with which I looked at the illustrations and read the description of them. These illustrations opened up before me a world which increased daily in breadth—a world adorned with towns, just like the towns of story-land. They showed me lofty hills and lovely seashores. Life developed wonderfully for me. The earth became more fascinating, rich in people, abounding in towns and all kinds of things. Now when I gazed into the distance beyond the Volga, I knew that it was not space which lay beyond, but before that, when I had looked, it used to make me feel oddly miserable. The meadows lay flat, bushes grew in clumps, and where the meadows ended, rose the indented black wall of the forest. Above the meadows it was dull, cold blue. The earth seemed an empty, solitary place. And my heart also was empty. A gentle sorrow nipped it; all desires had departed, and I thought of nothing. All I wanted was to shut my eyes. This melancholy emptiness promised me nothing, and sucked out of my heart all that there was in it.

The description of the illustrations told me in language which I could understand about other countries, other peoples. It spoke of various incidents of the past and present, but there was a lot which I did not understand, and that worried me. Sometimes strange words stuck in my brain, like "metaphysics," "chiliasm," "chartist." They were a source of great anxiety to me, and seemed to grow into monsters obstructing my vision. I thought that I should never understand anything. I did not succeed in finding out the meaning of those words. In fact, they stood like sentries on the threshold of all secret knowledge. Often whole phrases stuck in my memory for a long time, like a splinter in my finger, and hindered me from thinking of anything else.

I remembered reading these strange verses:

> "All clad in steel, through the unpeopled land,
> Silent and gloomy as the grave,
> Rides the Czar of the Huns, Attilla.
> Behind him comes a black mass of warriors, crying,
> 'Where, then, is Rome; where is Rome the mighty?'"

That Rome was a city, I knew; but who on earth were the Huns? I simply had to find that out. Choosing a propitious moment, I asked my master. "The Huns?" he cried in amazement. "The devil knows who they are. Some trash, I expect."

And shaking his head disapprovingly, he said:

"That head of yours is full of nonsense. That is very bad, Pyeshkov."

Bad or good, I wanted to know.

I had an idea that the regimental chaplain, Soloviev, ought to know who the Huns were, and when I caught him in the yard, I asked him. The pale, sickly, always disagreeable man, with red eyes, no eyebrows, and a yellow beard, pushing his black staff into the earth, said to me:

"And what is that to do with you, eh?"

Lieutenant Nesterov answered my question by a ferocious:

"What-a-t?"

Then I concluded that the right person to ask about the Huns was the dispenser at the chemist's. He always looked at me kindly. He had a clever face, and gold glasses on his large nose.

"The Huns," said the dispenser, "were a nomad race, like the people of Khirgiz. There are no more of these people now. They are all dead."

I felt sad and vexed, not because the Huns were dead, but because the meaning of the word that had worried me for so long was quite simple, and was also of no use to me.

But I was grateful to the Huns after my collision with the word ceased to worry me so much, and thanks to Attilla, I made the acquaintance of the dispenser Goldberg.

This man knew the literal meaning of all words of wisdom. He had the keys to all knowledge. Setting his glasses straight with two fingers, he looked fixedly into my eyes and said, as if he were driving small nails into my forehead:

"Words, my dear boy, are like leaves on a tree. If we want to find out why the leaves take one form instead of another, we must learn how the tree grows. We must study books, my dear boy. Men are like a good garden in which everything grows, both pleasant and profitable."

I often had to run to the chemist's for soda-water and magnesia for the adults of the family, who were continually suffering from heartburn, and for castor-oil and purgatives for the children.

The short instructions which the dispenser gave me instilled into my mind a still deeper regard for books. They gradually became as necessary to me as vodka to the drunkard. They showed me a new life, a life of noble sentiments and strong desires which incite people to deeds of heroism and crimes. I saw that the people about me were fitted for neither heroism nor crime. They lived apart from everything that I read about in books, and it was hard to imagine what they found interesting in their lives. I had no desire to live such a life. I was quite decided on that point. I would not.

From the letterpress which accompanied the drawings I had learned that in Prague, London, and Paris there are no open drains in the middle of the city, or dirty gulleys choked with refuse. There were straight, broad streets, and different kinds of houses and churches. There they did not have a six-months-long winter, which shuts people up in their houses, and no great fast, when only fermenting cabbage, pickled mushrooms, oatmeal, and potatoes cooked in disgusting vegetable oil can be eaten. During the great fast books are forbidden, and they took away the "Review of Painting" from me, and that empty, meager life again closed about me. Now that I could compare it with the life pictured in books, it seemed more wretched and ugly than ever. When I could read I felt well and strong; I worked well and quickly, and had an object in life. The sooner I was finished, the more time I should have for reading. Deprived of books, I became lazy, and drowsy, and became a victim to forgetfulness, to which I had been a stranger before.

I remember that even during those dull days something mysterious happened. One evening when we had all gone to bed the bell of the cathedral suddenly rang out, arousing every one in the house at once. Half-dressed people rushed to the windows, asking one another:

"Is it a fire? Is that the alarm-bell?"

In the other flats one could hear the same bustle going on. Doors slammed; some one ran across the yard with a horse ready saddled. The old mistress shrieked that the cathedral had been robbed, but the master stopped her.

"Not so loud, Mamasha! Can't you hear that that is not an alarm-bell?"

"Then the archbishop is dead."

Victorushka climbed down from the loft, dressed himself, and muttered:

"I know what has happened. I know!"

The master sent me to the attic to see if the sky was red. I ran up-stairs and climbed to the roof through the dormer-window. There was no red light in the sky. The bell tolled slowly in the quiet frosty air. The town lay sleepily on the earth. In the darkness invisible people ran about, scrunching the snow under their feet. Sledges squealed, and the bell wailed ominously. I returned to the sitting-room.

"There is no red light in the sky."

"Foo, you! Good gracious!" said the master, who had on his greatcoat and cap. He pulled up his collar and began to put his feet into his goloshes undecidedly.

The mistress begged him:

"Don't go out! Don't go out!"

"Rubbish!"

Victorushka, who was also dressed, teased them all.

"I know what has happened."

When the brothers went out into the street the women, having sent me to get the samovar ready, rushed to the window. But the master rang the street door-bell almost directly, ran up the steps silently, shut the door, and said thickly:

"The Czar has been murdered!"

"How murdered?" exclaimed the old lady.

"He has been murdered. An officer told me so. What will happen now?"

Victorushka rang, and as he unwillingly took off his coat said angrily:

"And I thought it was war!"

Then they all sat down to drink tea, and talked together calmly, but in low voices and cautiously. The streets were quiet now, the bells had given up tolling. For two days they whispered together mysteriously, and went to and fro. People also came to see them, and related some event in detail. I tried hard to understand what had happened, but they hid the newspapers from me. When I asked Sidorov why they had killed the Czar he answered, softly:

"It is forbidden to speak of it."

But all this soon wore away. The old empty life was resumed, and I soon had a very unpleasant experience.

On one of those Sundays when the household had gone to early mass I set the samovar ready and turned my attention to tidying the rooms. While I was so occupied the eldest child rushed into the kitchen, removed the tap from the samovar, and set himself under the table to play with it. There was a lot of charcoal in the pipe of the samovar, and when the water had all trickled away from it, it came unsoldered. While I was doing the other rooms, I heard an unusual noise. Going into the kitchen, I saw with horror that the samovar was all blue. It was shaking, as if it wanted to jump from the floor. The broken handle of the tap was drooping miserably, the lid was all on one side, the pewter was melted and running away drop by drop. In fact the purplish blue samovar looked as if it had drunken shivers. I poured water over it. It hissed, and sank sadly in ruins on the floor.

The front door-bell rang. I went to open the door. In answer to the old lady's question as to whether the samovar was ready, I replied briefly:

"Yes; it is ready."

These words, spoken, of course, in my confusion and terror, were taken for insolence. My punishment was doubled. They half killed me. The old lady beat me with a bunch of fir-twigs, which did not hurt much, but left under the skin of my back a great many splinters, driven in deeply. Before night my back was swollen like a pillow, and by noon the next day the master was obliged to take me to the hospital.

When the doctor, comically tall and thin, examined me, he said in a calm, dull voice:

"This is a case of cruelty which will have to be investigated."

My master blushed, shuffled his feet, and said something in a low voice to the doctor, who looked over his head and said shortly:

"I can't. It is impossible."

Then he asked me:

"Do you want to make a complaint?"

I was in great pain, but I said:

"No, make haste and cure me."

They took me into another room, laid me on a table, and the doctor pulled out the splinters with pleasantly cold pincers. He said, jestingly:

"They have decorated your skin beautifully, my friend; now you will be waterproof."

When he had finished his work of pricking me unmercifully, he said:

"Forty-two splinters have been taken out, my friend. Remember that. It is something to boast of! Come back at the same time to-morrow to have the dressing replaced. Do they often beat you?"

I thought for a moment, then said:

"Not so often as they used to."

The doctor burst into a hoarse laugh.

"It is all for the best, my friend, all for the best." When he took me back to my master he said to him:

"I hand him over to you; he is repaired. Bring him back to-morrow without fail. I congratulate you. He is a comical fellow you have there."

When we were in the cab my master said to me:

"They used to beat me too, Pyeshkov. What do you think of that? They did beat me, my lad! And you have me to pity you; but I had no one, no one. People are very hard everywhere; but one gets no pity—no, not from any one. Ekh! Wild fowl!"

He grumbled all the way home. I was very sorry for him, and grateful to him for treating me like a man.

They welcomed me at the house as if it had been my name-day. The women insisted on hearing in detail how the doctor had treated me and what he had said. They listened and sighed, then kissed me tenderly, wrinkling their brows. This intense interest in illness, pain, and all kinds of unpleasantness always amazed me.

I saw that they were pleased with me for not complaining of them, and I took advantage of the moment to ask if I might have some books from the tailor's wife. They did not have the heart to refuse me. Only the old lady cried in surprise:

"What a demon he is!"

The next day I stood before the tailor's wife, who said to me kindly:

"They told me that you were ill, and that you had been taken to hospital. You see what stories get about."

I was silent. I was ashamed to tell her the truth. Why should she know of such sad and coarse things? It was nice to think that she was different from other people.

Once more I read the thick books of Dumas *père*, Ponson de Terraille, Montepaine, Zakonier, Gaboriau, and Bourgobier. I devoured all these books quickly, one after the other, and I was happy. I felt myself to be part of a life which was out of the ordinary, which stirred me sweetly and aroused my courage. Once more I burned my improvised candle, and read all through the night till the morning, so that my eyes began to hurt me a little. The old mistress said to me kindly:

"Take care, bookworm. You will spoil your sight and grow blind!"

However, I soon realized that all these interestingly complicated books, despite the different incidents, and the various countries and towns about which they were written, had one common theme: good people made unhappy and oppressed by bad people, the latter were always more successful and clever than the good, but in the end something unexpected always overthrowing the wicked, and the good winning. The "love," of which both men and women spoke in the same terms, bored me. In fact, it was not only uninteresting to me, but it aroused a vague contempt.

Sometimes from the very first chapters I began to wonder who would win or who would be vanquished, and as soon as the course of the story became clear, I would set myself to unravel the skein of events by the aid of my own fancy. When I was not reading I was thinking of the books I had on hand, as one would think about the problems in an arithmetic. I became more skilful every day in guessing which of the characters would enter into the paradise of happiness and which would be utterly confounded.

But through all this I saw the glimmer of living and, to me, significant truths, the outlines of another life, other standards. It was clear to me that in Paris the cabmen, working men, soldiers, and all "black people"[1] were not at all as they were in Nijni, Kazan, or Perm. They dared to speak to gentlefolk, and behaved toward them more simply and independently than our people. Here, for example, was a soldier quite unlike any I had known, unlike Sidorov, unlike the Viatskian on the boat, and still more unlike Ermokhin. He was more human than any of these. He had something of Smouri about him, but he was not so savage and coarse. Here was a shopkeeper, but he was much better than any of the shopkeepers I had known. And the priests in books were not like the priests I knew. They had more feeling, and seemed to enter more into the lives of their flocks. And in general it seemed to me that life abroad, as it appeared in books, was more interesting, easier, better than the life I knew. Abroad, people did not behave so brutally. They never jeered at other human creatures as cruelly as the Viatskian soldier had been jeered at, nor prayed to God as importunately as the old mistress did. What I noticed particularly was that, when villains, misers, and low characters were depicted in books, they did not show that incomprehensible cruelty, that inclination to jeer at humanity, with which I was acquainted, and which was often brought to my notice. There was method in the cruelty of these bookish villains. One could almost always understand why they were cruel; but the cruelty which I witnessed was aimless, senseless, an amusement from which no one expected to gain any advantage.

[1] The common people.

With every book that I read this dissimilarity between Russian life and that of other countries stood out more clearly, causing a perplexed feeling of irritation within me, strengthening my suspicion of the veracity of the old, well-read pages with their dirty "dogs'-ears."

And then there fell into my hands Goncourt's novel, "The Brothers Zemganno." I read it through in one night, and, surprised at the new experience, read the simple, pathetic story over again. There was nothing complicated about it, nothing interesting at first sight. In fact, the first pages seemed dry, like the lives of the saints. Its language, so precise and stripped of all adornment, was at first an unpleasant surprise to me; but the paucity of words, the strongly constructed phrases, went straight to the heart. It so aptly described the drama of the acrobat brothers that my hands trembled with the enjoyment of reading the book. I wept bitterly as I read how the unfortunate artist, with his legs broken, crept up to the loft where his brother was secretly engaged in his favorite art.

When I returned this glorious book to the tailor's wife I begged her to give me another one like it.

"How do you mean like that?" she asked, laughing.

This laugh confused me, and I could not explain what I wanted. Then she said:

"That is a dull book. Just wait! I will give you another more interesting."

In the course of a day or two she gave me Greenwood's "The True History of a little Waif." The title of the book at first turned me against it, but the first pages called up a smile of joy, and still smiling, I read it from beginning to end, re-reading some of the pages two or three times.

So in other countries, also, boys lived hard and harassing lives! After all, I was not so badly off; I need not complain.

Greenwood gave me a lot of courage, and soon after that I was given a "real" book, "Eugénie Grandet."

Old Grandet reminded me vividly of grandfather. I was annoyed that the book was so small, and surprised at the amount of truth it contained. Truths which were familiar and boring to me in life were shown to me in a different light in this book, without malice and quite calmly. All the books which I had read before Greenwood's, condemned people as severely and noisily as my employers did, often arousing my sympathy for the villain and a feeling of irritation with the good people. I was always sorry to see that despite enormous expenditure of intelligence and willpower, a man still failed to obtain his desires. The good characters stood awaiting events from first to last page, as immovable as stone pillars, and although all kinds of evil plots were formed against these stone pillars, stones do not arouse sympathy. No matter how beautiful and strong a wall may be, one does not love it if one wants to get the apple on the tree on the other side of it. It always seemed to me that all that was most worth having, and vigorous was hidden behind the "good" people.

In Goncourt, Greenwood, and Balzac there were no villains, but just simple people, wonderfully alive. One could not doubt that, whatever they were alleged to have said and done, they really did say and do, and they could not have said and done anything else.

In this fashion I learned to understand what a great treat a "good and proper" book can be. But how to find it? The tailor's wife could not help me in this.

"Here is a good book," she said, laying before me Arsène Huissier's "Hands full of Roses, Gold, and Blood." She also gave me the novels of Beyle, Paul de Kock and Paul Féval, and I read them all with relish. She liked the novels of Mariette and Vernier, which to me appeared dull. I did not care for Spielhagen, but I was much taken with the stories of Auerbach. Sue and Huga, also, I did not like, preferring Walter Scott. I wanted books which excited me, and made me feel happy, like wonderful Balzac.

I did not care for the porcelain woman as much as I had done at first. When I went to see her, I put on a clean shirt, brushed my hair, and tried to appear good-looking. In this I was hardly successful. I always hoped that, seeing my good looks, she would speak to me in a simple and friendly manner, without that hsh-like smile on her frivolous face. But all she did was to smile and ask me in her sweet, tired voice:

"Have you read it? Did you like it?"

"No."

Slightly raising her eyebrows, she looked at me, and, drawing in her breath, spoke through her nose.

"But why?"

"I have read about all that before."

"Above what?"

"About love."

Her eyes twinkled, as she burst out into her honeyed laugh.

"*Ach*, but you see all books are written about love!"

Sitting in a big arm-chair, she swung her small feet, incased in fur slippers, to and fro, yawned, wrapped her blue dressing-gown around her, and drummed with her pink fingers on the cover of the book on her knee. I wanted to say to her:

"Why don't you leave this flat? The officers write letters to you, and laugh at you."

But I had not the audacity to say this, and went away, bearing with me a thick book on "Love," a sad sense of disenchantment in my heart.

They talked about this woman in the yard more evilly, derisively, and spitefully than ever. It offended me to hear these foul and, no doubt, lying stories. When I was away from her, I pitied the woman, and suffered for her; but when I was with her, and saw her small, sharp eyes, the cat-like flexibility of her small body, and that always frivolous face, pity and fear disappeared, vanished like smoke.

In the spring she suddenly went away, and in a few days her husband moved to new quarters.

While the rooms stood empty, awaiting a new tenant, I went to look at the bare walls, with their square patches where pictures had hung, bent nails, and wounds made by nails. Strewn about the stained floor were pieces of different-colored cloth, balls of paper, broken boxes from the chemist, empty scent-bottles. A large brass pin gleamed in one spot.

All at once I felt sad and wished that I could see the tailor's little wife once more to tell her how grateful I was to her.

CHAPTER X

Before the departure of the tailor's wife there had come to live under the flat occupied by my employers a black-eyed young lady, with her little girl and her mother, a gray-haired old woman, everlastingly smoking cigarettes in an amber mouthpiece. The young lady was very beautiful, imperious, and proud. She spoke in a pleasant, deep voice. She looked at every one with head held high and unblinking eyes, as if they were all far away from her, and she could hardly see them. Nearly every day her black soldier-servant, Tuphyaev, brought a thin-legged, brown horse to the steps of her flat. The lady came out in a long, steel-colored, velvet dress, wearing white gauntleted gloves and tan boots. Holding the train of her skirt and a whip with a lilac-colored stone in its handle in one hand, with the other little hand she lovingly stroked the horse's muzzle. He fixed his great eyes upon her, trembling all over, and softly trampled the soaked ground under his hoofs.

"Robaire, Robaire," she said in a low voice, and patted the beautiful, arched neck of the steed with a firm hand.

Then setting her foot on the knee of Tuphyaev, she sprang lightly into the saddle, and the horse, prancing proudly, went through the gateway. She sat in the saddle as easily as if she were part of it. She was beautiful with that rare kind of beauty which always seems new and wonderful, and always fills the heart with an intoxicating joy. When I looked at her I thought that Diana of Poitiers, Queen Margot, the maiden La Vallière, and other beauties, heroines of historical novels, were like her.

She was constantly surrounded by the officers of the division which was stationed in the town, and in the evenings they used to visit her, and play the piano, violin, guitar, and dance and sing. The most frequent of her visitors was Major Olessov, who revolved about her on his short legs, stout, red-faced, gray-haired, and as greasy as an engineer on a steamboat. He played the guitar well, and bore himself as the humble, devoted servant of the lady.

As radiantly beautiful as her mother was the little five-year-old, curly-haired, chubby girl. Her great, dark-blue eyes looked about her gravely, calmly expectant, and there was an air of thoughtfulness about her which was not at all childish.

Her grandmother was occupied with housekeeping from morning to night, with the help of Tuphyaev, a morose, taciturn man, and a fat, cross-eyed housemaid. There was no nursemaid, and the little girl lived almost without any notice being taken of her, playing about all day on the front steps or on a heap of planks near them. I often went out to play with her in the evenings, for I was very fond of her. She soon became used to me, and would fall asleep in my arms while I was telling her a story. When this happened, I used to carry her to bed. Before long it came about that she would not go to sleep, when she was put to bed, unless I went to say good night to her. When I went to her, she would hold out her plump hand with a grand air and say:

"Good-by till to-morrow. Grandmother, how ought I to say it?"

"God preserve you!" said the grandmother, blowing a cloud of dark-blue smoke from her mouth and thin nose.

"God preserve you till to-morrow! And now I am going to sleep," said the little girl, rolling herself up in the bedclothes, which were trimmed with lace.

The grandmother corrected her.

"Not till to-morrow, but for always."

"But does n't to-morrow mean for always?"

She loved the word "to-morrow," and whatever pleased her specially she carried forward into the future. She would stick into the ground flowers that had been plucked or branches that had been broken by the wind, and say:

"To-morrow this will be a garden."

"To-morrow, some time, I shall buy myself a horse, and ride on horseback like mother."

She was a clever child, but not very lively, and would often break off in the midst of a merry game to become thoughtful, or ask unexpectedly:

"Why do priests have hair like women?"

If she stung herself with nettles, she would shake her finger at them, saying:

"You wait! I shall pray God to do something vewy bady to you. God can do bad things to every one; He can even punish mama." Sometimes a soft, serious melancholy descended upon her. She would press close to me, gazing up at the sky with her blue, expectant eyes, and say:

"Sometimes grandmother is cross, but mama never; she on'y laughs. Every one loves her, because she never has any time. People are always coming to see her and to look at her because she is so beautiful. She is 'ovely, mama is. 'Oseph says so—'ovely!"

I loved to listen to her, for she spoke of a world of which I knew nothing. She spoke willingly and often about her mother, and a new life gradually opened out before me. I was again reminded of Queen Margot, which deepened my faith in books and also my interest in life. One day when I was sitting on the steps waiting for my people, who had gone for a walk, and the little girl had dozed off in my arms, her mother rode up on horseback, sprang lightly to the ground, and, throwing back her head, asked:

"What, is she asleep?"

"Yes."

"That's right."

The soldier Tuphyaev came running to her and took the horse. She stuck her whip into her belt and, holding out her arms, said:

"Give her to me!"

"I'll carry her in myself."

"Come on!" cried the lady, as if I had been a horse, and she stamped her foot on the step.

The little girl woke up, blinking, and, seeing her mother, held out her arms to her. They went away.

I was used to being shouted at, but I did not like this lady to shout at me. She had only to give an order quietly, and every one obeyed her.

In a few minutes the cross-eyed maid came out for me. The little girl was naughty, and would not go to sleep without saying good night.

It was not without pride in my bearing toward the mother that I entered the drawing-room, where the little girl was sitting on the knees of her mother, who was deftly undressing her.

"Here he is," she said. "He has come—this monster."

"He is not a monster, but my boy."

"Really? Very good. Well, you would like to give something to your boy, would n't you?"

"Yes, I should."

"A good idea! I will see to it, and you will go to bed."

"Good-by till to-morrow," said the little girl, holding out her hand to me. "God preserve you till to-morrow!"

The lady exclaimed in surprise:

"Who taught you to say that? Grandmother?"

"Ye-es."

When the child had left the room the lady beckoned to me.

"What shall we give you?"

I told her that I did not want anything; but could she let me have a book to read?

She lifted my chin with her warm, scented fingers, and asked, with a pleasant smile:

"So you are fond of reading? Yes; what books have you read?"

When she smiled she looked more beautiful than ever. I confusedly told her the names of several books.

"What did you find to like in them?" she asked, laying her hand on the table and moving her fingers slightly.

A strong, sweet smell of some sort of flowers came from her, mixed with the odor of horse-sweat. She looked at me through her long eyelashes, thoughtfully grave. No one had ever looked at me like that before.

The room was packed as tightly as a bird's nest with beautiful, soft furniture. The windows were covered with thick green curtains; the snowy white tiles of the stove gleamed in the half-light; beside the stove shone the glossy surface of a black piano; and from the walls, in dull-gold frames, looked dark writings in large Russian characters. Under each writing hung a large dark seal by a cord. Everything about her looked at that woman as humbly and timidly as I did.

I explained to her as well as I could that my life was hard and uninteresting and that reading helped me to forget it.

"Yes; so that's what it is," she said, standing up. "It is not a bad idea, and, in fact, it is quite right. Well, what shall we do? I will get some books for you, but just now I have none. But wait! You can have this one."

She took a tattered book with a yellow cover from the couch.

"When you have read this I will give you the second volume; there are four."

I went away with the "Secrets of Peterburg," by Prince Meshtcheski, and began to read the book with great attention. But before I had read many pages I saw that the Peterburgian "secrets" were considerably less interesting than those of Madrid, London, or Paris. The only part which took my fancy was the fable of *Svoboda* (Liberty) and *Palka* (stick).

"I am your superior," said *Svoboda*, "because I am cleverer."

But *Palka* answered her:

"No, it is I who am your superior, because I am stronger than you."

They disputed and disputed and fought about it. *Palka* beat *Svoboda*, and, if I remember rightly, *Svoboda* died in the hospital as the result of her injuries.

There was some talk of nihilists in this book. I remember that, according to Prince Meshtcheski, a nihilist was such a poisonous person that his very glance would kill a fowl. What he wrote about nihilists struck me as being offensive and rude, but I understood nothing else, and fell into a state of melancholy. It was evident that I could not appreciate good books; for I was convinced that it was a good book. Such a great and beautiful lady could never read bad books.

"Well, did you like it?" she asked me when I took back the yellow novel by Meshtcheski.

I found it very hard to answer no; I thought it would make her angry. But she only laughed, and going behind the *portière* which led into her sleeping-chamber, brought back a little volume in a binding of dark-blue morocco leather.

"You will like this one, only take care not to soil it."

This was a volume of Pushkin's poems. I read all of them at once, seizing upon them with a feeling of greed such as I experienced whenever I happened to visit a beautiful place that I had never seen before. I always tried to run all over it at once. It was like roaming over mossy hillocks in a marshy wood, and suddenly seeing spread before one a dry plain covered with flowers and bathed in sun-rays. For a second one gazes upon it enchanted, and then one begins to race about happily, and each contact of one's feet with the soft growth of the fertile earth sends a thrill of joy through one.

Pushkin had so surprised me with the simplicity and music of poetry that for a long time prose seemed unnatural to me, and it did not come easy to read it. The prologue to "Ruslan" reminded me of grandmother's best stories, all wonderfully compressed into one, and several lines amazed me by their striking truth.

> There, by ways which few observe,
> Are the trails of invisible wild creatures.

I repeated these wonderful words in my mind, and I could see those footpaths so familiar to me, yet hardly visible to the average being. I saw the mysterious footprints which had pressed down the grass, which had not had time to shake off the drops of dew, as heavy as mercury. The full, sounding lines of poetry were easily remembered. They adorned everything of which they spoke as if for a festival. They made me happy, my life easy and pleasant. The verses rang out like bells heralding me into a new life. What happiness it was to be educated!

The magnificent stories of Pushkin touched me more closely, and were more intelligible to me than anything I had read. When I had read them a few times I knew them by heart, and when I went to bed I whispered the verses to myself, with my eyes closed, until I fell asleep. Very often I told these stories to the orderlies, who listened and laughed, and abused me jokingly. Sidorov stroked my head and said softly:

"That's fine, is n't it? O Lord—"

The awakening which had come to me was noticed by my employers. The old lady scolded me.

"You read too much, and you have not cleaned the samovar for four days, you young monkey! I shall have to take the rolling-pin to you—"

What did I care for the rolling-pin? I took refuge in verses.

> Loving black evil with all thy heart,
> O old witch that thou art!

The lady rose still higher in my esteem. See what books she read! She was not like the tailor's porcelain wife.

When I took back the book, and handed it to her with regret, she said in a tone which invited confidence:

"Did you like it? Had you heard of Pushkin before?"

I had read something about the poet in one of the newspapers, but I wanted her to tell me about him, so I said that I had never heard of him.

Then she briefly told me the life and death of Pushkin, and asked, smiling like a spring day:

"Do you see how dangerous it is to love women?"

All the books I had read had shown me it was really dangerous, but also pleasant, so I said:

"It is dangerous, yet every one falls in love. And women suffer for love, too."

She looked at me, as she looked at every one, through her lashes, and said gravely:

"You think so? You understand that? Then the best thing I can wish you is that you may not forget it."

And then she asked me what verses I liked best.

I began to repeat some from memory, with gesticulations. She listened silently and gravely, then rose, and, walking up and down the room, said thoughtfully:

"We shall have to have you taught, my little wild animal. I must think about it. Your employers—are they relatives of yours?"

When I answered in the affirmative she exclaimed: "Oh!" as if she blamed me for it.

She gave me "The Songs of Béranger," a special edition with engravings, gilt edges, and a red leather binding. These songs made me feel giddy, with their strange mixture of bitter grief and boisterous happiness.

With a cold chill at my heart I read the bitter words of "The Old Beggar."

> Homeless worm, have I disturbed you?
> Crush me under your feet!
> Why be pitiful? Crush me quickly!
> Why is it that you have never taught me,
> Nor given me an outlet for my energy?
> From the grub an ant might have come.
> I might have died in the love of my fellows.
> But dying as an old tramp,
> I shall be avenged on the world!

And directly after this I laughed till I cried over the "Weeping Husband." I remembered especially the words of Béranger:

> A happy science of life
> Is not hard for the simple.

Béranger aroused me to moods of joyfulness, to a desire to be saucy, and to say something rude to people,—rude, sharp words. In a very short time I had become proficient in this art. His verses I learned by heart, and recited them with pleasure to the orderlies, running into the kitchen, where they sat for a few minutes at a time.

But I soon had to give this up because the lines,

> But such a hat is not becoming
> To a young girl of seventeen,

gave rise to an offensive conversation about girls that made me furiously disgusted, and I hit the soldier Ermokhin over the head with a saucepan. Sidorov and the other orderlies tore me away from his clumsy hands, but I made up my mind from that time to go no more to the officers' kitchen.

I was not allowed to walk about the streets. In fact, there was no time for it, since the work had so increased. Now, in addition to my usual duties as housemaid, yardman, and errand-boy, I had to nail calico to wide boards, fasten the plans thereto, and copy calculations for my master's architectural work. I also had to verify the contractor's accounts, for my master worked from morning to night, like a machine.

At that time the public buildings of the *Yarmarka*[1] were private property. Rows of shops were built very rapidly, and my master had the contracts for the reconstruction of old shops and the erection of new ones. He drew up plans for the rebuilding of vaults, the throwing out of a dormer-window, and such changes. I took the plans to an old architect, together with an envelop in which was hidden paper money to the value of twenty-five rubles. The architect took the money, and wrote under the plans: "The plans are correct, and the inspection of the work has been performed by me. Imraik." As a matter of fact, he had not seen the original of the plans, and he could not inspect the work, as he was always obliged to stay at home by reason of his malady.

[1] Market-place.

I used to take bribes to the inspector of the *Yarmarka* and to other necessary people, from whom I received what the master called papers, which permitted all kinds of illegalities. For this service I obtained the right to wait for my employers at the door on the front steps when they went out to see their friends in the evenings. This did not often happen, but when it did, they never returned until after midnight. I used to sit at the top of the steps, or on the heap of planks opposite them, for hours, looking into the windows of my lady's flat, thirstily listening to the gay conversation and the music.

The windows were open. Through the curtains and the screen of flowers I could see the fine figures of officers moving about the room. The rotund major waddled about, and she floated about, dressed with astonishing simplicity, but beautifully.

In my own mind I called her "Queen Margot."

"This is the gay life that they write about in French books," I thought, looking in at the window. And I always felt rather sad about it. A childish jealousy made it painful for me to see "Queen Margot" surrounded by men, who buzzed about her like bees over flowers.

Her least-frequent visitor was a tall, unhappy-looking officer, with a furrowed brow and deep-sunken eyes, who always brought his violin with him and played marvelously—so marvelously that the passers-by used to stop under the window, and all the dwellers in the street used to gather round. Even my employers, if they happened to be at home, would open the window, listen, and praise. I never remember their praising any one else except the subdeacon of the cathedral, and I knew that a fish-pie was more pleasing to them than any kind of music.

Sometimes this officer sang, or recited verses in a muffled voice, sighing strangely and pressing his hand to his brow. Once when I was playing under the window with the little girl and "Queen Margot" asked him to sing, he refused for a long time. Then he said clearly:

> "Only a song has need of beauty,
> While beauty has no need of songs."

I thought these lines were lovely, and for some reason I felt sorry for the officer.

What I liked best was to look at my lady when she sat at the piano, alone in the room, and played. Music intoxicated me, and I could see nothing but the window, and beyond that, in the yellow light of the lamp, the finely formed figure of the woman, with her haughty profile and her white hands hovering like birds over the keys. I gazed at her, listened to the plaintive music, and dreamed. If I could find some treasure, I would give it all to her, so that she should be rich. If I had been Skobelev, I would have declared war on the Turks again. I would have taken money for ransoms, and built a house for her on the Otkossa, the best site in the whole town, and made her a present of it. If only she would leave this street, where every one talked offensively about her. The neighbors, the servants belonging to our yard, and my employers more than all spoke about "Queen Margot" as evilly and spitefully as they had talked about the tailor's wife, though more cautiously, with lowered voices, and looking about them as they spoke.

They were afraid of her, probably because she was the widow of a very distinguished man. The writings on the walls of her rooms, too, were privileges bestowed on her husband's ancestors by the old Russian emperors Goudonov, Alexei, and Peter the Great. This was told me by the soldier Tuphyaev, a man of education, who was always reading the gospels. Or it may have been that people were afraid lest she should thrash them with her whip with the lilac-colored stone in the handle. It was said that she had once struck a person of position with it.

But words uttered under the breath are no better than words uttered aloud. My lady lived in a cloud of enmity—an enmity which I could not understand and which tormented me.

Now that I knew there was another life; that there were different people, feelings, and ideas, this house and all its tenants aroused in me a feeling of disgust that oppressed me more and more. It was entangled in the meshes of a dirty net of disgraceful tittle-tattle, there was not a single person in it of whom evil was not spoken. The regimental chaplain, though he was ill and miserable, had a reputation for being a drunkard and a rake; the officers and their wives were living, according to my employers, in a state of sin; the soldiers' conversation about women, which ran on the same lines, had become repulsive to me. But my employers disgusted me most of all. I knew too well the real value of their favorite amusement, namely, the merciless judgment of other people. Watching and commenting on the crimes of others was the only amusement in which they could indulge without paying for it. They amused themselves by putting those about them verbally on the rack, and, as it were, revenged themselves on others because they lived so piously, laboriously, and uninterestingly themselves.

When they spoke vilely about "Queen Margot" I was seized by a convulsion of feeling which was not childish at all. My heart swelled with hatred for the backbiters. I was overcome by an irresistible desire to do harm to every one, to be insolent, and sometimes a flood of tormenting pity for myself and every one else swept over me. That dumb pity was more painful than hatred.

I knew more about my queen than they did, and I was always afraid that they would find out what I knew.

On Sundays, when my employers had gone to the cathedral for high mass, I used to go to her the first thing in the morning. She would call me into her bedroom, and I sat in a small arm-chair, upholstered in gold-colored silk, with the little girl on my knee, and told the mother about the books I had read. She lay in a wide bed, with her cheek resting on her small hands, which were clasped together. Her body was hidden under a counterpane, gold in color, like everything else in the bedroom; her dark hair lay in a plait over her swarthy shoulder and her breast, and sometimes fell over the side of the bed till it touched the floor.

As she listened to me she looked into my face with her soft eyes and a hardly perceptible smile and said:

"That's right."

Even her kind smile was, in my eyes, the condescending smile of a queen. She spoke in a deep, tender voice, and it seemed to me that it said always:

"I know that I am immeasurably above all other people; no one of them is necessary to me."

Sometimes I found her before her mirror, sitting in a low chair and doing her hair, the ends of which lay on her knees, over the arms, and back of the chair, and fell almost to the floor. Her hair was as long and thick as grandmother's. She put on her stockings in my presence, but her clean nudity aroused in me no feeling of shame. I had only a joyful feeling of pride in her. A flowerlike smell always came from her, protecting her from any evil thoughts concerning her.

I felt sure that the love of the kitchen and the pantry was unknown to Queen Margot. She knew something different, a higher joy, a different kind of love.

But one day, late in the afternoon, on going into her drawing-room, I heard from the bedroom the ringing laugh of the lady of my heart. A masculine voice said:

"Wait a minute! Good Lord! I can't believe—"

I ought to have gone away. I knew that, but I could not.

"Who is that?" she asked. "You? Come in!"

The bedroom was heavy with the odor of flowers. It was darkened, for the curtains were drawn. Queen Margot lay in bed, with the bedclothes drawn up to her chin, and beside her, against the wall, sat, clad only in his shirt, with his chest bared, the officer violinist. On his breast was a scar which lay like a red streak from the right shoulder to the nipple and was so vivid that even in the half-light I could see it distinctly. The hair of the officer was ruffled comically, and for the first time I saw a smile on his sad, furrowed countenance. He was smiling strangely. His large, feminine eyes looked at the "queen" as if it were the first time he had gazed upon her beauty.

"This is my friend," said Queen Margot. I did not know whether she were referring to me or to him.

"What are you looking so frightened about?" I heard her voice as if from a distance. "Come here."

When I went to her she placed her hands on my bare neck and said:

"You will grow up and you will be happy. Go along!"

I put the book on the shelf, took another, and went away as best I could.

Something seemed to grate in my heart. Of course I did not think for a moment that my queen loved as other women nor did the officer give me reason to think so. I saw his face before me, with that smile. He was smiling for joy, like a child who has been pleasantly surprised, and his sad face was wonderfully transfigured. He had to love her. Could any one not love her? And she also had cause to bestow her love upon him generously. He played so wonderfully, and could quote poetry so touchingly.

But the very fact that I had to find these consolations showed me clearly that all was not well with my attitude toward what I had seen or even toward Queen Margot herself. I felt that I had lost something, and I lived for several days in a state of deep dejection. One day I was turbulently and recklessly insolent, and when I went to my lady for a book, she said to me sternly:

"You seem to be a desperate character from what I have heard. I did not know that."

I could not endure this, and I began to explain how nauseating I found the life I had to lead, and how hard it was for me to hear people speaking ill of her. Standing in front of me, with her hand on my shoulder, she listened at first attentively and seriously; but soon she was laughing and pushing me away from her gently.

"That will do; I know all about it. Do you understand? I know."

Then she took both my hands and said to me very tenderly:

"The less attention you pay to all that, the better for you. You wash your hands very badly."

She need not have said this. If she had had to clean the brasses, and wash the floor and the dirty cloths, her hands would not have been any better than mine, I think.

"When a person knows how to live, he is slandered; they are jealous of him. And if he doesn't know how to live, they despise him," she said thoughtfully, drawing me to her, and looking into my eyes with a smile. "Do you love me?"

"Yes."

"Very much?"

"Yes."

"But how?"

"I don't know."

"Thank you! You are a good boy. I like people to love me." She smiled, looked as if she were going to say something more, but remained silent, still keeping me in her arms. "Come oftener to see me; come whenever you can."

I took advantage of this, and she did me a lot of good. After dinner my employers used to lie down, and I used to run down-stairs. If she was at home, I would stay with her for an hour and sometimes even longer.

"You must read Russian books; you must know all about Russian life."

She taught me, sticking hair-pins into her fragrant hair with rosy fingers. And she enumerated the Russian authors, adding:

"Will you remember them?"

She often said thoughtfully, and with an air of slight vexation:

"We must have you taught, and I am always forgetting. *Ach*, my God!"

After sitting with her, I ran down-stairs with a new book in my hands, feeling as if I had been washed inside.

I had already read Aksakov's "Family Chronicle," the glorious Russian poem "In the Forests," the amazing "Memoirs of a Hunter," several volumes of Grebenkov and Solugub, and the poetry of Venevitinov, Odoevski, and Tutchev. These books laved my soul, washing away the husks of barren and bitter reality. I felt that these were good books, and realized that they were indispensable to me. One result of reading them was that I gained a firm conviction that I was not alone in the world, and the fact that I should not be lost took root in my soul.

When grandmother came to see me I used to tell her joyfully about Queen Margot, and she, taking a pinch of snuff with great enjoyment, said heartily:

"Well, well; that is very nice. You see, there are plenty of good people about. You only have to look for them, and then you will find them."

And one day she suggested:

"How would it be if I went to her and said thank you for what she does for you?"

"No; it is better not."

"Well, if you don't want me to——Lord! Lord! how good it all is! I would like to go on living for ever and ever!"

Queen Margot never carried out her project of having me taught, for an unpleasant affair happened on the feast of the Holy Trinity that nearly ruined me.

109

Not long before the holiday my eyelids became terribly swollen, and my eyes were quite closed up. My employers were afraid that I should go blind, and I also was afraid. They took me to the well-known doctor, Genrikh Rodzevich, who lanced my eyelids and for days I lay with my eyes bandaged, in tormenting, black misery. The day before the feast of the Trinity my bandages were taken off, and I walked about once more, feeling as if I had come back from a grave in which I had been laid alive. Nothing can be more terrible than to lose one's sight. It is an unspeakable injury which takes away a hundred worlds from a man.

The joyful day of the Holy Trinity arrived, and, as an invalid, I was off duty from noon and went to the kitchen to pay a visit to the orderlies. All of them, even the strict Tuphyaev, were drunk, and toward evening Ermokhin struck Sidorov on the head with a block of wood. The latter fell senseless to the ground, and Ermokhin, terrified, ran out to the causeway.

An alarming rumor that Sidorov had been murdered soon spread over the yard. People gathered on the steps and looked at the soldier stretched motionless across the threshold. There were whispers that the police ought to be sent for, but no one went to fetch them, and no one could be persuaded to touch the soldier.

Then the washerwoman Natalia Kozlovski, in a new, blue frock, with a white neckerchief, appeared on the scene. She pushed the people aside angrily, went into the entrance passage, squatted down, and said loudly:

"Fools! He is alive! Give me some water!"

They began to protest.

"Don't meddle with what is not your business!"

"Water, I tell you!" she cried, as if there were a fire. She lifted her new frock over her knees in a businesslike manner, spread out her underskirt, and laid the soldier's bleeding head on her knees.

The crowd dispersed, disapproving and fearful.

In the dim light of the passage I could see the eyes of the washerwoman full of tears, flashing angrily in her white, round face. I took her a pail of water, and she ordered me to throw it over the head and breast of Sidorov with the caution:

"Don't spill it over me. I am going to pay a visit to some friends."

The soldier came to himself, opened his dull eyes, and moaned.

"Lift him up," said Natalia, holding him under the armpits with her hands outstretched lest he should soil her frock. We carried the soldier into the kitchen and laid him on the bed. She wiped his face with a wet cloth, and went away, saying:

"Soak the cloth in water and hold it to his head. I will go and find that fool. Devils! I suppose they won't be satisfied until they have drunk themselves into prison."

She went out, after slipping her soiled underpetticoat to the floor, flinging it into a corner and carefully smoothing out her rustling, crumpled frock.

Sidorov stretched himself, hiccupped, sighed. Warm drops of thick blood fell on my bare feet from his head. This was unpleasant, but I was too frightened to move my feet away from those drops.

It was bitter. The sun shone festively out in the yard; the steps of the houses and the gate were decorated with young birch; to each pedestal were tied freshly cut branches of maple and mountain ash. The whole street was gay with foliage; everything was young, new. Ever since the morning I had felt that the spring holiday had come to stay, and that it had made life cleaner, brighter, and happier.

The soldier was sick. The stifling odor of warm vodka and green onion filled the kitchen. Against the window were pressed dull, misty, broad faces, with flattened noses, and hands held against their cheeks, which made them look hideous.

The soldier muttered as he recollected himself:

"What happened to me? Did I fall, Ermokhin? Go-o-od comrade!" Then he began to cough, wept drunken tears, and groaned, "My little sister! my little sister!"

He stood up, tottering, wet. He staggered, and, falling back heavily upon the bed, said, rolling his eyes strangely:

"They have quite killed me!"

This struck me as funny.

"What the devil are you laughing at?" he asked, looking at me dully. "What is there to laugh at? I am killed forever!"

He began to hit out at me with both hands, muttering:

"The first time was that of Elias the prophet; the second time, St. George on his steed; the third—Don't come near me! Go away, wolf!"

"Don't be a fool!" I said.

He became absurdly angry, roared, and stamped his feet.

"I am killed, and you—"

With his heavy, slow, dirty hand he struck me in the eyes. I set up a howl, and blindly made for the yard, where I ran into Natalia leading Ermokhin by the arm, crying: "Come along, horse! What is the matter with you?" she asked, catching hold of me.

"He has come to himself."

"Come to himself, eh?" she drawled in amazement. And drawing Ermokhin along, she said, "Well, werwolf, you may thank your God for this!"

I washed my eyes with water, and, looking through the door of the passage, saw the soldiers make their peace, embracing each other and crying. Then they both tried to embrace Natalia, but she hit out at them, shouting:

"Take your paws off me, curs! What do you take me for? Make haste and get to sleep before your masters come home, or there will be trouble for you!"

She made them lie down as if they were little children, the one on the floor, the other on the pallet-bed, and when they began to snore, came out into the porch.

"I am in a mess, and I was dressed to go out visiting, too! Did he hit you? What a fool! That's what it does—vodka! Don't drink, little fellow, never drink."

Then I sat on the bench at the gate with her, and asked how it was that she was not afraid of drunken people.

"I am not afraid of sober people, either. If they come near me, this is what they get!" She showed me her tightly clenched, red fist. "My dead husband was also given to drink too much, and once when he was drunk I tied his hands and feet. When he had slept it off, I gave him a birching for his health. 'Don't drink; don't get drunk when you are married,' I said. 'Your wife should be your amusement, and not vodka.' Yes, I scolded him until I was tired, and after that he was like wax in my hands."

"You are strong," I said, remembering the woman Eve, who deceived even God Himself.

Natalia replied, with a sigh:

"A woman needs more strength than a man. She has to have strength enough for two, and God has bestowed it upon her. Man is an unstable creature."

She spoke calmly, without malice, sitting with her arms folded over her large bosom, resting her back against the fence, her eyes fixed sadly on the dusty gutter full of rubbish. Listening to her clever talk, I forgot all about the time. Suddenly I saw my master coming along arm in arm with the mistress. They were walking slowly, pompously, like a turkey-cock with his hen, and, looking at us attentively, said something to each other.

I ran to open the front door for them, and as she came up the steps the mistress said to me, venomously:

"So you are courting the washerwoman? Are you learning to carry on with ladies of that low class?"

This was so stupid that it did not even annoy me but I felt offended when the master said, laughing:

"What do you expect? It is time."

The next morning when I went into the shed for the wood I found an empty purse, in the square hole which was made for the hook of the door. As I had seen it many times in the hands of Sidorov I took it to him at once.

"Where is the money gone?" he asked, feeling inside the purse with his fingers. "Thirty rubles there were! Give them here!"

His head was enveloped in a turban formed of a towel. Looking yellow and wasted, he blinked at me angrily with his swollen eyes, and refused to believe that I had found the purse empty.

Ermokhin came in and backed him up, shaking his head at me.

"It is he who has stolen it. Take him to his master. Soldiers do not steal from soldiers."

These words made me think that he had stolen the money himself and had thrown the purse into my shed. I called out to his face, without hesitation:

"Liar! You stole it yourself!"

I was convinced that I had guessed right when I saw his wooden face drawn crooked with fear and rage. As he writhed, he cried shrilly:

"Prove it!"

How could I prove it? Ermokhin dragged me, with a shout, across the yard. Sidorov followed us, also shouting. Several people put their heads out of the windows. The mother of Queen Margot looked on, smoking calmly. I realized that I had fallen in the esteem of my lady, and I went mad.

I remember the soldiers dragging me by the arms and my employers standing before them, sympathetically agreeing with them, as they listened to the complaint. Also the mistress saying:

"Of course he took it! He was courting the washerwoman at the gate last evening, and he must have had some money. No one gets anything from her without money."

"That's true," cried Ermokhin.

I was swept off my feet, consumed by a wild rage. I began to abuse the mistress, and was soundly beaten.

But it was not so much the beating which tortured me as the thought of what my Queen Margot was now thinking of me. How should I ever set myself right in her eyes? Bitter were my thoughts in that dreadful time. I did not strangle myself only because I had not the time to do so.

Fortunately for me, the soldiers spread the story over the whole yard, the whole street, and in the evening, as I lay in the attic, I heard the loud voice of Natalia Kozlovski below.

"No! Why should I hold my tongue? No, my dear fellow, get away! Get along with you! Go away, I say! If you don't, I will go to your gentleman, and he will give you something!"

I felt at once that this noise was about me. She was shouting near our steps; her voice rang out loudly and triumphantly.

"How much money did you show me yesterday? Where did you get it from? Tell us!"

Holding my breath with joy, I heard Sidorov drawl sadly:

"*Aie! aie!* Ermokhin—"

"And the boy has had the blame for it? He has been beaten for it, eh?"

I felt like running down to the yard, dancing there for joy, kissing the washerwoman out of gratitude; but at that moment, apparently from the window, my mistress cried:

"The boy was beaten because he was insolent. No one believed that he was a thief except you, you slut!"

"Slut yourself, madam! You are nothing better than a cow, if you will permit me to say so."

I listened to this quarrel as if it were music. My heart burned with hot tears of self-pity, and gratitude to Natalia. I held my breath in the effort to keep them back.

Then the master came slowly up to the attic, sat on a projecting beam near me, and said, smoothing his hair:

"Well, brother Pyeshkov, and so you had nothing to do with it?"

I turned my face away without speaking.

"All the same, your language was hideous," he went on. I announced quietly:

"As soon as I can get up I shall leave you."

He sat on in silence, smoking a cigarette. Looking fixedly at its end, he said in a low voice:

"What of it? That is your business. You are not a little boy any longer; you must look about and see what is the best thing for yourself."

Then he went away. As usual, I felt sorry for him.

Four days after this I left that house. I had a passionate desire to say good-by to Queen Margot, but I had not the audacity to go to her, though I confess I thought that she would have sent for me herself.

When I bade good-by to the little girl I said:

"Tell your mother that I thank her very much, will you?"

"Yes, I will," she promised, and she smiled lovingly and tenderly. "Good-by till to-morrow, eh? Yes?"

I met her again twenty years later, married to an officer in the *gendarmerie*.

CHAPTER XI

Once more I became a washer-up on a steamboat, the *Perm*, a boat as white as a swan, spacious, and swift. This time I was a "black" washer-up, or a "kitchen man." I received seven rubles a month, and my duties were to help the cook.

The steward, stout and bloated, was as bald as a billiard-ball. He walked heavily up and down the deck all day long with his hands clasped behind his back, like a boar looking for a shady corner on a sultry day. His wife flaunted herself in the buffet. She was a woman of about forty, handsome, but faded, and so thickly powdered that her colored dress was covered with the white, sticky dust that fell from her cheeks.

The kitchen was ruled over by an expensive cook, Ivan Ivanovich, whose surname was Medvyejenok. He was a small, stout man, with an aquiline nose and mocking eyes. He was a coxcomb, wore starched collars, and shaved every day. His cheeks were dark blue, and his dark mustaches curled upward. He spent all his spare moments in the arrangement of these mustaches, pulling at them with fingers stained by his work at the stove, and looking at them in a small handglass.

The most interesting person on the boat was the stoker, Yaakov Shumov, a broad-chested, square man. His snub-nosed face was as smooth as a spade; his coffee-colored eyes were hidden under thick eyebrows; his cheeks were covered with small, bristling hairs, like the moss which is found in marshes; and the same sort of hair, through which he could hardly pass his crooked fingers, formed a close-fitting cap for his head.

He was skilful in games of cards for money, and his greed was amazing. He was always hanging about the kitchen like a hungry dog, asking for pieces of meat and bones. In the evenings he used to take his tea with Medvyejenok and relate amazing stories about himself. In his youth he had been assistant to the town shepherd of Riazin. Then a passing monk lured him into a monastery, where he served for four years.

"And I should have become a monk, a black star of God," he said in his quick, comical way, "if a pilgrim had not come to our cloister from Penza. She was very entertaining, and she upset me. 'Eh, you 're a fine strong fellow,' says she, 'and I am a respectable widow and lonely. You shall come to me,' she says. 'I have my own house, and I deal in eider-down and feathers.' That suited me, and I went to her. I became her lover, and lived with her as comfortably as warm bread in a oven, for three years."

"You lie hardily," Medvyejenok interrupted him, anxiously examining a pimple on his nose. "If lies could make money, you would be worth thousands."

Yaakov hummed. The blue, bristling hairs moved on his impassive face, and his shaggy mustaches quivered. After he had heard the cook's remark he continued as calmly and quickly as before:

"She was older than I, and she began to bore me. Then I must go and take up with her niece, and she found it out, and turned me out by the scruff of the neck."

"And served you right, you did not deserve anything better," said the cook as easily and smoothly as Yaakov himself.

The stoker went on, with a lump of sugar in his cheek:

"I was at a loose end till I came across an old Volodimerzian peddler. Together we wandered all over the world. We went to the Balkan Hills to Turkey itself, to Rumania, and to Greece, to different parts of Austria. We visited every nation. Wherever there were likely to be buyers, there we went, and sold our goods."

"And stole others?" asked the cook, gravely.

"'No? no!' the old man said to me. 'You must act honestly in a strange land, for they are so strict here, it is said, that they will cut off your head for a mere nothing.' It is true that I did try to steal, but the result was not at all consoling. I managed to get a horse away from the yard of a certain merchant, but I had done no more than that when they caught me, knocked me about, and dragged me to the police station. There were two of us. The other was a real horse-stealer, but I did it only for the fun of the thing. But I had been working at the merchant's house, putting in a new stove for his bath, and the merchant fell ill, and had bad dreams about me, which alarmed him, so that he begged the magistrate, 'Let him go,'—that was me, you know,—'let him go; for I have had dreams about him, and if you don't let him off, you will never be well. It is plain that he is a wizard.' That was me, if you please—a wizard! However, the merchant was a person of influence, and they let me go."

"I should not have let you go. I should have let you lie in water for three days to wash the foolery out of you," said the cook.

Yaakov instantly seized upon his words.

"True, there is a lot of folly about me, and that is the fact—enough folly for a whole village."

Thrusting his fingers into his tight collar, the cook angrily dragged it up, and complained in a tone of vexation:

"Fiddlesticks! How a villain like you can live, gorge himself, drink, and stroll about the world, beats me. I should like to know what use you are."

Munching, the stoker, answered:

"I don't know myself. I live, and that is all I can say about it. One man lies down, and another walks about. A *chinovnik* leads a sedentary life, but every one must eat."

The cook was more incensed than ever.

"You are such a swine that you are absolutely unbearable. Really, pigs' food—"

"What are you in such a rage about?" asked Yaakov, surprised. "All men are acorns from the same oak. But don't you abuse me. It won't make me any better, you know."

This man attracted me and held me at once. I gazed at him with unbounded astonishment, and listened to him with open mouth. I had an idea that he possessed a deep knowledge of life. He said "thou" to every one, looked at every one from under his bushy brows with the same straight and independent glance, and treated every one—the captain, the steward, and the first-class passengers, who were very haughty—as if they were the equals of himself, the sailors, the waiters, and the deck passengers.

Sometimes he stood before the captain or the chief engineer, with his ape-like hands clasped behind his back, and listened while they scolded him for laziness, or for having unscrupulously won money at cards. He listened, but it was evident that scolding made not the slightest impression upon him, and that the threats to put him off the boat at the first stopping-place did not frighten him. There was something alien about him, as there had been about "Good Business." Evidently he was aware of his own peculiarities and of the fact that people could not understand him.

I never once knew this man to be offended, and, when I think of it, do not remember that he was ever silent for long. From his rough mouth and, as it were, despite himself, a stream of words always flowed. When he was being scolded or when he was listening to some interesting story, his lips moved just as if he were repeating what he heard to himself or simply continued speaking quietly to himself. Every day, when he had finished his watch, he climbed out of the stoke-hole, barefooted, sweating, smeared with naphtha, in a wet shirt without a belt, showing his bare chest covered with thick, curly hair, and that very minute his even, monotonous, deep voice could be heard across the deck. His words followed one another like drops of rain.

"Good morning, Mother! Where are you going? To Chistopol? I know it; I have been there. I lived in the house of a rich Tatar workman; his name was Usan Gubaildulin. The old man had three wives. A robust man he was, with a red face, and one of his wives was young. An amu-u-sing little Tatar girl she was."

He had been everywhere, and apparently had committed sin with all the women who had crossed his path. He spoke of every one without malice, calmly, as he had never in his life been hurt or scolded. In a few minutes his voice would be heard in the stern.

"Good people, who will have a game of cards? Just a little flutter, *ei?* Cards are a consolation. You can make money sitting down, a profitable undertaking."

I noticed that he hardly ever said that anything was good, bad, or abominable, but always that it was amusing, consoling, or curious. A beautiful woman was to him an amusing little female. A fine sunny day was a consoling little day. But more often than anything else he said:

"I spit upon it!"

He was looked upon as lazy, but it seemed to me that he performed his laborious task in that infernal, suffocating, and fetid heat as conscientiously as any of the others. I never remember that he complained of weariness or heat, as the other stokers did.

One day some one stole a purse containing money from one of the old women passengers. It was a clear, quiet evening; every one was amiable and peaceably inclined. The captain gave the old woman five rubles. The passengers also collected a small sum among themselves. When the old woman was given the money, she crossed herself, and bowed low, saying:

"Kind friends, you have given me three *greven* too much."

Some one cried gayly:

"Take it all, my good woman,—all that your eyes fall upon. Why do you talk nonsense? No one can have too much."

But Yaakov went to the old woman and said quite seriously:

"Give me what you don't want; I will play cards with it."

The people around laughed, thinking that the stoker was joking, but he went on urging the confused woman perseveringly:

"Come, give it to me, woman! What do you want the money for? To-morrow you will be in the churchyard."

They drove him away with abuse, but he said to me, shaking his head, and greatly surprised:

"How funny people are! Why do they interfere in what does not concern them? She said herself that she had more than she wanted. And three *greven* would have been very consoling to me."

The very sight of money evidently pleased him. While he was talking he loved to clean the silver and brass on his breeches, and would polish coins till they shone. Moving his eyebrows up and down, he would gaze at them, holding them in his crooked fingers before his snub-nosed face. But he was not avaricious.

One day he asked me to play with him, but I could not. "You don't know how?" he cried. "How is that? And you call yourself educated! You must learn. We will play for lumps of sugar."

He won from me half a pound of the best sugar, and hid every lump in his furry cheek. As soon as he found that I knew how to play he said:

"Now we will play seriously for money. Have you any money?"

"I have five rubles."

"And I have two."

As may be imagined, he soon won from me. Desiring to have my revenge, I staked my jacket, worth five rubles, and lost. Then I staked my new boots, and lost again. Yaakov said to me, unwillingly, almost crossly:

"No, you don't know how to play yet; you get too hot about it. You must go and stake everything, even your boots. I don't care for that sort of thing. Come, take back your clothes and your money,—four rubles,—and I will keep a ruble for teaching you. Agreed?"

I was very grateful to him.

"It is a thing to spit upon," he said in answer to my thanks. "A game is a game, just an amusement, you know; but you would turn it into a quarrel. And even in a quarrel it does n't do to get too warm. You want to calculate the force of your blows. What have you to get in a stew about? You are young; you must learn to hold yourself in. The first time you don't succeed; five times you don't succeed; the seventh time—spit! Go away, get yourself cool, and have another go! That is playing the game."

He delighted me more and more, and yet he jarred on me. Sometimes his stories reminded me of grandmother. There was a lot in him which attracted me, but his lifelong habit of dull indifference repelled me violently.

Once at sunset a drunken second-class passenger, a corpulent merchant of Perm, fell overboard, and was carried away, struggling on the red-gold waterway. The engineers hastily shut off steam, and the boat came to a standstill, sending off a cloud of foam from the wheel, which the red beams of the sun made look like blood. In that blood-red, seething, caldron a dark body struggled, already far away from the stern of the boat. Wild cries were heard from the river; one's heart shook. The passengers also screamed, and jostled one another, rolling about the deck, crowding into the stern. The friend of the drowning man, also drunk, red, and bald, hit out with his fists and roared:

"Get out of the way! I will soon get him!"

Two sailors had already thrown themselves into the water, and were swimming toward the drowning man. The boats were let down. Amid the shouts of the commander and the shrieks of the women Yaakov's deep voice rang out calmly and evenly:

"He will be drowned; he will certainly be drowned, because he has his clothes on. Fully dressed as he is, he must certainly drown. Look at women for example. Why do they always drown sooner than men? Because of their petticoats. A woman, when she falls into the water, goes straight to the bottom, like a pound weight. You will see that he will be drowned. I do not speak at random."

As a matter of fact, the merchant was drowned. They sought for him for two hours, and failed to find him. His companion, sobered, sat on the deck, and, panting heavily, muttered plaintively:

"We are almost there. What will happen when we arrive, eh? What will his family say? He had a family."

Yaakov stood in front of him, with his hands behind his back, and began to console him.

"There is nothing to worry about. No one knows when he is destined to die. One man will eat mushrooms, fall ill and die, while thousands of people can eat mushrooms and be all the better for them. Yet one will die. And what are mushrooms?"

Broad and strong, he stood like a rock in front of the merchant, and poured his words over him like bran. At first the merchant wept silently, wiping the tears from his beard with his broad palms, but when he had heard him out, he roared:

"What do you mean by torturing me like this? Fellow-Christians, take him away, or there will be murder!"

Yaakov went away, calmly saying:

"How funny people are! You go to them out of kindness, and all they do is to abuse you!"

Sometimes I thought the stoker a fool, but more often I thought that he purposely pretended to be stupid. I asked him straight out about his youth and his wanderings around the world. The result was not what I meant it to be. Throwing his head back, almost closing his dark, copper-colored eyes, he stroked his mossy face with his hand and drawled:

"People everywhere, Brother,—everywhere,—are simple as ants! And where there are people, there is always trouble, I tell you! The greater number, of course, are peasants. The earth is absolutely strewn with *muzhiks*,—like autumn leaves, as we say. I have seen the Bulgars, and Greeks, too, and those—what do you call them?—Serbians; Rumanians also, and all kinds of Gipsies. Are there many different sorts? What sort of people? What do you mean by that? In the towns they are townspeople, and in the country—why, they are just like the country people among us. They resemble them in many ways. Some of them even speak our tongue, though badly, as, for instance, the Tatars and the Mordovans. The Greeks cannot speak our language. They chatter whatever comes into their heads, and it sounds like words; but what they say or about what it is impossible to understand. You have to talk on your fingers to them. But my old man managed to talk so that even the Greeks understood him. He muttered something, and they knew what he meant. An artful old man he was. He knew how to work upon them. Again you want to know what sort of people? You funny fellow! What should people be like? They were black, of course; and the Rumanians, too, were of the same faith. The Bulgars are also black, but they hold the same religion as ourselves. As for the Greeks, they are of the same race as the Turks."

It seemed to me that he was not telling me all he knew; that there was something which he did not wish to tell. From illustrations in the magazines I knew that the capital of Greece was Athens, an ancient and most beautiful town. But Yaakov shook his head doubtfully as he rejected the idea.

"They have been telling you lies, my friend. There is no place called Athens, but there is a place called Athon; only it is not a town, but a hill with a monastery on it, and that is all. It is called the Holy Hill of Athon. There are pictures of it; the old man used to sell them. There is a town called Byelgorod, which stands on the Dounai River, built in the style of Yaroslav or Nijni. Their towns are nothing out of the ordinary, but their villages, that is another matter. Their women, too—well, they are absolutely killingly pleasant. I very nearly stayed there altogether for the sake of one. What the deuce was her name?"

He rubbed his perspiring face hard with the palms of his hands, and his coarse hair clicked softly. In his throat, somewhere deep down, rumbled his laugh, like the rattle of a drum.

"How forgetful a man can be! And yet, you know, we were—When she said good-by to me—she cried, and I cried, too. Good—go-o—" Calmly and with an entire absence of reticence, he began to instruct me in the way to behave to women.

We were sitting on the deck. The warm moonlight night swam to meet us; the meadow-land of the shore was hardly visible beyond the silver water. In the heavens twinkled yellow lights; these were certain stars which had been captivated by the earth. All around there was movement, sleeplessly palpitating, quiet; but real life was going on. Into this pleasant, melancholy silence fell the hoarse words:

"And so we let go of each other's hands and parted."

Yaakov's stories were immodest, but not repulsive, for they were neither boastful nor cruel, and there was a ring of artlessness and sorrow in them. The moon in the sky was also shamelessly naked, and moved me in the same way, setting me fretting for I knew not what. I remembered only what was good, the very best thing in my life—Queen Margot and the verses, unforgettable in their truth:

> Only a song has need of beauty,
> While beauty has no need of songs.

Shaking off this dreamy mood as if it had been a light doze, I again asked the stoker about his life and what he had seen.

"You 're a funny fellow," he said. "What am I to tell you? I have seen everything. You ask have I seen a monastery? I have. *Traktirs?* I have seen them also. I have seen the life of a gentleman and the life of a peasant. I have lived well-fed, and I have lived hungry."

Slowly, as if he were crossing a deep stream by a shaky, dangerous bridge, he recalled the past.

"For instance, I was sitting in the police station after the horse-stealing affair. 'They will send me to Siberia,' I was thinking when the constable began to rage because the stove in his new house smoked. I said to him, 'This is a business which I can set right for you, your Honor,' He shut me up. 'It is a thing,' he grumbled, 'which the cleverest workman could not manage.' Then I said to him, 'Sometimes a shepherd is cleverer than a general.' I felt very brave toward every one just then. Nothing mattered now, with Siberia before me. 'All right; try,' he said, 'but if it smokes worse afterwards I will break all your bones for you.' In two days I had finished the work. The constable was astonished. '*Ach!* he cried, 'you fool, you blockhead! Why, you are a skilled workman, and you steal horses! How is it?' I said to him, 'That was simply a piece of foolery, your Honor.' 'That's true,' he said, 'it was foolery. I am sorry for you.' 'Yes, I am sorry,' he repeated. Do you see? A man in the police force, carrying out his duties without remorse, and yet he was sorry for me."

"Well, what happened then?" I asked him.

"Nothing. He was sorry for me. What else should happen?"

"What was the use of pitying you? You are like a stone."

Yaakov laughed good-naturedly.

"Funny fellow! A stone, you say? Well, one may feel for stones. A stone also serves in its proper place; streets are paved with stones. One ought to pity all kinds of materials; nothing is in its place by chance. What is soil? Yet little blades of grass grow in it."

When the stoker spoke like this, it was quite clear to me that he knew something more than I could grasp.

"What do you think of the cook?" I asked him.

"Of Medvyejenok?" said Yaakov, calmly. "What do I think of him? There is nothing to think about him at all."

That was true. Ivan Ivanovich was so strictly correct and smooth that one's thoughts could get no grip on him. There was only one interesting thing about him: he loved the stoker, was always scolding him, and yet always invited him to tea.

One day he said to him:

"If you had been my serf and I had been your master, I would have flogged you seven times each week, you sluggard!"

Yaakov replied in a serious tone:

"Seven times? That's rather a lot!"

Although he abused the stoker, the cook for some reason or other fed him with all kinds of things. He would throw a morsel to him roughly and say:

"There. Gobble it up!"

Yaakov would devour it without any haste, saying:

"I am accumulating a reserve of strength through you, Ivan Ivanovich."

"And what is the use of strength to you, lazy-bones?"

"What is the use? Why, I shall live all the longer for it."

"Why should you live, useless one?"

"But useless people go on living. Besides, you know, it is very amusing to be alive, is n't it? Living, Ivan Ivanovich, is a very comforting business."

"What an idiot!"

"Why do you say that?"

"I-di-ot!"

"There's a way of speaking!" said Yaakov in amazement, and Medvyejenok said to me:

"Just think of it! We dry up our blood and roast the marrow out of our bones in that infernal heat at the stoves while he guzzles like a boar!"

"Every one must work out his own fate," said the stoker, masticating.

I knew that to stoke the furnaces was heavier and hotter work than to stand at the stove, for I had tried several times at night to stoke with Yaakov, and it seemed strange to me that he did not enlighten the cook with regard to the heaviness of his labors. Yes, this man certainly had a peculiar knowledge of his own.

They all scolded him,—the captain, the engineer, the first mate, all of those who must have known he was not lazy. I thought it very strange. Why did they not appraise him rightly? The stokers behaved considerably better to him than the rest although they made fun of his incessant chatter and his love of cards.

I asked them: "What do you think of Yaakov? Is he a good man?"

"Yaakov? He's all right. You can't upset him whatever you do, even if you were to put hot coals in his chest."

What with his heavy labor at the boilers, and his appetite of a horse, the stoker slept but little. Often, when the watches were changed, without changing his clothes, sweating and dirty, he stayed the whole night on deck, talking with the passengers, and playing cards.

In my eyes he was like a locked trunk in which something was hidden which I simply must have, and I obstinately sought the key by which I might open it.

"What you are driving at, little brother, I cannot, for the life of me, understand," he would say, looking at me with his eyes almost hidden under his eyebrows. "It is a fact that I have traveled about the world a lot. What about it? Funny fellow! You had far better listen to a story I have to tell you about what happened to me once———"

And he told me how there had lived, somewhere in one of the towns he had passed through, a young consumptive lawyer who had a German wife—a fine, healthy woman, without children. And this German woman was in love with a dry-goods merchant. The merchant was married, and his wife was beautiful and had three children. When he discovered that the German woman was in love with him, he planned to play a practical joke on her. He told her to meet him in the garden at night, and invited two of his friends to come with him, hiding them in the garden among the bushes.

"Wonderful! When the German woman came, he said, 'Here she is, all there!' And to her, he said, 'I am no use to you, lady; I am married. But I have brought two of my friends to you. One of them is a widower, and the other a bachelor.' The German woman—ach! she gave him such a slap on the face that he fell over the garden bench, and then she trampled his ugly mug and his thick head with her heel! I had brought her there, for I was *dvornik* at the lawyer's house. I looked through a chink in the fence, and saw how the soup was boiling. Then the friends sprang out upon her, and seized her by the hair, and I dashed over the fence, and beat them off. 'You must not do this, Mr. Merchants!' I said. The lady had come trustfully, and he had imagined that she had evil intentions. I took her away, and they threw a brick at me, and bruised my head. She was overcome with grief, and almost beside herself. She said to me, as we crossed the yard: 'I shall go back to my own people, the Germans, as soon as my husband dies!' I said to her, 'Of course you must go back to them.' And when the lawyer died, she went away. She was very kind, and so clever, too! And the lawyer was kind, too,—God rest his soul!"

Not being quite sure that I had understood the meaning of this story, I was silent. I was conscious of something familiar, something which had happened before, something pitiless and blind about it. But what could I say?

"Do you think that is a good story?" asked Yaakov.

I said something, making some confused objections, but he explained calmly:

"People who have more than is necessary are easily amused, but sometimes, when they want to play a trick on some one, it turns out not to be fun at all. It does n't come off as they expected. Merchants are brainy people, of course. Commerce demands no little cleverness, and the life of clever persons is very dull, you see, so they like to amuse themselves."

Beyond the prow, all in a foam, the river rushed swiftly. The seething, running water was audible, the dark shore gliding slowly along with it. On the deck lay snoring passengers. Among the benches, among the sleeping bodies, a tall faded woman in a black frock, with uncovered gray head, moved quietly, coming towards us. The stoker, nudging me, said softly:

"Look—she is in trouble!"

And it seemed to me that other people's griefs were amusing to him. He told me many stories, and I listened greedily. I remember his stories perfectly, but I do not remember one of them that was happy. He spoke more calmly than books. In books, I was often conscious of the feelings of the writer,—of his rage, his joy, his grief, his mockery; but the stoker never mocked, never judged. Nothing excited either his disgust or his pleasure to any extent. He spoke like an impartial witness at a trial, like a man who was a stranger alike to accuser, accused, and judge. This equanimity aroused in me an ever-increasing sense of irritated sorrow, a feeling of angry dislike for Yaakov.

Life burned before his eyes like the flame of the stove beneath the boilers. He stood in front of the stove with a wooden mallet in his pock-marked, coffee-colored hands, and softly struck the edge of the regulator, diminishing or increasing the heat.

"Hasn't all this done you harm?"

"Who would harm me? I am strong. You see what blows I can give!"

"I am not speaking of blows, but has not your soul been injured?"

"The soul cannot be hurt. The soul does not receive injuries," he said. "Souls are not affected by any human agency, by anything external."

The deck passengers, the sailors, every one, in fact, used to speak of the soul as often and as much as they spoke of the land, of their work, of food and women. "Soul" is the tenth word in the speech of simple people, a word expressive of life and movement.

I did not like to hear this word so habitually on people's slippery tongues, and when the peasants used foul language, defiling their souls, it struck me to the heart.

I remember so well how carefully grandmother used to speak of the soul,—that secret receptacle of love, beauty, and joy. I believed that, after the death of a good person, white angels carried his soul to the good God of my grandmother, and He greeted it with tenderness.

"Well, my dear one, my pure one, thou hast suffered and languished below."

And He would give the soul the wings of seraphim—six white wings. Yaakov Shumov spoke of the soul as carefully, as reluctantly, and as seldom as grandmother. When he was abused, he never blasphemed, and when others discussed the soul he said nothing, bowing his red, bull-like neck. When I asked him what the soul was like, he replied:

"The soul is the breath of God."

This did not enlighten me much, and I asked for more; upon which the stoker, inclining his head, said:

"Even priests do not know much about the soul, little brother; that is hidden from us."

He held my thoughts continually, in a stubborn effort to understand him, but it was an unsuccessful effort. I saw nothing else but him. He shut out everything else with his broad figure.

The stewardess bore herself towards me with suspicious kindness. In the morning, I was deputed to take hot water for washing to her, although this was the duty of the second-class chambermaid, Lusha, a fresh, merry girl. When I stood in the narrow cabin, near the stewardess, who was stripped to the waist, and looked upon her yellow body, flabby as half-baked pastry, I thought of the lissom, swarthy body of "Queen Margot," and felt disgusted. And the stewardess talked all the time, now complainingly and scolding, now crossly and mockingly.

I did not grasp the meaning of her speech, although I dimly guessed at it—at its pitiful, low, shameful meaning. But I was not disturbed by it. I lived far away from the stewardess, and from all that went on in the boat. I lived behind a great rugged rock, which hid from me all that world. All that went on during those days and nights flowed away into space.

"Our Gavrilovna is quite in love with you." I heard the laughing words of Lusha as in a dream. "Open your mouth, and take your happiness."

And not only did she make fun of me, but all the dining-room attendants knew of the weakness of their mistress. The cook said, with a frown:

"The woman has tasted everything, and now she has a fancy for pastry! People like that——! You look, Pyeshkov, before you leap."

And Yaakov also gave me paternal advice.

"Of course, if you were a year or two older, I should give you different advice, but at your age, it is better for you to keep yourself to yourself. However, you must do as you like."

"Shut up!" said I. "The whole thing is disgusting."

"Of course it is."

But almost immediately after this, trying to make the limp hair on his head stand up with his fingers, he said tersely, in well-rounded periods:

"Well, one must look at it from her point of view, too. She has a miserable, comfortless job. Even a dog likes to be stroked, and how much more a human being. A female lives by caresses, as a mushroom by moisture. She ought to be ashamed of herself, but what is she to do?"

I asked, looking intently into his elusive eyes:

"Do you begrudge her that, then?"

"What is she to me? Is she my mother? And if she were——But you are a funny fellow!"

He laughed in a low voice, like the beating of a drum.

Sometimes when I looked at him, I seemed to be falling into silent space, into a bottomless pit full of twilight.

"Every one is married but you, Yaakov. Why have n't you ever married?"

"Why? I have always been a favorite with the women, thank God, but it's like this. When one is married, one has to live in one place, settle down on the land. My land is very poor, a very small piece, and my uncle has taken even that from me. When my young brother came back from being a soldier, he fell out with our uncle, and was brought before the court for punching his head. There was blood shed over the matter, in fact. And for that they sent him to prison for a year and a half. When you come out of prison, son, there is only one road for you; and that leads back to prison again. His wife was such a pleasant young woman—but what is the use of talking about it? When one is married, one ought to be master of one's own stable. But a soldier is not even master of his own life."

"Do you say your prayers?"

"You fun—n—y—y fellow, of course I do!"

"But how?"

"All kinds of ways."

"What prayers do you say?"

"I know the night prayers. I say quite simply, my brother: 'Lord Jesus, while I live, have mercy on me, and when I am dead give me rest. Save me, Lord, from sickness——' and one or two other things I say."

"What things?"

"Several things. Even what you don't say, gets to Him."

His manner to me was kind, but full of curiosity, as it might have been to a clever kitten which could perform amusing tricks. Sometimes, when I was sitting with him at night, when he smelt of naphtha, burning oil, and onions, for he loved onions and used to gnaw them raw, like apples, he would suddenly ask:

"Now, Olekha, lad, let's have some poetry."

I knew a lot of verse by heart, besides which I had a large notebook in which I had copied my favorites. I read "Rousslan" to him,' and he listened without moving, like a deaf and dumb man, holding his wheezy breath. Then he said to me in a low voice:

"That's a pleasant, harmonious, little story. Did you make it up yourself? There is a gentleman called Mukhin Pushkin. I have seen him."

"But this man was killed ever so long ago."

"What for?"

I told him the story in short words, as "Queen Margot" had told it to me. Yaakov listened, and then said calmly:

"Lots of people are ruined by women."

I often told him similar stories which I had read in books. They were all mixed up, effervescing in my mind into one long story of disturbed, beautiful lives, interspersed with flames of passion. They were full of senseless deeds of heroism, blue-blooded nobility, legendary feats, duels and deaths, noble words and mean actions. Rokambol was confused with the knightly forms of Lya-Molya and Annibal Kokonna, Ludovic XI took the form of the Père Grandet, the Comet Otletaev was mixed up with Henry IV. This story, in which I changed the character of the people and altered events according to my inspiration, became a whole world to me. I lived in it, free as grand-father's God, Who also played with every one as it pleased Him. While not hindering me from seeing the reality, such as it was, nor cooling my desire to understand living people, nevertheless this bookish chaos hid me by a transparent but impenetrable cloud from much of the infectious obscenity, the venomous poison of life. Books rendered many evils innocuous for me. Knowing how people loved and suffered, I could never enter a house of ill fame. Cheap depravity only roused a feeling of repulsion and pity for those to whom it was sweet. Rokambol taught me to be a Stoic, and not be conquered by circumstances. The hero of Dumas inspired me with the desire to give myself for some great cause. My favorite hero was the gay monarch, Henry IV, and it seemed to me that the glorious songs of B?ranger were written about him.

> He relieved the peasants of their taxes,
> And himself he loved to drink.
> Yes, and if the whole nation is happy,
> Why should the king not drink?

Henry IV was described in novels as a kind man, in touch with his people. Bright as the sun, he gave me the idea that France—the most beautiful country in the whole world, the country of the knights—was equally great, whether represented by the mantle of a king or the dress of a peasant. Ange Piutou was just as much a knight as D'Artagnan. When I read how Henry was murdered, I cried bitterly, and ground my teeth with hatred of Ravaillac. This king was nearly always the hero of the stories I told the stoker, and it seemed to me that Yaakov also loved France and "Khenrik."

"He was a good man was King 'Khenrik,' whether he was punishing rebels, or whatever he was doing," he said.

He never exclaimed, never interrupted my stories with questions, but listened in silence, with lowered brows and immobile face, like an old stone covered with fungus growth. But if, for some reason, I broke off my speech, he at once asked:

"Is that the end?"

"Not yet."

"Don't leave off, then!"

Of the French nation he said, sighing:

"They had a very easy time of it!"

"What do you mean?"

"Well, you and I have to live in the heat. We have to labor, while they lived at ease. They had nothing to do but to sing and walk about—a very consoling life!"

"They worked, too!"

"It doesn't say so in your stories," observed the stoker with truth, and I suddenly realized clearly that the greater number of the books which I had read hardly ever spoke of the heroes working, or of the hardships they had to encounter.

"Now I am going to sleep for a short time," said Yaakov, and falling back where he lay, he was soon snoring peacefully.

In the autumn, when the shores of the Kama were turning red, the leaves were taking a golden tinge, and the crosswise beams of the sun grew pallid, Yaakov unexpectedly left the boat. The day before, he had said to me:

"The day after to-morrow, you and I, my lad, will be in Perm. We will go to the bath, steam ourselves to our hearts' content, and when we have finished will go together to a Traktir. There is music and it is very pleasant. I like to see them playing on those machines."

But at Sarapulia there came on the boat a stout man with a flabby, womanish face. He was beardless and whiskerless. His long warm cloak, his cap with ear flaps of fox fur, increased his resemblance to a woman. He at once engaged a small table near the kitchen, where it was warmest, asked for tea to be served to him, and began to drink the yellow boiling liquid. As he neither unfastened his coat nor removed his cap, he perspired profusely.

A fine rain fell unweariedly from the autumn mist. It seemed to me that when this man wiped the sweat from his face with his checked handkerchief, the rain fell less, and in proportion as he began to sweat again, it began to rain harder.

Very soon Yaakov appeared, and they began to look at a map together. The passenger drew his finger across it, but Yaakov said:

"What's that? Nothing! I spit upon it!"

"All right," said the passenger, putting away the map in a leather bag which lay on his knees. Talking softly together, they began to drink tea.

Before Yaakov went to his watch, I asked him what sort of a man this was. He replied, with a laugh:

"To see him, he might be a dove. He is a eunuch, that's what he is. He comes from Siberia—a long way off! He is amusing; he lives on a settlement."

Setting his black strong heels on the deck, like hoofs, once again he stopped, and scratched his side.

"I have hired myself to him as a workman. So when we get to Perm, I shall leave the boat, and it will be good-by to you, lad? We shall travel by rail, then by river, and after that by horses. For five weeks we shall have to travel, to get to where the man has his colony."

"Did you know him before?" I asked, amazed at his sudden decision.

"How should I know him? I have never seen him before. I have never lived anywhere near him."

In the morning Yaakov, dressed in a short, greasy fur-coat, with sandals on his bare feet, wearing Medvyejenok's tattered, brimless straw hat, took hold of my arm with his iron grasp, and said:

"Why don't you come with me, eh? He will take you as well, that dove, if you only tell him you want to go. Would you like to? Shall I tell him? They will take away from you something which you will not need, and give you money. They make a festival of it when they mutilate a man, and they reward him for it."

The eunuch[1] stood on board, with a white bundle under his arm, 2nd looked stubbornly at Yaakov with his dull eyes, which were heavy and swollen, like those of a drowned person. I abused him in a low voice, and the stoker once more took hold of my arm.

"Let him alone! There's no harm in him. Every one has his own way of praying. What business is it of ours? Well, good-by. Good luck, to you!" And Yaakov Shumov went away, rolling from side to side like a bear, leaving in my heart an uneasy, perplexed feeling. I was sorry to lose the stoker, and angry with him. I was, I remember, a little jealous and I thought fearfully, "Fancy a man going away like that, without knowing where he is going!"

[1]Skoptsi, or eunuchs, form a sect in Russia, or rather part of the schism known as the Old Believers. Sexual purity being enjoined on its members, and the practice of it being found to be lax, mutilation was resorted to.

And what sort of a man was he—Yaakov Shumov?

CHAPTER XII

Late in the autumn, when the steamboat voyages finished, I went as pupil in the workshop of an icon painter. But in a day or two my mistress, a gentle old lady given to tippling, announced to me in her Vladimirski speech:

"The days are short now and the evenings long, so you will go to the shop in the mornings, and be shop-boy. In the evenings you will learn."

She placed me under the authority of a small, swift-footed shopman, a young fellow with a handsome, false face. In the mornings, in the cold twilight of dawn, I went with him right across the town, up the sleepy mercantile street, Ilnik, to the Nijni bazaar, and there, on the second floor of the Gostini Dvor, was the shop. It had been converted from a warehouse into a shop, and was dark, with an iron door, and one small window on the terrace, protected by iron bars. The shop was packed with icons of different sizes, with image-cases, and with highly finished books in church Slav characters, bound in yellow leather. Beside our shop there was another, in which were also sold icons and books, by a black-bearded merchant, kinsman to an Old Believer valuer. He was celebrated beyond the Volga as far as the boundaries of Kirjinski, and was assisted by his lean and lively son, who had the small gray face of in old man, and the restless eyes of a mouse.

When I had opened the shop, I had to run to the tavern for boiling water, and when I had finished breakfast, I had to set the shop in order, dust the goods, and then go out on the terrace and watch with vigilant eyes, lest customers should enter the neighboring shop.

"Customers are fools," said the shopman forcibly to me. "They don't mind where they buy, so long as it is cheap, and they do not understand the value of the goods."

Lightly tapping the wooden surface of an icon, he aired his slight knowledge of the business to me. He instructed me:

"This is a clever piece of work—very cheap—three or four vershoks—stands by itself. Here is another—six or seven vershoks—stands by itself. Do you know about the saints? Remember Boniface is a protection against drink; Vvaara, the great martyr, against toothache and death by accident; Blessed Vassili, against fevers. Do you know all about Our Lady? Look! This is Our Lady of Sorrows, and Our Lady of Abalak, Most Renowned. Do not weep for me, Mother. Assuage my griefs. Our lady of Kazan, of Pokrove; Our Lady of Seven Dolors."

I soon remembered the prices of the icons, according to their size and the work on them, and learned to distinguish between the different images of Our Lady. But to remember the significations of the various saints was difficult.

Sometimes I would be standing at the door of the shop, dreaming, when the shopman would suddenly test my knowledge.

"Who is the deliverer from painful childbirth?"

If I answered wrongly, he would ask scornfully:

"What is the use of your head?"

Harder still was it for me to tout for customers. The hideously painted icons did not please me at all, and I did not like having to sell them. According to grandmother's stories, I had imagined Our Lady as young, beautiful, and good, just as she was in pictures. in the magazines, but the icons represented her as old and severe, with a long crooked nose, and wooden hands.

On market days, Wednesdays and Fridays, business was brisk. Peasants, old women, and sometimes whole families together, appeared on the terrace,—all old Ritualists from Zavoljia, suspicious and surly people of the forests. I would see, perhaps, coming along slowly, almost timidly, across the gallery, a ponderous man wrapped in sheepskin and thick, homemade cloth, and I would feel awkward and ashamed at having to accost him. At last by a great effort I managed to intercept him, and revolving about his feet in their heavy boots, I chanted in a constrained, buzzing voice:

"What can we do for you, your honor? We have psalters with notes and comments, the books of Ephrem Siren, Kyrillov, and all the canonical books and breviaries. Please come and look at them. All kinds of icons, whatever you want, at various prices. Only the best work,—dark colors! We take orders, too, if you wish it, for all kinds of saints and madonnas. Perhaps you would like to order something for a Name Day, or for your family? This is the best workshop in Russia! Here are the best goods in the town!"

The impervious and inscrutable customer would look at me for a long time in silence. Suddenly pushing me aside with an arm like a piece of wood, he would go into the shop next door, and my shopman, rubbing his large ears, grumbled angrily:

"You have let him go! You're a nice salesman!"

In the next shop could be heard a soft, sweet voice, pouring forth a speech which had the effect of a narcotic.

"We don't sell sheepskins or boots, my friend, but the blessing of God, which is of more value than silver or gold; which, in fact, is priceless."

"The devil!" whispered our shopman, full of envy and almost beside himself with rage. "A curse on the eyes of that muzhik! You must learn! You must learn!"

I did honestly try to learn, for one ought to do well whatever one has to do. But I was not a success at enticing the customers in, nor as a salesman. These gruff men, so sparing of their words, those old women who looked like rats, always for some reason timid and abject, aroused my pity, and I wanted to tell them on the quiet the real value of the icons, and not ask for the extra two *greven*.

They amazed me by their knowledge of books, and of the value of the painting on the icons. One day a gray-haired old man whom I had herded into the shop said to me shortly:

"It is not true, my lad, that your image workshop is the best in Russia—the best is Rogoshin's in Moscow."

In confusion I stood aside for him to pass, and he went to another shop, not even troubling to go next door.

"Has he gone away?" asked the shopman spitefully.

"You never told me about Rogoshin's workshop."

He became abusive.

"They come in here so quietly, and all the time they know all there is to know, curse them! They understand all about the business, the dogs!"

Handsome, overfed, and selfish, he hated the peasants. When he was in a good humor, he would complain to me:

"I am clever! I like cleanliness and scents, incense, and eau-de-Cologne, and though I set such a value on myself, I am obliged to bow and scrape to some peasant, to get five copecks' profit out of him for the mistress. Do you think it is fair? What is a peasant, after all? A bundle of foul wool, a winter louse, and yet——"

And he fell into an indignant silence.

I liked the peasants. There was something elusive about each one of them which reminded me of Yaakov.

Sometimes there would climb into the shop a miserable-looking figure in a *chapan*, put on over a short, fur-coat. He would take off his shaggy cap, cross himself with two fingers, look into the corner where the lamp glimmered, yet try not to, lest his eyes rest on the unblessed icons. Then glancing around, without speaking for some time, he would manage at length to say:

"Give me a psalter with a commentary."

Tucking up the sleeves of his *chapan*, he would read the pages, as he turned them over with clumsy movement, biting his lips the while.

"Haven't you any more ancient than this?"

"An old one would cost a thousand rubles, as you know."

"I know."

The peasant moistened his finger as he turned over the leaves, and there was left a dark fingerprint where he had touched them. The shopman, gazing with an evil expression at the back of his head, said:

"The Holy Scriptures are all of the same age; the word of God does not change."

"We know all about that; we have heard that! God did not change it, but Nikon[1] did."

Closing the book, he went out in silence.

[1] The Nikonites are the followers of Nikon, patriarch of Moscow, who objected to the innovation of Peter the Great in suppressing the patriarchate of Moscow, and establishing a State Church upon the lines of the old patriarchal church. They are also termed the Old Believers, who are split up into several extraordinary schisms which existed before and after the suppression of the patriarchate, but who, in the main, continue their orthodoxy.

Sometimes these forest people disputed with the shopman, and it was evident to me that they knew more about the sacred writings than he did.

"Outlandish heathen!" grumbled the shopman.

I saw also that, although new books were not to the taste of the peasants, they looked upon a new book with awe, handling it carefully, as if it were a bird which might fly out of their hands. This was very pleasant to me to see, because a book was a miracle to me. In it was inclosed the soul of the writer, and when I opened it, I set this soul free, and it spoke to me in secret.

Often old men and women brought books to sell printed in the old characters of the pre-Nikonovski period, or copies of such books, beautifully made by the monks of Irgiz and Kerjentz. They also brought copies of missals uncorrected by Dmitry Rostovski, icons with ancient inscriptions, crosses, folding icons with brass mountings, and silver, eucharist spoons given by the Muscovite princes to their hosts as keepsakes. All these were offered secretly, from their hoards under the floor.

Both my shopman and his neighbor kept a very sharp lookout for such vendors, each trying to take them away from the other. Having bought antiques for anything up to ten rubles, they would sell them on the market-place to rich Old Ritualists for hundreds of rubles.

"Mind you look out for those were-wolves, those wizards! Look for them with all your eyes; they bring luck with them."

When a vendor of this kind appeared, the shopman used to send me to fetch the valuer, Petr Vassilich, a connoisseur in old books, icons, and all kind of antiques.

He was a tall old man with a long beard, like Blessed Vassili, with intelligent eyes in a pleasant face. The tendon of one of his legs had been removed, and he walked lame, with a long stick. Summer and winter he wore a light garment, like a cassock, and a velvet cap of a strange shape, which looked like a saucepan. Usually brisk and upright, when he entered the shop, he let his shoulders droop, and bent his back, sighing gently and crossing himself often, muttering prayers and psalms to himself all the time. This pious and aged feebleness at once inspired the vendor with confidence in the valuer.

"What is the matter? Has something gone wrong?" the old man would ask.

"Here is a man who has brought an icon to sell. He says it is a Stroganovski."

"What!"

"A Stroganovski."

"Aha, my hearing is bad. The Lord has stopped my ears against the abomination of the Nikonites."

Taking off his cap, he held the icon horizontally, looked at the inscription lengthways, sideways, straight up, examined the knots in the wood, blinked, and murmured:

"The godless Nikonites, observing our love of ancient beauties, and instructed by the devil, have maliciously made forgeries. In these days it is very easy to make holy images,—oh, very easy! At first sight, this might be a real Stroganovski, or an Ustiujcki painting, or even a Suzdulski, but when you look into it, it is a forgery."

If he said "forgery," it meant, "This icon is precious and rare."

By a series of pre-arranged signs, he informed the shopman how much he was to give for the icon or book. I knew that the words "melancholy" and "affliction" meant ten rubles. "Nikon the tiger" meant twenty-five. I felt ashamed to see how they deceived the sellers, but the skilful by-play of the valuer amused me.

"Those Nikonites, black children of Nikon the tiger, will do anything,—led by the Devil as they are! Look! Even this signature looks real, and the bas-relief as if it were painted by the one hand. But look at the face—that was not done by the same brush. An old master like Pimen Ushakov, although he was a heretic, did the whole icon himself. He did the bas-relief, the face, and even the chasing very carefully, and sketched in the inscription, but the impious people of our day cannot do anything like it! In old times image painting was a holy calling, but now they make what concerns God merely a matter of art."

At length he laid the icon down carefully on the counter, and putting on his hat, said:

"It is a sin!"

This meant "buy it."

Overwhelmed by his flow of sweet words, astounded by the old man's knowledge, the client would ask in an impressed tone:

"Well, your honor, what is your opinion of the icon?"

"The icon was made by Nikonite hands."

"That cannot be! My grandfather and my grandmother prayed before it!"

"Nikon lived before your grandfather lived."

The old man held the icon close to the face of the seller, and said sternly:

"Look now what a joyous expression it has! Do you call that an icon? It is nothing more than a picture—a blind work of art, a Nikonski joke—there is no soul in it! Would I tell you what is not true? I, an old man, persecuted for the sake of the truth! I shall soon have to go to God. I have nothing to gain by acting unfairly."

He went out from the shop onto the terrace, languid with the feebleness of old age, offended by the doubt cast upon his valuation. The shopman paid a few rubles for the picture, the seller left, bowing low to Petr Vassilich, and they sent me to the tavern to get boiling water for the tea. When I returned, I would find the valuer brisk and cheerful, looking lovingly at the purchase, and thus instructing the shopman:

"Look, this icon has been very carefully done! The painting is very fine, done in the fear of God. Human feelings had no part in it."

"And whose work is it?" asked the shopman, beaming and jumping about for joy.

"It is too soon for you to know that."

"But how much would connoisseurs give for it?" "That I could not say. Give it to me, and I will show it to some one."

"Och, Petr Vassilich."

"And if I sell it, you shall have half the hundred rubles. Whatever there is over, that is mine!"

"Och!"

"You need not keep on saying 'Och'!"

They drank their tea, bargaining shamelessly, looking at one another with the eyes of conspirators. That the shopman was completely under the thumb of the old man was plain, and when the latter went away, he would say to me:

"Now don't you go chattering to the mistress about this deal."

When they had finished talking about the sale of the icon, the shopman would ask:

"And what news is there in the town, Petr Vassilich?"

Smoothing his beard with his yellow fingers, laying bare his oily lips, the old man told stories of the lives of the merchants. He spoke of commercial successes, of feasts, of illnesses, of weddings, and of the infidelities of husbands and wives. He served up these greasy stories quickly and skilfully, as a good cook serves up pancakes, with a sauce of hissing laughter. The shopman's round face grew dark with envy and rapture. His eyes were wide with dreamy wistfulness, as he said complainingly:

"Other people live, and here am I!"

"Every one has his appointed destiny," resounded the deep voice. "Of one, the fate is heralded by angels with little silver hammers, and of another, by devils with the butt-end of an ax."

This strong, muscular, old man knew everything—the whole life of the town, all the secrets of the merchants, chinovniks, priests, and citizens. He was keensighted as a bird of prey, and with this had some of the qualities of the wolf and fox. I always wanted to make him angry, but he looked at me from afar, almost as if through a fog. He seemed to me to be surrounded by a limitless space. If one went closer to him, one seemed to be falling. I felt in him some affinity to the stoker Shumov.

Although the shopman went into ecstasies over his cleverness, both to his face and behind his back, there were times when, like me, he wanted to provoke or offend the old man.

"You are a deceiver of men," he would say, suddenly looking heatedly into the old man's face.

The latter, smiling lazily, answered:

"Only the Lord lives without deceit, and we live among fools, you see. Can one meet fools, and not deceive them? Of what use would they be, then?"

The shopman lost his temper.

"Not all the peasants are fools. The merchants themselves came from the peasantry!"

"We are not talking about merchants. Fools do not live as rogues do. A fool is like a saint—his brains are asleep."

The old man drawled more and more lazily, and this was very irritating. It seemed to me that he was standing on a hillock in the midst of a quagmire. It was impossible to make him angry. Either he was above rage, or he was able to hide it very successfully.

But he often happened to be the one to start a dispute with me. He would come quite close to me, and smiling into his beard, remark:

"What do you call that French writer—Ponoss?" I was desperately angry at this silly way of turning the names upside down. But holding myself in for the time, I said:

"Ponson de Terrail."

"Where was he lost?"[LLL]

"Don't play the fool. You are not a child." "That is true. I am not a child. What are you reading?"

"'Ephrem Siren.'"

"And who writes best. Your foreign authors? or he?"

I made no reply.

"What do the foreign ones write about most?"

"About everything which happens to exist in life."

[1] Terryat in Russian means "to lose."

"That is to say, about dogs and horses—whichever may happen to come their way."

The shopman laughed. I was enraged. The atmosphere was oppressive, unpleasant to me. But if I attempted to get away, the shopman stopped me.

"Where are you going?"

And the old man would examine me.

"Now, you learned man, gnaw this problem. Suppose you had a thousand naked people standing before you, five hundred women and five hundred men, and among them Adam and Eve. How would you tell which were Adam and Eve?"

He kept asking me this, and at length explained triumphantly:

"Little fool, don't you see that, as they were not born, but were created, they would have no navels!" The old man knew an innumerable quantity of these "problems." He could wear me out with them.

During my early days at the shop, I used to tell the shopman the contents of some of the books I had read. Now these stories came back to me in an evil form. The shopman retold them to Petr Vassilich, considerably cut up, obscenely mutilated. The old man skilfully helped him in his shameful questions. Their slimy tongues threw the refuse of their obscene words at Eugénie Grandet, Ludmilla, and Henry IV.

I understood that they did not do this out of ill-nature, but simply because they wanted something to do. All the same, I did not find it easy to bear.

Having created the filth, they wallowed in it, like hogs, and grunted with enjoyment when they soiled what was beautiful, strange, unintelligible, and therefore comical to them.

The whole Gostinui Dvor, the whole of its population of merchants and shopmen, lived a strange life, full of stupid, puerile, and always malicious diversions. If a passing peasant asked which was the nearest way to any place in the town, they always gave him the wrong direction. This had become such a habit with them that the deceit no longer gave them pleasure. They would catch two rats, tie their tails together, and let them go in the road. They loved to see how they pulled in different directions, or bit each other, and sometimes they poured paraffin-oil over the rats, and set fire to them. They would tie an old iron pail on the tail of a dog, who, in wild terror, would tear about, yelping and growling, while they all looked on, and laughed.

There were many similar forms of recreation, "and it seemed to me that all kinds of people, especially country people, existed simply for the amusement of the Gostinui Dvor. In their relations to other people, there was a constant desire to make fun of them, to give them pain, and to make them uncomfortable. It was strange that the books I had read were silent on the subject of this unceasing, deep-seated tendency of people to jeer at one another.

One of the amusements of the Gostinui Dvor seemed to me peculiarly offensive and disgusting.

Underneath our shop there was a dealer in woolen and felt footwear, whose salesman amazed the whole of Nijni by his gluttony. His master used to boast of this peculiarity of his employee, as one boasts of the fierceness of a dog, or the strength of a horse. He often used to get the neighboring shopkeepers to bet.

"Who will go as high as ten rubles? I will bet that Mishka devours, ten pounds of ham in two hours!"

But they all knew that Mishka was well able to do that, and they said:

"We won't take your bet, but buy the ham and let him eat it, and we will look on."

"Only let it be all meat and no bones!"

They would dispute a little and lazily, and then out of the dark storehouse crept a lean, beardless fellow with high cheek-bones, in a long cloth coat girdled with a red belt all stuck round with tufts of wool. Respectfully removing his cap from his small head, he gazed in silence, with a dull expression in his deep-set eyes, at the round face of his master which was suffused with purple blood. The latter was saying in his thick harsh voice:

"Can you eat a gammon of ham?"

"How long shall I have for it?" asked Mishka practically, in his thin voice.

"Two hours."

"That will be difficult."

"Where is the difficulty?"

"Well, let me have a drop of beer with it."

"All right," said his master, and he would boast:

"You need not think that he has an empty stomach. No! In the morning he had two pounds of bread, and dinner at noon, as you know."

They brought the ham, and the spectators took their places. All the merchants were tightly enveloped in their thick fur-coats and looked like gigantic weights. They were people with big stomachs, but they all had small eyes and some had fatty tumors. An unconquerable feeling of boredom oppressed them all.

With their hands tucked into their sleeves, they surrounded the great glutton in a narrow circle, armed with knives and large crusts of rye bread. He crossed himself piously, sat down on a sack of wool and placed the ham on a box at his side, measuring it with his vacant eyes.

Cutting off a thin slice of bread and a thick one of meat, the glutton folded them together carefully, and held the sandwich to his mouth with both hands. His lips trembled; he licked them with his thin and long canine tongue, showing his small sharp teeth, and with a dog-like movement bent his snout again over the meat.

"He has begun!"

"Look at the time!"

All eyes were turned in a business-like manner on the face of the glutton, on his lower jaw, on the round protuberances near his ears; they watched the sharp chin rise and fall regularly, and drowsily uttered their thoughts.

"He eats cleanly—like a bear."

"Have you ever seen a bear eat?"

"Do I live in the woods? There is a saying, 'he gobbles like a bear.'"

"Like a pig, it says."

"Pigs don't eat pig."

They laughed unwillingly, and soon some one knowingly said:

"Pigs eat everything—little pigs and their own sisters."

The face of the glutton gradually grew darker, his ears became livid, his running eyes crept out of their bony pit, he breathed with difficulty, but his chin moved as regularly as ever.

"Take it easy, Mikhail, there is time!" they encouraged him.

He uneasily measured the remains of the meat with his eyes, drank some beer, and once more began to munch. The spectators became more animated. Looking more often at the watch in the hand of Mishka's master, they suggested to one another:

"Don't you think he may have put the watch back? Take it away from him! Watch Mishka in case he should put any meat up his sleeve! He won't finish it in the time!"

Mishka's master cried passionately:

"I'll take you on for a quarter of a ruble! Mishka, don't give way!"

They began to dispute with the master, but no one would take the bet.

And Mishka went on eating and eating; his face began to look like the ham, his sharp grisly nose whistled plaintively. It was terrible to look at him. It seemed to me that he was about to scream, to wail:

"Have mercy on me!"

At length he finished it all, opened his tipsy eyes wide, and said in a hoarse, tired voice:

"Let me go to sleep."

But his master, looking at his watch, cried angrily:

"You have taken four minutes too long, you wretch!"

The others teased him:

"What a pity we did not take you on; you would have lost."

"However, he is a regular wild animal, that fellow."

"Ye—e—es, he ought to be in a show."

"You see what monsters the Lord can make of men, eh?"

"Let us go and have some tea, shall we?"

And they swam like barges to the tavern.

I wanted to know what stirred in the bosoms of these heavy, iron-hearted people that they should gather round the poor fellow because his unhealthy gluttony amused them.

It was dark and dull in that narrow gallery closely packed with wool, sheepskins, hemp, ropes, felt, boots, and saddlery. It was cut off. from the pavement by pillars of brick, clumsily thick, weather-beaten, and spattered with mud from the road. All the bricks and all the chinks between them, all the holes made by the fallen-away mortar, had been mentally counted by me a thousand times, and their hideous designs were forever heavily imprinted on my memory.

The foot-passenger dawdled along the pavement; hackney carriages and sledges loaded with goods passed up the road without haste. Beyond the street, in a red-brick, square, two-storied shop, was the marketplace, littered with cases, straw, crumpled paper, covered with dirt and trampled snow.

All this, together with the people and the horses, in spite of the movement, seemed to be motionless, or lazily moving round and round in one place to which it was fastened by invisible chains. One felt suddenly that this life was almost devoid of sound, or so poor in sounds that it amounted to dumbness. The sides of the sledges squeaked, the doors of the shops slammed, sellers of pies and honey cried their wares, but their voices sounded unhappy, unwilling. They were all alike; one quickly became used to them, and ceased to pay attention to them.

The church-bells tolled funerally. That melancholy sound was always in my ears. It seemed to float in the air over the market-place without ceasing from morning to night; it was mingled with all my thoughts and feelings; it lay like a copper veneer over all my impressions.

Tedium, coldness, and want breathed all around: from the earth covered with dirty snow, from the gray snow-drift on the roof, from the flesh-colored bricks of the buildings; tedium rose from the chimneys in a thick gray smoke, and crept up to the gray, low, empty sky; with tedium horses sweated and people sighed. They had a peculiar smell of their own, these people—the oppressive dull smell of sweat, fat, hemp oil, hearth-cakes, and smoke. It was an odor which pressed upon one's head like a warm close-fitting cap, and ran down into one's breast, arousing a strange feeling of intoxication, a vague desire to shut one's eyes, to cry out despairingly, to run away somewhere and knock one's head against the first wall.

I gazed into the faces of the merchants, over-nourished, full-blooded, frost-bitten, and as immobile as if they were asleep. These people often yawned, opening their mouths like fish which have been cast on dry land.

In winter, trade was slack and there was not in the eyes of the dealer that cautious, rapacious gleam which somehow made them bright and animated in the summer. The heavy fur coats hampered their movements, bowed them to the earth. As a rule they spoke lazily, but when they fell into a passion, they grew vehement. I had an idea that they did this purposely, in order to show one another that they were alive.

It was perfectly clear to me that tedium weighed upon them, was killing them, and the unsuccessful struggle against its overwhelming strength was the only explanation I could give of their cruelty and senseless amusements at the expense of others.

Sometimes I discussed this with Petr Vissilich.

Although as a rule he behaved to me scornfully and jeeringly, he liked me for my partiality for books, and at times he permitted himself to talk to me instructively, seriously.

"I don't like the way these merchants live," I said.

Twisting a strand of his beard in his long fingers, he said:

"And how do you know how they live? Do you then often visit them at their houses? This is merely a street, my friend, and people do not live in a street; they simply buy and sell, and they get through that as quickly as they can, and then go home again! People walk about the streets with their clothes on, and you do not know what they are like under their clothes.

What a man really is is seen in his own home, within his own four walls, and how he lives there—that you know nothing about!"

"Yes, but they have the same ideas whether they are here or at home, don't they?"

"And how can any one know what ideas his neighbors have?" said the old man, making his eyes round. "Thoughts are like lice; you cannot count them. It may be that a man, on going to his home, falls on his knees and, weeping, prays to God: 'Forgive me, Lord, I have defiled Thy holy day!' It may be that his house is a sort of monastery to him, and he lives there alone with his God. You see how it is! Every spider knows its own corner, spins its own web, and understands its own position, so that it may hold its own."

When he spoke seriously, his voice went lower and lower to a deep base, as if he were communicating secrets.

"Here you are judging others, and it is too soon for you; at your age one lives not by one's reason but by one's eyes. What you must do is to look, remember, and hold your tongue. The mind is for business, but faith is for the soul. It is good for you to read books, but there must be moderation in all things, and some have read themselves into madness and godlessness."

I looked upon him as immortal; it was hard for me to believe that he might grow older and change. He liked to tell stories about merchants and coiners who had become notorious. I had heard many such stories from grandfather, who told them better than the valuer, but the underlying theme was the same—that riches always lead to sin towards God and one's fellow-creatures. Petr Vassilich had no pity for human creatures, but he spoke of God with warmth of feeling, sighing and covering his eyes.

"And so they try to cheat God, and He, the Lord Jesus Christ, sees it all and weeps. 'My people, my people, my unhappy people, hell is being prepared for you!'"

Once I jokingly reminded him:

"But you cheat the peasants yourself."

He was not offended by this.

"Is that a great matter as far as I am concerned?" he said. "I may rob them of from three to five rubles, and that is all it amounts to!"

When he found me reading, he would take the book out of my hands and ask me questions about what I had read, in a fault-finding manner. With amazed incredulity he would say to the shopman:

"Just look at that now; he understands books, the young rascal!"

And he would give me a memorable, intelligent lecture:

"Listen to what I tell you now; it is worth your while. There were two Kyrills, both of them bishops; one Kyrill of Alexandria, and the other Kyrill of Jerusalem. The first warred against the cursed heretic, Nestorius, who taught obscenely that Our Lady was born in original sin and therefore could not have given birth to God; but that she gave birth to a human being with the name and attributes of the Messiah, the Saviour of the world, and therefore she should be called not the God-Bearer, but the Christ-Bearer. Do you understand? That is called heresy! And Kyrill of Jerusalem fought against the Arian heretics."

I was delighted with his knowledge of church history, and he, stroking his beard with his well-cared-for, priest-like hands, boasted:

"I am a past master in that sort of thing. When I was in Moscow, I was engaged in a verbal debate against the poisonous doctrines of the Nikonites, with both priests and seculars. I, my little one, actually conducted discussions with professors, yes! To one of the priests I so drove home the verbal scourge that his nose bled infernally, that it did!"

His cheeks were flushed; his eyes shone.

The bleeding of the nose of his opponent was evidently the highest point of his success, in his opinion; the highest ruby in the golden crown of his glory, and he told the story voluptuously.

"A ha—a—andsome, wholesome-looking priest he was! He stood on the platform and drip, drip, the blood came from his nose. He did not see his shame. Ferocious was the priest as a desert lion; his voice was like a bell. But very quietly I got my words in between his ribs, like saws. He was really as hot as a stove, made red-hot by heretical malice—ekh—that was a business!"

Occasionally other valuers came. These were Pakhomi, a man with a fat belly, in greasy clothes, with one crooked eye who was wrinkled and snarling; Lukian, a little old man, smooth as a mouse, kind and brisk; and with him came a big, gloomy man looking like a coachman, black bearded, with a deathlike face, unpleasant to look upon, but handsome, and with eyes which never seemed to move. Almost always they brought ancient books, icons and thuribles to sell, or some kind of bowl. Sometimes they brought the vendors—an old man or woman from the Volga. When their business was finished, they sat on the counter, looking just like crows on a furrow, drank tea with rolls and lenten sugar, and told each other about the persecutions of the Nikonites.

Here a search had been made, and books of devotion had been confiscated; there the police had closed a place of worship, and had contrived to bring its owner to justice under Article 103. This Article 103 was frequently the theme of their discussions, but they spoke of it calmly, as of something unavoidable, like the frosts of winter. The words police, search, prison, justice, Siberia—these words, continually recurring in their conversations about the persecutions for religious beliefs, fell on my heart like hot coals, kindling sympathy and fellow feeling for these Old Believers. Reading had taught me to look up to people who were obstinate in pursuing their aims, to value spiritual steadfastness.

I forgot all the bad which I saw in these teachers of life. I felt only their calm stubbornness, behind which, it seemed to me, was hidden an unwavering belief in the teachings of their faith, for which they were ready to suffer all kinds of torments.

At length, when I had come across many specimens of these guardians of the old faith, both among the people and among the intellectuals, I understood that this obstinacy was the oriental passivity of people who never moved from the place whereon they stood, and had no desire to move from it, but were bound by strong ties to the ways of the old words, and worn-out ideas. They were steeped in these words and ideas. Their wills were stationary, incapable of looking forward, and when some blow from without cast them out of their accustomed place, they mechanically and without resistance let themselves roll down, like a stone off a hill. They kept their own fasts in the graveyards of lived-out truths, with a deadly strength of memory for the past, and an insane love of suffering and persecution; but if the possibility of suffering were taken away from them, they faded away, disappeared like a cloud on a fresh winter day.

The faith for which they, with satisfaction and great self-complacency, were ready to suffer is incontestably a strong faith, but it resembles well-worn clothes, covered with all kinds of dirt, and for that very reason is less vulnerable to the ravages of time. Thought and feeling become accustomed to the narrow and oppressive envelope of prejudice and dogma, and although wingless and mutilated, they live in ease and comfort.

This belief founded on habits is one of the most grievous and harmful manifestations of our lives. Within the domains of such beliefs, as within the shadows of stone walls, anything new is born slowly, is deformed, and grows anaemic. In that dark faith there are very few of the beams of love, too many causes of offense, irritations, and petty spites which are always friendly with hatred. The flame of that faith is the phosphorescent gleam of putrescence.

But before I was convinced of this, I had to live through many weary years, break up many images in my soul, and cast them out of my memory. But at the time when I first came across these teachers of life, in the midst of tedious and sordid realities, they appeared to me as persons of great spiritual strength, the best people in the world. Almost every one of them had been persecuted, put in prison, had been banished from different towns, traveling by stages with convicts. They all lived cautious, hidden lives.

However, I saw that while pitying the "narrow spirit" of the Nikonites, these old people willingly and with great satisfaction kept one another within narrow bounds.

Crooked Pakhomie, when he had been drinking, liked to boast of his wonderful memory with regard to matters of the faith. He had several books at his finger-ends, as a Jew has his Talmud. He could put his finger on his favorite page, and from the word on which he had placed his finger, Pakhomie could go on reciting by heart in his mild, snuffling voice. He always looked on the floor, and his solitary eye ran over the floor disquietingly, as if he were seeking some lost and very valuable article.

The book with which he most often performed this trick was that of Prince Muishetzki, called "The Russian Vine," and the passage he best knew was, "The long suffering and courageous suffering of wonderful and valiant martyrs," but Petr Vassilitch was always trying to catch him in a mistake.

"That's a lie! That did not happen to Cyprian the Mystic, but to Denis the Chaste."

"What other Denis could it be? You are thinking of Dionysius."

"Don't shuffle with words!"

"And don't you try to teach me!"

In a few moments both, swollen with rage, would be looking fixedly at one another, and saying:

"Perverter of the truth! Away, shameless one!"

Pakhomie answered, as if he were adding up accounts:

"As for you, you are a libertine, a goat, always hanging round the women."

The shopman, with his hands tucked into his sleeves, smiled maliciously, and, encouraging the guardians of the ancient religion, cried, just like a small boy:

"Th—a—at's right! Go it!"

One day when the old men were quarreling, Petr Vassilitch slapped his comrade on the face with unexpected swiftness, put him to flight, and, wiping the sweat from his face, called after the fugitive:

"Look out; that sin lies to your account! You led my hand into sin, you accursed one; you ought to be ashamed of yourself!"

He was especially fond of reproaching his comrades in that they were wanting in firm faith, and predicting that they would fall away into "Protestantism."

"That is what troubles you, Aleksasha—the sound of the cock crowing!"

Protestantism worried and apparently frightened him, but to the question, "What is the doctrine of that sect?" he answered, not very intelligibly:

"Protestantism is the most bitter heresy; it acknowledges reason alone, and denies God! Look at the Bible Christians, for example, who read nothing but the Bible, which came from a German, from Luther, of whom it was said: He was rightly called Luther, for if you make a verb of it, it runs: Lute bo, lubo luto![1] And all that comes from the west, from the heretics of that part of the world."

Stamping his mutilated foot, he would say coldly and heavily:

"Those are they whom the new Ritualists will have to drive out, whom they will have to watch,—yes, and burn too! But not us—we are of the true faith. Eastern, we are of the faith, the true, eastern, original Russian faith, and all the others are of the west, spoiled by free will! What good has ever come from the Germans, or the French? Look what they did in the year 12—."

Carried away by his feelings, he forgot that it was a boy who stood before him, and with his strong hands he took hold of me by the belt, now drawing me to him, now pushing me away, as he spoke beautifully, emotionally, hotly, and youthfully:

"The mind of man wanders in the forest of its own thoughts. Like a fierce wolf it wanders, the devil's assistant, putting the soul of man, the gift of God, on the rack! What have they imagined, these servants of the devil? The Bogomuili,[2] through whom Protestantism came, taught thus: Satan, they say, is the son of God, the elder brother of Jesus Christ, That is what they have come to! They taught people also not to obey their superiors, not to work, to abandon wife and children; a man needs nothing, no property whatever in his life; let him live as he chooses, and the devil shows him how. That Aleksasha has turned up here again."

[1]From Lutui which means hard, violent.

[2]Another sect of Old Believers.

At this moment the shopman set me to do some work, and I left the old man alone in the gallery, but he went on talking to space:

"O soul without wings! O blind-born kitten, whither shall I run to get away from you?"

And then, with bent head and hands resting on his knees, he fell into a long silence, gazing, intent and motionless, up at the gray winter sky.

He began to take more notice of me, and his manner was kinder. When he found me with a book, he would glance over my shoulder, and say:

"Read, youngster, read; it is worth your while! It may be that you are clever; it is a pity that you think so little of your elders. You can stand up to any one, you think, but where will your sauciness land you in the end? It will lead you nowhere, youngster, but to a convict's prison. Read by all means; but remember that books are books, and use your own brains! Danilov, the founder of the Xlist sect, came to the conclusion that neither old nor new books were necessary, and he put them all in a sack, and threw them in the water. Of course that was a stupid thing to do, but——And now that cur, Aleksasha, must come disturbing us."

He was always talking about this Aleksasha, and one day he came into the shop, looking preoccupied and stern, and explained to the shopman:

"Aleksander Vassiliev is here in the town; he came yesterday. I have been looking for him for a long time, but he has hidden himself somewhere!"

The shopman answered in an unfriendly tone:

"I don't know anything about him!"

Bending his head, the old man said:

"That means that for you, people are either buyers or sellers, and nothing more! Let us have some tea."

When I brought in the big copper tea-pot, there were visitors in the shop. There was old Lukian, smiling happily, and behind the door in a dark corner sat a stranger dressed in a dark overcoat and high felt boots, with a green belt, and a cap set clumsily over his brows. His face was indistinct, but he seemed to be quiet and modest, and he looked somewhat like a shopman who had just lost his place and was very dejected about it.

Petr Vassilich, not glancing in his direction, said something sternly and ponderously, and he pulled at his cap all the time, with a convulsive movement of his right hand. He would raise his hand as if he were about to cross himself, and push his cap upwards, and he would do this until he had pushed it as far back as his crown, when he would again pull it over his brows. That convulsive movement reminded me of the mad beggar, Igosha, "Death in his pocket."

"Various kinds of reptiles swim in our muddy rivers, and make the water more turbid than ever," said Petr Vassilich.

The man who resembled a shopman asked quietly and gently:

"Do you mean that for me?"

"And suppose I do mean it for you?"

Then the man asked again, not loudly but very frankly:

"Well, and what have you to say about yourself, man?"

"What I have to say about myself, I say to God—that is my business."

"No, man, it is mine also," said the new-comer solemnly and firmly. "Do not turn away your face from the truth, and don't blind yourself deliberately; that is the great sin towards God and your fellow-creatures———"

I liked to hear him call Petr Vassilich "man," and his quiet, solemn voice stirred me. He spoke as a good priest reads, "Lord and Master of my life," and bending forward, got off his chair, spreading his hands before his face:

"Do not judge me; my sins are not more grievous than yours."

The samovar boiled and hissed, the old valuer spoke contemptuously, and the other continued, refusing to be stopped by his words:

"Only God knows who most befouls the source of the Holy Spirit. It may be your sin, you book-learned, literary people. As for me, I am neither book-learned nor literary; I am a man of simple life."

"We know all about your simplicity—we have heard of it—more than we want to hear!"

"It is you who confuse the people; you break up the true faith, you scribes and Pharisees. I— what shall I say? Tell me—"

"Heresy," said Petr Vassilich. The man held his hands before his face, just as if he were reading something written on them, and said warmly: "Do you think that to drive people from one hole to another is to do better than they? But I say no! I say: Let us be free, man! What is the good of a house, a wife, and all your belongings, in the sight of God? Let us free ourselves, man, from all that for the sake of which men fight and tear each other to pieces— from gold and silver and all kinds of property, which brings nothing but corruption and uncleanness! Not on earthly fields is the soul saved, but in the valleys of paradise! Tear yourself away from it all, I say; break all ties, all cords; break the nets of this world. They are woven by antichrist. I am going by the straight road; I do not juggle with my soul'; the dark world has no part in me."

"And bread, water, clothes—do you have any part in them? They are worldly, you know," said the valuer maliciously.

But these words had no effect on Aleksander. He talked all the more earnestly, and although his voice was so low, it had the sound of a brass trumpet.

"What is dear to you, man? The one God only should be dear to you. I stand before Him, cleansed from every stain. Remove the ways of earth from your heart and see God; you alone—He alone! So you will draw near to God; that is the only road to Him. That is the way of salvation—to leave father and mother—to leave all, and even thine eye, if it tempts thee— pluck it out! For God's sake tear yourself from things and save your soul; take refuge in the spirit, and your soul shall live for ever and ever."

"Well, it is a case with you, of the dog returning to his vomit," said Petr Vassiliev, rising, "I should have thought that you would have grown wiser since last year, but you are worse than ever."

The old man went swaying from the shop onto the terrace, which action disturbed Aleksander. He asked amazedly and hastily:

"Has he gone? But—why?"

Kind Lukian, winking consolingly, said:

"That's all right—that's all right!"

Then Aleksander fell upon him:

"And what about you, worldling? You are also sewing rubbishy words, and what do they mean? Well—a threefold alleluia—a double——"

Lukian smiled at him and then went out on the terrace also, and Aleksander, turning to the shopman, said in a tone of conviction:

"They can't stand up to me, they simply can't! They disappear like smoke before a flame."

The shopman looked at him from under his brows, and observed dryly:

"I have not thought about the matter."

"What! Do you mean you have not thought about it? This is a business which demands to be thought about."

He sat for a moment in silence, with drooping head. Then the old men called him, and they all three went away.

This man had burst upon me like a bonfire in the night. He burned brightly, and when he was extinguished, left me feeling that there was truth in his refusal to live as other men.

In the evening, choosing a good time, I spoke about him excitedly to the head icon-painter. Quiet and kind Ivan Larionovich listened to what I had to say, and explained:

"He belongs to the Byegouns,[1] a sort of sect; they acknowledge no authority."

"How do they live?"

"Like fugitives they wander about the earth; that is why they have been given the name Byegoun. They say that no one ought to have land, or property. And the police look upon them as dangerous, and arrest them."

Although my life was bitter, I could not understand how any one could run away from everything pleasant. In the life which went on around me at that time, there was much that was interesting and precious to me, and Aleksander Vassiliev soon faded from my mind.

[1]Byegouns, or wanderers, still another sect of Old Believers.

But from time to time, in hours of darkness, he appeared to me. He came by the fields, or by the gray road to the forest, pushed his cap aside with a convulsive movement of his white hands, unsoiled by work, and muttered:

"I am going on the straight road; I have no part in this world; I have broken all ties."

In conjunction with him I remembered my father, as grandmother had seen him in her dream, with a walnut stick in his hand, and behind him a spotted dog running, with its tongue hanging out.

CHAPTER XIII

The icon-painting workshop occupied two rooms in a large house partly built of stone. One room had three windows overlooking the yard and one overlooking the garden; the other room had one window overlooking the garden and another facing the street. These windows were small and square, and their panes, irisated by age, unwillingly admitted the pale, diffused light of the winter days. Both rooms were closely packed with tables, and at every table sat the bent figures of icon-painters. From the ceilings were suspended glass balls full of water, which reflected the light from the lamps and threw it upon the square surfaces of the icons in white cold rays.

It was hot and stifling in the workshop. Here worked about twenty men, icon-painters, from Palekh, Kholia, and Mstir. They all sat down in cotton overalls with unfastened collars. They had drawers made of ticking, and were barefooted, or wore sandals. Over their heads stretched, like a blue veil, the smoke of cheap tobacco, and there was a thick smell of size, varnish, and rotten eggs. The melancholy Vlandimirski song flowed slowly, like resin:

> How depraved the people have now become;
> The boy ruined the girl, and cared not who knew.

They sang other melancholy songs, but this was the one they sang most often. Its long-drawn-out movement did not hinder one from thinking, did not impede the movement of the fine brush, made of weasel hair, over the surface of the icons, as it painted in the lines of the figure, and laid upon the emaciated faces of the saints the fine lines of suffering. By the windows the chaser, Golovev, plied his small hammer. He was a drunken old man with an enormous blue nose. The lazy stream of song was punctuated by the ceaseless dry tap of the hammer; it was like a worm gnawing at a tree. Some evil genius had divided the work into a long series of actions, bereft of beauty and incapable of arousing any love for the business, or interest in it. The squinting joiner, Panphil, ill-natured and malicious, brought the pieces of cypress and lilac-wood of different sizes, which he had planed and glued; the consumptive lad, Davidov, laid the colors on; his comrade, Sorokin, painted in the inscription; Milyashin outlined the design from the original with a pencil; old Golovev gilded it, and embossed the pattern in gold; the finishers drew the landscape, and the clothes of the figures; and then they were stood with faces or hands against the wall, waiting for the work of the face-painter.

It was very weird to see a large icon intended for an iconastasis, or the doors of the altar, standing against the wall without face, hands, or feet,—just the sacerdotal vestments, or the armor, and the short garments of archangels. These variously painted tablets suggested death. That which should have put life into them was absent, but it seemed as if it had been there, and had miraculously disappeared, leaving only its heavy vestments behind.

When the features had been painted in by the face-painter, the icon was handed to the workman, who filled in the design of the chaser. A different workman had to do the lettering, and the varnish was put on by the head workman himself Ivan Larionovich, a quiet man. He had a gray face; his beard, too, was gray, the hair fine and silky; his gray eyes were peculiarly deep and sad. He had a pleasant smile, but one could not smile at him. He made one feel awkward, somehow. He looked like the image of Simon Stolpnik, just as lean and emaciated, and his motionless eyes looked far away in the same abstracted manner, through people and walls.

Some days after I entered the workshop, the banner-worker, a Cossack of the Don, named Kapendiukhin, a handsome, mighty fellow, arrived in a state of intoxication. With clenched teeth and his gentle, womanish eyes blinking, he began to smash up everything with his iron fist, without uttering a word. Of medium height and well built, he cast himself on the workroom like a cat chasing rats in a cellar. The others lost their presence of mind, and hid themselves away in the corners, calling out to one another:

"Knock him down!"

The face-painter, Evgen Sitanov, was successful in stunning the maddened creature by hitting him on the head with a small stool. The Cossack subsided on the floor, and was immediately held down and tied up with towels, which he began to bite and tear with the teeth of a wild beast. This infuriated Evgen. He jumped on the table, and with his hands pressed close to his sides, prepared to jump on the Cossack. Tall and stout as he was, he would have inevitably crushed the breast-bone of Kapendiukhin by his leap, but at that moment Larionovich appeared on the scene in cap and overcoat, shook his finger at Sitanov, and said to the workmen in a quiet and business-like tone:

"Carry him into the vestibule, and leave him there till he is sober."

They dragged the Cossack out of the workshop, set the chairs and tables straight, and once again set to work, letting fall short remarks on the strength of their comrade, prophesying that he would one day be killed by some one in a quarrel.

"It would be a difficult matter to kill him," said Sitanov very calmly, as if he were speaking of a business which he understood very well.

I looked at Larionovich, wondering perplexedly why these strong, pugilistic people were so easily ruled by him. He showed every one how he ought to work; even the best workmen listened willingly to his advice; he taught Kapendiukhin more, and with more words, than the others.

"You, Kapendiukhin, are what is called a painter—that is, you ought to paint from life in the Italian manner. Painting in oils requires warm colors, and you have introduced too much white, and made Our Lady's eyes as cold as winter. The cheeks are painted red, like apples, and the eyes do not seem to belong to them. And they are not put in right, either; one is looking over the bridge of the nose, and the other has moved to the temple; and the face has not come out pure and holy, but crafty, wintry. You don't think about your work, Kapendiukhin."

The Cossack listened and made a wry face. Then smiling impudently with his womanish eyes, he said in his pleasant voice, which was rather hoarse with so much drinking:

"Ekh! I—va—a—n Larionovich, my father, that is not my trade. I was born to be a musician, and they put me among monks."

"With zeal, any business may be mastered."

"No; what do you take me for? I ought to have been a coachman with a team of gray horses, eh?" And protruding his Adam's apple, he drawled despairingly:

> "Eh, i-akh, if I had a leash of grayhounds
> And dark brown horses,
> Och, when I am in torment on frosty nights
> I would fly straight, straight to my love!"

Ivan Larionovich, smiling mildly, set his glasses straight on his gray, sad, melancholy nose, and went away. But a dozen voices took up the song in a friendly spirit, and there flowed forth a mighty stream of song which seemed to raise the whole work-shop into the air and shake it with measured blows:

> "By custom the horses know
> Where the little lady lives."

The apprentice, Pashka Odintzov, threw aside his work of pouring off the yolks of the eggs, and holding the shells in his hand, led the chorus in a masterly manner. Intoxicated by the sounds, they all forgot themselves, they all breathed together as if they had but one bosom, and were full of the same feelings, looking sideways at the Cossack. When he sang, the workshop acknowledged him as its master; they were all drawn to him, followed the brief movements of his hands; he spread his arms out as if he were about to fly. I believe that if he had suddenly broken off his song and cried, "Let us smash up everything," even the most serious of the workmen would have smashed the workshop to pieces in a few moments.

He sang rarely, but the power of his tumultuous songs was always irresistible and all-conquering. It was as if these people were not very strongly made, and he could lift them up and set them on fire; as if everything was bent when it came within the warm influence of that mighty organ of his.

As for me, these songs aroused in me a hot feeling of envy of the singer, of his admirable power over people. A painful emotion flowed over my heart, making it feel as if it would burst. I wanted to weep and call out to the singers:

"I love you!"

Consumptive, yellow Davidov, who was covered with tufts of hair, also opened his mouth, strangely resembling a young jackdaw newly burst out of the egg.

These happy, riotous songs were only sung when the Cossack started them. More often they sang the sad, drawn-out one about the depraved people, and another about the forests, and another about the death of Alexander I, "How our Alexander went to review his army." Sometimes at the suggestion of our best face painter, Jikharev, they tried to sing some church melodies, but it was seldom a success. Jikharev always wanted one particular thing; he had only one idea of harmony, and he kept on stopping the song.

He was a man of forty-five, dry, bald, with black, curly, gipsy-like hair, and large black brows which looked like mustaches. His pointed, thick beard was very ornamental to his fine, swarthy, un-Russian face, but under his protuberant nose stuck out ferocious-looking mustaches, superfluous when one took his brows into consideration. His blue eyes did not match, the left being noticeably larger than the right.

"Pashka," he cried in a tenor voice to my comrade, the apprentice, "come along now, start off: 'Praise—'Now people, listen!"

Wiping his hands on his apron, Pashka led off:

"Pr—a—a—ise—"

"The Name of the Lord," several voices caught it up, but Jikharev cried fussily:

"Lower, Evgen! Let your voice come from the very depths of the soul."

Sitanov, in a voice so deep that it sounded like the rattle of a drum, gave forth:

"R—rabi Gospoda (slaves of the Lord)—"

"Not like that! That part should be taken in such a way that the earth should tremble and the doors and windows should open of themselves!"

Jikharev was in a state of incomprehensible excitement. His extraordinary brows went up and down on his forehead, his voice broke, his fingers played on an invisible dulcimer.

"Slaves of the Lord—do you understand?" he said importantly. "You have got to feel that right to the kernel of your being, right through the shell. Slaves, praise the Lord! How is it that you—living people—do not understand that?"

"We never seem to get it as you say it ought to be," said Sitanov quietly.

"Well, let it alone then!"

Jikharev, offended, went on with his work. He was the best workman we had, for he could paint faces in the Byzantine manner, and artistically, in the new Italian style. When he took orders for iconostasis, Larionovich took counsel with him. He had a fine knowledge of all original image-paintings; all the costly copies of miraculous icons, Theodorovski, Kazanski, and others, passed through his hands. But when he lighted upon the originals, he growled loudly:

"These originals tie us down; there is no getting away from that fact."

In spite of his superior position in the workshop, he was less conceited than the others, and was kind to the apprentices—Pavl and me. He wanted to teach us the work, since no one else ever bothered about us.

He was difficult to understand; he was not usually cheerful, and sometimes he would work for a whole week in silence, like a dumb man. He looked on every one as at strangers who amazed him, as if it were the first time he had come across such people. And although he was very fond of singing, at such times he did not sing, nor did he even listen to the songs. All the others watched him, winking at one another. He would bend over the icon which stood sideways, his tablet on his knees, the middle resting on the edge of the table, while his fine brush diligently painted the dark, foreign face. He was dark and foreign-looking himself. Suddenly he would say in a clear, offended tone:

"Forerunner—what does that mean? *Tech* means in ancient language 'to go.' A forerunner is one who goes before,—and that is all."

The workshop was very quiet; every one was glancing askance at Jikharev, laughing, and in the stillness rang out these strange words:

"He ought to be painted with a sheepskin and wings."

"Whom are you talking to?" I asked.

He was silent, either not hearing my question or not caring to answer it. Then his words again fell into the expectant silence:

"The lives of the saints are what we ought to know! What do we know? We live without wings. Where is the soul? The soul—where is it? The originals are there—yes—but where are the souls?"

This thinking aloud caused even Sitanov to laugh derisively, and almost always some one whispered with malicious joy:

"He will get drunk on Saturday."

Tall, sinewy Sitanov, a youngster of twenty-two years, with a round face without whiskers or eyebrows, gazed sadly and seriously into the corner.

I remember when the copy of the Theodorovski Madonna, which I believe was Kungur, was finished. Jikharev placed the icon on the table and said loudly, excitedly:

"It is finished, Little Mother! Bright Chalice, Thou! Thou, bottomless cup, in which are shed the bitter tears from the hearts of the world of creatures!"

And throwing an overcoat over his shoulders, he went out to the tavern. The young men laughed and whistled, the elder ones looked after him with envious sighs, and Sitanov went to his work. Looking at it attentively, he explained:

"Of course he will go and get drunk, because he is sorry to have to hand over his work. That sort of regret is not given to all."

Jikharev's drinking bouts always began on Saturday, and his, you must understand, was not the usual alcoholic fever of the workman. It began thus: In the morning he would write a note and sent Pavl somewhere with it, and before dinner he would say to Larionovich:

"I am going to the bath to-day."

"Will you be long?"

"Well, Lord—"

"Please don't be gone over Tuesday!"

Jikharev bowed his bald cranium in assent; his brows twitched. When he returned from the baths, he attired himself fashionably in a false shirt-front and a cravat, attached a long silver chain to his satin waistcoat, and went out without speaking, except to say to Pavl and me:

"Clean up the workshop before the evening; wash the large table and scrape it."

Then a kind of holiday excitement showed itself in every one of them. They braced themselves up, cleaned themselves, ran to the bath, and had supper in a hurry. After supper Jikharev appeared with light refreshments, beer, and wine, and following him came a woman so exaggerated in every respect that she was almost a monstrosity. She was six feet five inches in height. All our chairs and stools looked like toys when she was there, and even tall Sitanov looked undersized beside her. She was well formed, but her bosom rose like a hillock to her chin, and her movements were slow and awkward. She was about forty years of age, but her mobile face, with its great horse-like eyes, was fresh and smooth, and her small mouth looked as if it had been painted on, like that of a cheap doll. She smiled, held out her broad hand to everyone, and spoke unnecessary words:

"How do you do? There is a hard frost to-day. What a stuffy smell there is here! It is the smell of paint. How do you do?"

To look at her, so calm and strong, like a large river at high tide, was pleasant, but her speech had a soporific influence, and was both superfluous and wearisome. Before she uttered a word, she used to puff, making her almost livid cheeks rounder than ever. The young ones giggled, and whispered among themselves:

"She is like an engine!"

"Like a steeple!"

Pursing her lips and folding her hands under her bosom, she sat at the cloth-covered table by the samovar, and looked at us all in turn with a kind expression in her horse-like eyes.

Every one treated her with great respect, and the younger ones were even rather afraid of her. The youths looked at that great body with eager eyes, but when they met her all-embracing glance, they lowered their own eyes in confusion. Jikharev was also respectful to his guest, addressed her as "you," called her "little comrade," and pressed hospitality upon her, bowing low the while.

"Now don't you put yourself out," she drawled sweetly. "What a fuss you are making of me, really!"

As for herself, she lived without hurry; her arms moved only from the elbow to the wrist, while the elbows themselves were pressed against her sides. From her came an ardent smell, as of hot bread. Old Golovev, stammering in his enthusiasm, praised the beauty of the woman, like a deacon chanting the divine praises. She listened, smiling affably, and when he had become involved in his speech, said of herself:

"We were not a bit handsome when we were young; this has all come through living as a woman. By the time we were thirty, we had become so remarkable that even the nobility interested themselves in us, and one district commander actually promised a carriage with a pair of horses."

Kapendiukhin, tipsy and dishevelled, looked at her with a glance of hatred, and asked coarsely:

"What did he promise you that for?"

"In return for our love, of course," explained the guest.

"Love," muttered Kapendiukhin, "what sort of love?"

"Such a handsome young man as you are must know all about love," answered the woman simply.

The workshop shook with laughter, and Sitanov growled to Kapendiukhin:

"A fool, if no worse, she is! People only love that way through a great passion, as every one knows."

He was pale with the wine he had drunk; drops of sweat stood on his temples like pearls; his intelligent eyes burned alarmingly.

But old Golovev, twitching his monstrous nose, wiped the tears from his eyes with his fingers, and asked:

"How many children did you have?"

"Only one."

Over the table hung a lamp; over the stove, another. They gave a feeble light; thick shadows gathered in the corners of the workshop, from which looked half-painted headless figures. The dull, gray patches in place of hands and heads look weird and large, and, as usual, it seemed to me that the bodies of the saints had secretly disappeared from the painted garments. The glass balls, raised right up to the ceiling, hung there on hooks in a cloud of smoke, and gleamed with a blue light.

Jikharev went restlessly round the table, pressing hospitality on every one. His broad, bald skull inclined first to one and then to another, his thin fingers always were on the move. He was very thin, and his nose, which was like that of a bird of prey, seemed to have grown sharper; when he stood sideways to the light, the shadow of his nose lay on his cheek.

"Drink and eat, friends," he said in his ringing tenor.

"Why do you worry yourself, comrade? They all have hands, and every one has his own hands and his own appetite; more than that no one can eat, however much they may want to!"

"Rest yourself, people," cried Jikharev in a ringing voice. "My friends, we are all the slaves of God; let us sing, 'Praise His Name.'"

The chant was not a success; they were all enervated and stupefied by eating and vodka-drinking. In Kapendiukhin's hands was a harmonica with a double keyboard; young Victor Salautin, dark and serious as a young crow, took up a drum, and let his fingers wander over the tightly stretched skin, which gave forth a deep sound; the tambourines tinkled.

"The Russian dance!" commanded Jikharev, "little comrade, please."

"Ach!" sighed the woman, rising, "what a worry you are!"

She went to the space which had been cleared, and stood there solidly, like a sentry. She wore a short brown skirt, a yellow batiste blouse, and a red handkerchief on her head.

The harmonica uttered passionate lamentations; its little bells rang; the tambourines tinkled; the skin of the drum gave forth a heavy, dull, sighing sound. This had an unpleasant effect, as if a man had gone mad and was groaning, sobbing, and knocking his head against the wall.

Jikharev could not dance. He simply moved his feet about, and setting down the heels of his brightly polished boots, jumped about like a goat, and that not in time with the clamorous music. His feet seemed to belong to some one else; his body writhed unbeautifully; he struggled like a wasp in a spider's web, or a fish in a net. It was not at all a cheerful sight. But all of them, even the tipsy ones, seemed to be impressed by his convulsions; they all watched his face and arms in silence. The changing expressions of his face were amazing. Now he looked kind and rather shy, suddenly he became proud, and frowned harshly; now he seemed to be startled by something, sighed, closed his eyes for a second, and when he opened them, wore a sad expression. Clenching his fists he stole up to the woman, and suddenly stamping his feet, fell on his knees in front of her with arms outspread and raised brows, smiling ardently. She looked down upon him with an affable smile, and said to him calmly:

"Stand up, comrade."

She tried to close her eyes, but those eyes, which were in circumference like a three copeck piece, would not close, and her face wrinkled and assumed an unpleasant expression.

She could not dance either, and did nothing but move her enormous body from side to side, noiselessly transferring it from place to place. In her left hand was a handkerchief which she waved languidly; her right was placed on her hip. This gave her the appearance of a large pitcher.

And Jikharev moved round this massive woman with so many different changes of expression that he seemed to be ten different men dancing, instead of one. One was quiet and humble, another proud and terrifying; in the third movement he was afraid, sighing gently, as if he desired to slip away unnoticed from the large, unpleasant woman. But still another person appeared, gnashing his teeth and writhing convulsively like a wounded dog. This sad, ugly dance reminded me of the soldiers, the laundresses, and the cooks, and their vile behavior.

Sitanov's quiet words stuck in my memory:

"In these affairs every one lies; that's part of the business. Every one is ashamed; no one loves any one—but it is simply an amusement."

I did not wish to believe that "every one lied in these affairs." How about Queen Margot, then? And of course Jikharev was not lying. And I knew that Sitanov had loved a "street" girl, and she had deceived him. He had not beaten her for it, as his comrades advised him to do, but had been kind to her.

The large woman went on rocking, smiling like a corpse, waving her handkerchief. Jikharev jumped convulsively about her, and I looked on and thought: "Could Eve, who was able to deceive God, have been anything like this horse?" I was seized by a feeling of dislike for her.

The faceless images looked from the dark walls; the dark night pressed against the window-panes. The lamps burned dimly in the stuffy workshop; if one listened, one could hear above the heavy trampling and the din of voices the quick dropping of water from the copper wash-basin into the tub.

How unlike this was to the life I read of in books! It was painfully unlike it. At length they all grew weary of this, and Kapendiukhin put the harmonica into Salautin's hands, and cried:

"Go on! Fire away!"

He danced like Vanka Tzigan, just as if he was swimming in the air. Then Pavl Odintzov and Sorokhin danced passionately and lightly after him. The consumptive Davidov also moved his feet about the floor, and coughed from the dust, smoke, and the strong odor of vodka and smoked sausage, which always smells like tanned hide.

They danced, and sang, and shouted, but each remembered that they were making merry, and gave each other a sort of test—a test of agility and endurance.

Tipsy Sitanov asked first one and then another:

"Do you think any one could really love a woman like that?"

He looked as if he were on the verge of tears.

Larionovich, lifting the sharp bones of his shoulders, answered:

"A woman is a woman—what more do you want?"

The two of whom they spoke disappeared unnoticed. Jikharev reappeared in the workshop in two or three days, went to the bath, and worked for two weeks in his corner, without speaking, pompous and estranged from every one.

"Have they gone?" asked Sitanov of himself, looking round the workshop with sad blue-gray eyes. His face was not handsome, for there was something elderly about it, but his eyes were clear and good. Sitanov was friendly to me—a fact which I owed to my thick note-book in which I had written poetry. He did not believe in God, but it was hard to understand who in the workshop, beside Larionovich, loved God and believed in Him. They all spoke of Him with levity, derisively, just as they liked to speak of their mistresses. Yet when they dined, or supped, they all crossed themselves, and when they went to bed, they said their prayers, and went to church on Sundays and feast days.

Sitanov did none of these things, and he was counted as an unbeliever.

"There is no God," he said.

"Where did we all come from, then?"

"I don't know."

When I asked him how God could possibly not be, he explained:

"Don't you see that God is height!"

He raised his long arm above his head, then lowered it to an arshin from the floor, and said:

"And man is depth! Is that true? And it is written: Man was created in the image and likeness of God,—as you know! And what is Golovev like?"

This defeated me. The dirty and drunken old man, in spite of his years, was given to an unmentionable sin. I remembered the Viatski soldier, Ermokhin, and grandmother's sister. Where was God's likeness in them?

"Human creatures are swine—as you know," said Sitanov, and then he tried to console me. "Never mind, Maxim, there are good people; there are!"

He was easy to get on with; he was so simple. When he did not know anything, he said frankly:

"I don't know; I never thought about it!"

This was something unusual. Until I met him, I had only come across people who knew everything and talked about everything. It was strange to me to see in his note-book, side by side with good poetry which touched the soul, many obscene verses which aroused no feeling but that of shame. When I spoke to him about Pushkin, he showed me "Gavrialad," which had been copied in his book.

"What is Pushkin? Nothing but a jester, but that Benediktov—he is worth paying attention to."

And closing his eyes he repeated softly:

> "Look at the bewitching bosom
> Of a beautiful woman."

For some reason he was especially partial to the three lines which he quoted with joyful pride:

"Not even the orbs of an eagle
Into that warm cloister can penetrate
And read that heart."

"Do you understand that?"

It was very uncomfortable to me to have to acknowledge that I did not understand what he was so pleased about.

CHAPTER XIV

My duties in the workshop were not complicated.

In the morning when they were all asleep, I had to prepare the samovar for the men, and while they drank tea in the kitchen, Pavl and I swept and dusted the workshop, set out red, yellow, or white paints, and then I went to the shop. In the evening I had to grind up colors and "watch" the work. At first I watched with great interest, but I soon realized that all the men who were engaged on this handicraft which was divided up into so many processes, disliked it, and suffered from a torturing boredom.

The evenings were free. I used to tell them stories about life on the steamer and different stories out of books, and without noticing how it came about, I soon held a peculiar position in the workshop as story-teller and reader.

I soon found out that all these people knew less than I did; almost all of them had been stuck in the narrow cage of workshop life since their childhood, and were still in it. Of all the occupants of the workshop, only Jikharev had been in Moscow, of which he spoke suggestively and frowningly:

"Moscow does not believe in tears; there they know which side their bread is buttered."

None of the rest had been farther than Shuya, or Vladimir. When mention was made of Kazan, they asked me:

"Are there many Russians there? Are there any churches?"

For them, Perm was in Siberia, and they would not believe that Siberia was beyond the Urals.

"Sandres come from the Urals; and sturgeon—where are they found? Where do they get them? From the Caspian Sea? That means that the Urals are on the sea!"

Sometimes I thought that they were laughing at me when they declared that England was on the other side of the Atlantic, and that Bonaparte belonged by birth to a noble family of Kalonga. When I told them stories of what I had seen, they hardly believed me, but they all loved terrible tales intermixed with history. Even the men of mature years evidently preferred imagination to the truth. I could see very well that the more improbable the events, the more fantastic the story, the more attentively they listened to me. On the whole, reality did not interest them, and they all gazed dreamily into the future, not wishing to see the poverty and hideousness of the present.

This astonished me so much the more, inasmuch as I had felt keenly enough the contradiction existing between life and books. Here before me were living people, and in books there were none like them—no Smouri, stoker Yaakov, fugitive Aleksander Vassiliev, Jikharev, or washerwoman Natalia.

In Davidov's trunk a torn copy of Golitzinski's stories was found—"Ivan Vuijigin," "The Bulgar," "A Volume of Baron Brambeuss." I read all these aloud to them, and they were delighted. Larionovich said:

"Reading prevents quarrels and noise; it is a good thing!"

I began to look about diligently for books, found them, and read almost every evening. Those were pleasant evenings. It was as quiet as night in the workshop; the glass balls hung over the tables like white cold stars, their rays lighting up shaggy and bald heads. I saw round me at the table, calm, thoughtful faces; now and again an exclamation of praise of the author, or hero was heard. They were attentive and benign, quite unlike themselves. I liked them very much at those times, and they also behaved well to me. I felt that I was in my right place.

"When we have books it is like spring with us; when the winter frames are taken out and for the first time we can open the windows as we like," said Sitanov one day.

It was hard to find books. We could not afford to subscribe to a library, but I managed to get them somehow, asking for them wherever I went, as a charity. One day the second officer of the fire brigade gave me the first volume of "Lermontov," and it was from this that I felt the power of poetry, and its mighty influence over people. I remember even now how, at the first lines of "The Demon," Sitanov looked first at the book and then at my face, laid down his brush on the table, and, embracing his knee with his long arms, rocked to and fro, smiling.

"Not so much noise, brothers," said Larionovich, and also laying aside his work, he went to Sitanov's table where I was reading. The poem stirred me painfully and sweetly; my voice was broken; I could hardly read the lines. Tears poured from my eyes. But what moved me still more was the dull, cautious movement of the workmen. In the workshop everything seemed to be diverted from its usual course—drawn to me as if I had been a magnet. When I had finished the first part, almost all of them were standing round the table, closely pressing against one another, embracing one another, frowning and laughing.

"Go on reading," said Jikharev, bending my head over the book.

When I had finished reading, he took the book, looked at the title, put it under his arm, and said:

"We must read this again! We will read it to-morrow! I will hide the book away."

He went away, locked "Lermontov" in his drawer, and returned to his work. It was quiet in the workshop; the men stole back to their tables. Sitanov went to the window, pressed his forehead against the glass, and stood there as if frozen. Jikharev, again laying down his brush, said in a stern voice:

"Well, such is life; slaves of God—yes—ah!"

He shrugged his shoulders, hid his face, and went on:

"I can draw the devil himself; black and rough, with wings of red flame, with red lead, but the face, hands, and feet—these should be bluish-white, like snow on a moonlight night."

Until close upon supper-time he revolved about on his stool, restless and unlike himself, drumming with his fingers and talking unintelligibly of the devil, of women and Eve, of paradise, and of the sins of holy men.

"That is all true!" he declared. "If the saints sinned with sinful women, then of course the devil may sin with a pure soul."

They listened to him in silence; probably, like me, they had no desire to speak. They worked unwillingly, looking all the time at their watches, and as soon as it struck ten, they put away their work altogether.

Sitanov and Jikharev went out to the yard, and I went with them. There, gazing at the stars, Sitanov said:

> "Like a wandering caravan
> Thrown into space, it shone."

"You did not make that up yourself!"

"I can never remember words," said Jikharev, shivering in the bitter cold. "I can't remember anything; but he, I see—It is an amazing thing—a man who actually pities the devil! He has made you sorry for him, hasn't he?"

"He has," agreed Sitanov.

"There, that is a real man!" exclaimed Jikharev reminiscently. In the vestibule he warned me: "You, Maxim, don't speak to any one in the shop about that book, for of course it is a forbidden one."

I rejoiced; this must be one of the books of which the priest had spoken to me in the confessional.

We supped languidly, without the usual noise and talk, as if something important had occurred and we could not keep from thinking about it, and after supper, when we were going to bed, Jikharev said to me, as he drew forth the book:

"Come, read it once more!"

Several men rose from their beds, came to the table, and sat themselves round it, undressed as they were, with their legs crossed.

And again when I had finished reading, Jikharev said, strumming his fingers on the table:

"That is a living picture of him! Ach, devil, devil—that's how he is, brothers, eh?"

Sitanov leaned over my shoulder, read something, and laughed, as he said:

"I shall copy that into my own note-book." Jikharev stood up and carried the book to his own table, but he turned back and said in an offended, shaky voice:

"We live like blind puppies—to what end we do not know. We are not necessary either to God or the devil! How are we slaves of the Lord? The Jehovah of slaves and the Lord Himself speaks with them! With Moses, too! He even gave Moses a name; it means 'This is mine'—a man of God. And we—what are we?"

He shut up the book and began to dress himself, asking Sitanov:

"Are you coming to the tavern?"

"I shall go to my own tavern," answered Sitanov softly.

When they had gone out, I lay down on the floor by the door, beside Pavl Odintzov. He tossed about for a long time, snored, and suddenly began to weep quietly.

"What is the matter with you?"

"I am sick with pity for all of them," he said. "This is the fourth year of my life with them, and I know all about them."

I also was sorry for these people. We did not go to sleep for a long time, but talked about them in whispers, finding goodness, good traits in each one of them, and also something which increased our childish pity.

I was very friendly with Pavl Odintzov. They made a good workman of him in the end, but it did not last long; before the end of three years he had begun to drink wildly, later on I met him in rags on the Khitrov market-place in Moscow, and not long ago I heard that he had died of typhoid. It is painful to remember how many good people in my life I have seen senselessly ruined. People of all nations wear themselves out, and to ruin themselves comes natural but nowhere do they wear themselves out so terribly quickly, so senselessly, as in our own Russia.

Then he was a round-headed boy two years older than myself; he was lively, intelligent, and upright; he was talented, for he could draw birds, cats, and dogs excellently, and was amazingly clever in his caricatures of the workmen, always depicting them as feathered. Sitanov was shown as a sad-looking woodcock standing on one leg, Jikharev as a cock with a torn comb and no feathers on his head; sickly Davidov was an injured lapwing. But best of all was his drawing of the old chaser, Golovev, representing him as a bat with large whiskers, ironical nose, and four feet with six nails on each. From the round, dark face, white, round eyes gazed forth, the pupils of which looked like the grain of a lentil. They were placed crossways, thus giving to the face a lifelike and hideous expression.

The workmen were not offended when Pavl showed them the caricatures, but the one of Golovev made an unpleasant impression on them all, and the artist was sternly advised:

"You had better tear it up, for if the old man sees it, he will half kill you!"

The dirty, putrid, everlastingly drunk old man was tiresomely pious, and inextinguishably malicious. He vilified the whole workshop to the shopman whom the mistress was about to marry to her niece, and who for that reason felt himself to be master of the whole house and the workpeople. The workmen hated him, but they were afraid of him, and for the same reason were afraid of Golovev, too.

Pavl worried the chaser furiously and in all manner of ways, just as if he had set before himself the aim of never allowing Golovev to have a moment's peace. I helped him in this with enthusiasm, and the workshop amused itself with our pranks, which were almost always pitilessly coarse. But we were warned:

"You will get into trouble, children! Kouzka-Juchek will half kill you!"

Kouzka-Juchek was the nickname of the shopman, which was given to him on the quiet by the workshop.

The warning did not alarm us. We painted the face of the chaser when he was asleep. One day when he was in a drunken slumber we gilded his nose, and it was three days before he was able to get the gold out of the holes in his spongy nose. But every time that we succeeded in infuriating the old man, I remembered the steamboat, and the little Viatski soldier, and I was conscious of a disturbance in my soul. In spite of his age, Golovev was so strong that he often beat us, falling upon us unexpectedly; he would beat us and then complain of us to the mistress.

She, who was also drunk every day, and for that reason always kind and cheerful, tried to frighten us, striking her swollen hands on the table, and crying: "So you have been saucy again, you wild beast? He is an old man, and you ought to respect him! Who was it that put photographic solution in his glass, instead of wine?"

"We did."

The mistress was amazed.

"Good Lord, they actually admit it! Ah, accursed ones, you ought to respect old men!"

She drove us away, and in the evening she complained to the shopman, who spoke to me angrily:

"How can you read books, even the Holy Scriptures, and still be so saucy, eh? Take care, my brother!"

The mistress was solitary and touchingly sad. Sometimes when she had been drinking sweet liqueurs, she would sit at the window and sing:

> "No one is sorry for me,
> And pity have I from none;
> What my grief is no one knows;
> To whom shall I tell my sorrow."

And sobbingly she drawled in the quavering voice of age:

"U—oo—oo—"

One day I saw her going down the stairs with a jug of warm milk in her hands, but suddenly her legs gave way under her. She sat down, and descended the stairs, sadly bumping from step to step, and never letting the jug out of her hand. The milk splashed over her dress, and she, with her hands outstretched, cried angrily to the jug:

"What is the matter with you, satyr? Where are you going?"

Not stout, but soft to flabbiness, she looked like an old cat which had grown beyond catching mice, and, languid from overfeeding, could do no more than purr, dwelling sweetly on the memories of past triumphs and pleasures.

"Here," said Sitanov, frowning thoughtfully, "was a large business, a fine workshop, and clever men labored at this trade; but now that is all done with, all gone to ruin, all directed by the paws of Kuzikin! It is a case of working and working, and all for strangers! When one thinks of this, a sort of spring seems to break in one's head. One wants to do nothing,—a fig for any kind of work!—just to lie on the roof, lie there for the whole summer and look up into the sky."

Pavl Odintzov also appropriated these thoughts of Sitanov, and smoking a cigarette which had been given him by his elders, philosophized about God, drunkenness, and women. He enlarged on the fact that all work disappears; certain people do it and others destroy it, neither valuing it nor understanding it.

At such times his sharp, pleasant face frowned, aged. He would sit on his bed on the floor, embracing his knees, and look long at the blue square of the window, at the roof of the shed which lay under a fall of snow, and at the stars in the winter sky.

The workmen snored, or talked in their sleep; one of them raved, choking with words; in the loft, Davidov coughed away what was left of his life. In the corner, body to body, wrapped in an iron-bound sleep of intoxication, lay those "slaves of God"—Kapendiukhin, Sorokhin, Pershin; from the walls icons without faces, hands, or feet looked forth. There was a close smell of bad eggs, and dirt, which had turned sour in the crevices of the floor.

"How I pity them all!" whispered Pavl. "Lord!"

This pity for myself and others disturbed me more and more. To us both, as I have said before, all the workmen seemed to be good people, but their lives were bad, unworthy of them, unbearably dull. At the time of the winter snowstorms, when everything on the earth—the houses, the trees—was shaken, howled, and wept, and in Lent, when the melancholy bells rang out, the dullness of it all flowed over the workshop like a wave, as oppressive as lead, weighing people down, killing all that was alive in them, driving them to the tavern, to women, who served the same purpose as vodka in helping them to forget.

On such evenings books were of no use, so Pavl and I tried to amuse the others in our own way: smearing our faces with soot and paint, dressing ourselves up and playing different comedies composed by ourselves, heroically fighting against the boredom till we made them laugh. Remembering the "Account of how the soldier saved Peter the Great," I turned this book into a conversational form, and climbing on to Davidov's pallet-bed, we acted thereon cheerfully, cutting off the head of an imaginary Swede. Our audience burst out laughing.

They were especially delighted with the legend of the Chinese devil, Sing-U-Tongia. Pashka represented the unhappy devil who had planned to do a good deed, and I acted all the other characters—the people of the field, subjects, the good soul, and even the stones on which the Chinese devil rested in great pain after each of his unsuccessful attempts to perform a good action.

Our audience laughed loudly, and I was amazed when I saw how easily they could be made to laugh. This facility provoked me unpleasantly.

"Ach, clowns," they cried. "Ach, you devils!"

But the further I went, the more I was troubled with the thought that sorrow appealed more than joy to the hearts of these people. Gaiety has no place in their lives, and as such has no value, but they evoke it from under their burdens, as a contrast to the dreamy Russian sadness. The inward strength of a gaiety which lives not of itself not because it wishes to live, but because it is aroused by the call of sad days, is suspect. And too often Russian gaiety changes suddenly into cruel tragedy. A man will be dancing as if he were breaking the shackles which bound him. Suddenly a ferocious wild beast is let loose in him, and with the unreasoning anguish of a wild beast he will throw himself upon all who come in his way, tear them in pieces, bite them, destroy them.

This intense joy aroused by exterior forces irritated me, and stirred to self-oblivion, I began to compose and act suddenly created fantasies—for I wanted so much to arouse a real, free, and unrestrained joy in these people. I succeeded in some measure. They praised me, they were amazed at me, but the sadness which I had almost succeeded in shaking off, stole back again, gradually growing denser and stronger, harassing them.

Gray Larionovich said kindly:

"Well, you are an amusing fellow, God bless you!"

"He is a boon to us," Jikharev seconded him.

"You know, Maxim, you ought to go into a circus, or a theater; you would make a good clown."

Out of the whole workshop only two went to the theaters, on Christmas or carnival weeks, Kapendiukhin and Sitanov, and the older workmen seriously counseled them to wash themselves from this sin in the baptismal waters of the Jordan. Sitanov particularly would often urge me:

"Throw up everything and be an actor!"

And much moved, he would tell me the "sad" story of the life of the actor, Yakolev.

"There, that will show you what may happen!"

He loved to tell stories about Marie Stuart, whom he called "the rogue," and his peculiar delight was the "Spanish nobleman."

"Don Cæsar de Bazan was a real nobleman. Maximich! Wonderful!"

There was something of the "Spanish nobleman" about himself.

One day in the market-place, in front of the fire-station, three firemen were amusing themselves by beating a peasant. A crowd of people, numbering about forty persons, looked on and cheered the soldiers. Sitanov threw himself into the brawl. With swinging blows of his long arms he struck the firemen, lifted the peasant, and carried him into the crowd, crying:

"Take him away!"

But he remained behind himself, one against three. The yard of the fire-station was only about ten steps away; they might easily have called others to their aid and Sitanov would have been killed. But by good luck the firemen were frightened and ran away into the yard.

"Dogs!" he cried after them.

On Sunday the young people used to attend boxing-matches held in the Tyessni yard behind the Petropavlovski churchyard, where sledge-drivers and peasants from the adjacent villages assembled to fight with the workmen. The wagoners put up against the town an eminent boxer, a Mordovan giant with a small head, and large eyes always full of tears. Wiping away the tears with the dirty sleeve of his short *caftan*, he stood before his backers with his legs planted widely apart, and challenged good-naturedly:

"Come on, then; what is the matter with you? Are you cold?"

Kapendiukhin was set up against him on our side, and the Mordovan always beat him. But the bleeding, panting Cossack said:

"I 'll lick that Mordovan if I die for it!"

In the end, that became the one aim of his life. He even went to the length of giving up vodka, rubbed his body with snow before he went to sleep, ate a lot of meat, and to develop his muscles, crossed himself many times every evening with two pound weights. But this did not avail him at all. Then he sewed a piece of lead inside his gloves, and boasted to Sitanov:

"Now we will finish the Mordovan!"

Sitanov sternly warned him:

"You had better throw it away, or I will give you away before the fight."

Kapendiukhin did not believe him, but when the time for the fight arrived, Sitanov said abruptly to the Mordovan:

"Step aside, Vassili Ivanich; I have something to say to Kapendiukhin first!"

The Cossack turned purple and roared:

"I have nothing to do with you; go away!"

"Yes, you have!" said Sitanov, and approaching him, he looked into the Cossack's face with a compelling glance.

Kapendiukhin stamped on the ground, tore the gloves from his hands, thrust them in his breast, and went quickly away from the scene of his fight.

Both our side and the other were unpleasantly surprised, and a certain important personage said angrily to Sitanov:

"That is quite against the rules, brother,—to bring private affairs to be settled in the world of the prize ring!"

They fell upon Sitanov from all sides, and abused him. He kept silence for a long time, but at length he said to the important personage:

"Am I to stand by and see murder done?"

The important personage at once guessed the truth, and actually taking off his cap said:

"Then our gratitude is due to you!"

"Only don't go and spread it abroad, uncle!"

"Why should I? Kapendiukhin is hardly ever the victor, and ill-success embitters a man. We understand! But in future we will have his gloves examined before the contest."

"That is your affair!"

When the important personage had gone away, our side began to abuse Kapendiukhin:

"You have made a nice mess of it. He would have killed his man, our Cossack would, and now we have to stay on the losing side!"

They abused him at length, captiously, to their hearts' content.

Sitanov sighed and said:

"Oh, you guttersnipes!"

And to the surprise of everyone he challenged the Mordovan to a single contest. The latter squared up and flourishing his fists said jokingly:

"We will kill each other."

A good number of persons, taking hands, formed a wide, spacious circle. The boxers, looking at each other keenly, changed over, the right hand held out, the left on their breasts. The experienced people noticed at once that Sitanov's arms were longer than those of the Mordovan. It was very quiet; the snow crunched under the feet of the boxers. Some one, unable to restrain his impatience, muttered complainingly and eagerly:

"They ought to have begun by now."

Sitanov flourished his right hand, the Mordovan raised his left for defense, and received a straight blow under the right arm from Sitanov's left hand. He gasped, retired, and exclaimed in a tone of satisfaction:

"He is young, but he is no fool!"

They began to leap upon one another, striking each other's breasts with blows from their mighty fists. In a few minutes not only our own people, but strangers began to cry excitedly:

"Get your blows in quicker, image-painter! Fix him up, embosser."

The Mordovan was a little stronger than Sitanov, but as he was considerably the heavier, he could not deal such swift blows, and received two or three to every one he gave. But his seasoned body apparently did not suffer much, and he was laughing and exclaiming all the time, when, suddenly, with a heavy upward blow he put Sitanov's right arm out of joint from the shoulder.

"Part them; it is a draw!" cried several voices, and, breaking the circle, the crowd gathered round the pugilists.

"He is not very strong but he is skilful, the image-painter," said the Mordovan good-naturedly. "He will make a good boxer, and that I say before the whole world!"

The elder persons began a general wrestling match, and I took Sitanov to the Feldsher bone-setter. His deed had raised him still higher in my esteem, had increased my sympathy with him, and his importance in my eyes.

He was, in the main, very upright and honorable, and he felt that he had only done his duty, but the graceless Kapendiukhin made fun of him lightly.

"Ekh, Genya, you live for show! You have polished up your soul like a samovar before a holiday, "and you go about boasting, 'look how brightly it shines!' But your soul is really brass, and a very dull affair, too."

Sitanov remained calmly silent, either working hard or copying Lermontov's verses into his note-book. He spent all his spare time in this copying, and when I suggested to him:

"Why, when you have plenty of money, don't you buy the book?" he answered:

"No, it is better in my own handwriting."

Having written a page in his pretty, small handwriting, he would read softly while he was waiting for the ink to dry:

> "Without regret, as a being apart,
> You will look down upon this earth,
> Where there is neither real happiness
> Nor lasting beauty."

And he said, half-closing his eyes:

"That is true. Ekh! and well he knows the truth, too!"

The behavior of Sitanov to Kapendiukhin always amazed me. When he had been drinking, the Cossack always tried to pick a quarrel with his comrade, and Sitanov would go on for a long time bearing it, and saying persuasively:

"That will do, let me alone!"

And then he would start to beat the drunken man so cruelly that the workmen, who regarded internal dissensions amongst themselves merely as a spectacle, interfered between the friends, and separated them.

"If we did n't stop Evgen in time, he would beat any one to death, and he would never forgive himself," they said.

When he was sober Kapendiukhin ceaselessly jeered at Sitanov, making fun of his passion for poetry and his unhappy romance, obscenely, but unsuccessfully trying to arouse jealousy. Sitanov listened to the Cossack's taunts in silence, without taking offense, and he sometimes even laughed with Kapendiukhin at himself.

They slept side by side, and at night they would hold long, whispered conversations about something. These conversations gave me no peace, for I was anxious to know what these two people who were so unlike each other found to talk about in such a friendly manner. But when I went near them, the Cossack yelled:

"What do you want?"

But Sitanov did not seem to see me.

However, one day they called me, and the Cossack asked:

"Maximich, if you were rich, what would you do?"

"I would buy books."

"And what else?"

"I don't know."

"Ekh!" said Kapendiukhin, turning away from me in disgust, but Sitanov said calmly:

"You see; no one knows that, whether they be old or young. I tell you that riches in themselves are worth nothing, unless they are applied to some special purpose."

I asked them, "What are you talking about?"

"We don't feel inclined to sleep, and so we are talking," answered the Cossack.

Later, listening to them, I found that they were discussing by night those things which other people discussed by day—God, truth, happiness, the stupidity and cunning of women, the greediness of the rich, and the fact that life is complicated and incomprehensible.

I always listened to their conversations eagerly; they excited me. I was pleased to think that almost every one had arrived at the same conclusion; namely, that life is evil, and that we ought to have a better form of existence! But at the same time I saw that the desire to live under better conditions would have no effect, would change nothing in the lives of the work-people, in their relations one with another. All these talks, throwing a light upon my life as it lay before me, revealed at the same time, beyond it, a sort of melancholy emptiness; and in this emptiness, like specks of dust in a pond ruffled by the wind, floated people, absurdly and exasperatingly, among them those very people who had said that such a crowd was devoid 'of sense. Always ready to give their opinion, they were always passing judgment on others, repeating, bragging, and starting bitter quarrels about mere trifles. They were always seriously offending one another. They tried to guess what would happen to them after death; while on the threshold of the workshop where the washstand stood, the floor-boards had rotted away. From that damp, fetid hole rose the cold, damp smell of sour earth, and it was this that made one's feet freeze. Pavl and I stopped up this hole with straw and cloths. We often said that the boards should be renewed, but the hole grew larger and larger, and in bad weather fumes rose from it as from a pipe. Every one caught cold, and coughed. The tin ventilator in the fortochka squeaked, and when some one had oiled it, though they had all been grumbling at it, Jikharev said:

"It is dull, now that the fortochka has stopped squeaking."

To come straight from the bath and lie down on a dirty, dusty bed, in the midst of dirt and bad smells, did not revolt any one of them. There were many insignificant trifles which made our lives unbearable, which might easily have been remedied, but no one took the trouble to do anything.

They often said:

"No one has any mercy upon human creatures,—neither God nor we ourselves."

But when Pavl and I washed dying Davidov, who was eaten up with dirt and insects, a laugh was raised against us. They took off their shirts and invited us to search them, called us blockheads, and jeered at us as if we had done something shameful and very ludicrous.

From Christmas till the beginning of Lent drew near, Davidov lay in the loft, coughing protractedly, spitting blood, which, if it did not fall into the wash-hand basin, splashed on the floor. At night he woke the others with his delirious shrieks.

Almost every day they said:

"We must take him to the hospital!"

But it turned out that Davidov's passport had expired. Then he seemed better, and they said:

"It is of no consequence after all; he will soon be dead!"

And he would say to himself:

"I shall soon be gone!"

He was a quiet humorist and also tried to relieve the dullness of the workshop by jokes, hanging down his dark bony face, and saying in a wheezy voice:

"Listen, people, to the voice of one who ascended to the loft.

> "In the loft I live,
> Early do I wake;
> Asleep or awake
> Cockroaches devour me."

"He is not downhearted!" exclaimed his audience.

Sometimes Pavl and I went to him, and he joked with difficulty.

"With what shall I regale you, my dear guests? A fresh little spider—would you like that?"

He died slowly, and he grew very weary of it. He said with unfeigned vexation:

"It seems that I can't die, somehow; it is really a calamity!"

His fearlessness in the face of death frightened Pavl very much. He awoke me in the night and whispered:

"Maximich, he seems to be dying. Suppose he dies in the night, when we are lying beneath him—Oh, Lord! I am frightened of dead people."

Or he would say:

"Why was he born? Not twenty-two years have passed over his head and he is dying."

Once, on a moonlight night he awoke, and gazing with wide-open, terrified eyes said:

"Listen!"

Davidov was croaking in the loft, saying quickly and clearly:

"Give it to me—give—"

Then he began to hiccup.

"He is dying, by God he is; you see!" said Pavl agitatedly.

I had been carrying snow from the yard into the fields all day, and I was very sleepy, but Pavl begged me:

"Don't go to sleep, please; for Christ's sake don't go to sleep!"

And suddenly getting on to his knees, he cried frenziedly:

"Get up! Davidov is dead!"

Some of them awoke; several figures rose from the beds; angry voices were raised, asking questions.

Kapendiukhin climbed up into the loft and said in a tone of amazement:

"It is a fact; he is dead, although he is still warm." It was quiet now. Jikharev crossed himself, and wrapping himself round in his blanket, said:

"Well, he is in the Kingdom of Heaven now!" Some one suggested:

"Let us carry him into the vestibule."

Kapendiukhin climbed down from the loft and glanced through the window.

"Let him lie where he is till the morning; he never hurt any one while he was alive."

Pavl, hiding his head under the pillow, sobbed.

But Sitanov did not even wake!

CHAPTER XV

The snow melted away from the fields; the wintry clouds in the sky passed away; wet snow and rain fell upon the earth; the sun was slower and slower in performing his daily journey; the air grew warmer; and it seemed that the joyful spring had already arrived, sportively hiding herself behind the fields, and would soon burst upon the town itself. In the streets there was brown mud; streams ran along the gutters; in the thawed places of Arestantski Square the sparrows hopped joyfully. And in human creatures, also, was apparent the same excitement as was shown by the sparrows. Above the sounds of spring, almost uninterruptedly from morning to night, rang out the Lenten bells, stirring one's heart with their muffled strokes. In that sound, as in the speech of an old man, there was hidden something of displeasure, as if the bells had said with cold melancholy:

"Has been, this has been, has been—"

On my name-day the workmen gave me a small, beautifully painted image of Alexei, the man of God, and Jikharev made an impressive, long speech, which I remember very well.

"What are you?" said he, with much play of finger and raising of eyebrows. "Nothing more than a small boy, an orphan, thirteen years old—and I, nearly four times your age, praise you and approve of you, because you always stand with your face to people and not sideways! Stand like that always, and you will be all right!"

He spoke of the slaves of God, and of his people, but the difference between people and slaves I could never understand, and I don't believe that he understood it himself. His speech was long-winded, the workshop was laughing at him, and I stood, with the image in my hand, very touched and very confused, not knowing what I ought to do. At length Kapendiukhin called out irritably:

"Oh, leave off singing his praises; his ears are already turning blue!"

Then clapping me on the shoulder, he began to praise me himself:

"What is good in you is what you have in common with all human creatures, and not the fact that it is difficult to scold and beat you when you have given cause for it!"

They all looked at me with kind eyes, making good-natured fun of my confusion. A little more and I believe I should have burst out crying from the unexpected joy of finding myself valued by these people. And that very morning the shopman had said to Petr Vassilich, nodding his head toward me:

"An unpleasant boy that, and good for nothing!"

As usual I had gone to the shop in the morning, but at noon the shopman had said to me:

"Go home and clear the snow off the roof of the warehouse, and clean out the cellar."

That it was my name-day he did not know, and I had thought that no one knew it. When the ceremony of congratulations had finished in the workshop, I changed my clothes and climbed up to the roof of the shed to throw off the smooth, heavy snow which had accumulated during that winter. But being excited, I forgot to close the door of the cellar, and threw all the snow into it. When I jumped down to the ground, I saw my mistake, and set myself at once to get the snow away from the door. Being wet, it lay heavily; the wooden, spade moved it with difficulty; there was no iron one, and I broke the spade at the very moment when the shopman appeared at the yard-gate. The truth of the Russian proverb, "Sorrow follows on the heels of joy," was proved to me.

"So—o—o!" said the shopman derisively, "you are a fine workman, the devil take you! If I get hold of your senseless blockhead—" He flourished the blade of the shovel over me.

I move away, saying angrily:

"I was n't engaged as a yardman, anyhow."

He hurled the stick against my legs. I took up a snowball and threw it right in his face. He ran away snorting, and I left off working, and went into the workshop. In a few minutes his fiancée came running downstairs. She was an agile maiden, with pimples on her vacant face.

"Maximich, you are to go upstairs!"

"I am not going!" I said.

Larionich asked in an amazed undertone:

"What is this? You are not going?"

I told him about the affair. With an anxious frown he went upstairs, muttering to me:

"Oh, you impudent youngster—"

The workshop resounded with abuse of the shopman, and Kapendiukhin said:

"Well, they will kick you out this time!"

This did not alarm me. My relations with the shopman had already become unbearable. His hatred of me was undisguised and became more and more acute, while, for my part, I could not endure him. But what I wanted to know was: why did he behave so absurdly to me? He would throw coins about the floor of the shop, and when I was sweeping, I found them, and laid them on the counter in the cup which contained the small money kept for beggars. When I guessed what these frequent finds meant I said to him:

"You throw money about in my way on purpose!" He flew out at me and cried incautiously:

"Don't you dare to teach me! I know what I am doing!"

But he corrected himself immediately:

"And what do you mean by my throwing it about purposely? It falls about itself."

He forbade me to read the books in the shop, saying:

"That is not for you to trouble your head about! What! Have you an idea of becoming a valuer, sluggard?"

He did not cease his attempts to catch me in the theft of small money, and I realised that if, when I was sweeping the floor, the coin should roll into a crevice between the boards, he would declare that I had stolen it. Then I told him again that he had better give up that game, but that same day, when I returned from the tavern with the boiling water, I heard him suggesting to the newly engaged assistant in the neighboring shop:

"Egg him on to steal psalters. We shall soon be having three hampers of them."

I knew that they were talking about me, for when I entered the shop they both looked confused; and besides these signs, I had grounds for suspecting them of a foolish conspiracy against me.

This was not the first time that that assistant had been in the service of the man next door. He was accounted a clever salesman, but he suffered from alcoholism; in one of his drinking bouts the master had dismissed him, but had afterwards taken him back. He was an anaemic, feeble person, with cunning eyes. Apparently amiable and submissive to the slightest gesture of his master, he smiled a little, clever smile in his beard all the time, was fond of uttering sharp sayings, and exhaled the rotten smell which comes from people with bad teeth, although his own were white and strong.

One day he gave me a terrible surprise; he came towards me smiling pleasantly, but suddenly seized my cap off my head and took hold of my hair. We began to struggle. He pushed me from the gallery into the shop, trying all the time to throw me against the large images which stood about on the floor. If he had succeeded in this, I should have broken the glass, or chipped the carving, and no doubt scratched some of the costly icons. He was very weak, and I soon overcame him; when to my great amazement the bearded man sat on the floor and cried bitterly, rubbing his bruised nose.

The next morning when our masters had both gone out somewhere and we were alone, he said to me in a friendly manner, rubbing the lump on the bridge of his nose and under his eyes with his finger:

"Do you think that it was of my own will or desire that I attacked you? I am not a fool, you know, and I knew that you would be more than a match for me. I am a man of little strength, a tippler. It was your master who told me to do it. 'Lead him on,' he said, 'and get him to break something in the shop while he is fighting you. Let him damage something, anyhow!' I should never have done it of my own accord; look how you have ornamented my phiz for me."

I believed him, and I began to be sorry for him. I knew that he lived, half-starved, with a woman who knocked him about. However, I asked him:

"And if he told you to poison a person, I suppose you would do it?"

"He might do that," said the shopman with a pitiful smile; "he is capable of it."

Soon after this he asked me:

"Listen, I have not a farthing; there is nothing to eat at home; my missus nags at me. Couldn't you take an icon out of your stock and give it to me to sell, like a friend, eh? Will you? Or a breviary?"

I remembered the boot-shop, and the beadle of the church, and I thought: "Will this man give me away?" But it was hard to refuse him, and I gave him an icon. To steal a breviary worth several rubles, that I could not do; it seemed, to me a great crime. What would you have? Arithmetic always lies concealed in ethics; the holy ingenuousness of "Regulations for the Punishment of Criminals" clearly gives away this little secret, behind which the great lie of property hides itself.

When I heard my shopman suggesting that this miserable man should incite me to steal psalters I was afraid. It was clear that he knew how charitable I had been on the other's behalf, and that the man from next door had told him about the icon.

The abominableness of being charitable at another person's expense, and the realization of the rotten trap that had been set for me—both these things aroused in me a feeling of indignation and disgust with myself and every one else. For several days I tormented myself cruelly, waiting for the arrival of the hamper with the books. At length they came, and when I was putting them away in the store-room, the shopman from next door came to me and asked me to give him a breviary.

Then I asked him:

"Did you tell my master about the icon?"

"I did," he answered in a melancholy voice; "I can keep nothing back, brother."

This utterly confounded me, and I sat on the floor staring at him stupidly, while he muttered hurriedly, confusedly, desperately miserable:

"You see your man guessed—or rather, mine guessed and told yours—"

I thought I was lost. These people had been conspiring against me, and now there was a place ready for me in the colony for youthful criminals! If that were so, nothing mattered! If one must drown, it is better to drown in a deep spot. I put a breviary into the hands of the shopman; he hid it in the sleeves of his greatcoat and went away. But he returned suddenly, the breviary fell at my feet, and the man strode away, saying:

"I won't take it! It would be all over with you." I did not understand these words. Why should it be all over with me? But I was very glad that he had not taken the book. After this my little shopman began to regard me with more disfavor and suspicion than ever.

I remembered all this when Larionich went upstairs. He did not stay there long, and came back more depressed and quiet than usual, but before supper he said to me privately:

"I tried to arrange for you to be set free from the shop, and given over to the workshop, but it was no good. Kouzma would not have it. You are very much out of favor with him."

I had an enemy in the house, too—the shopman's fiancée, an immoderately sportive damsel. All the young fellows in the workshop played about with her; they used to wait for her in the vestibule and embrace her. This did not offend her; she only squeaked like a little dog. She was chewing something from morning to night; her pockets were always full of gingerbread or buns; her jaws moved ceaselessly. To look at her vacant face with its restless gray eyes was unpleasant. She used to ask Pavl and me riddles which always concealed some coarse obscenity, and repeated catchwords which, being said very quickly, became improper words.

One day one of the elderly workmen said to her:

"You are a shameless hussy, my girl!"

To which she answered swiftly, in the words of a ribald song:

> "If a maiden is too modest,
> She'll never be a woman worth having."

It was the first time I had ever seen such a girl. She disgusted and frightened me with her coarse playfulness, and seeing that her antics were not agreeable to me, she became more and more spiteful toward me.

Once when Pavl and I were in the cellar helping her to steam out the casks of kvass and cucumbers she suggested:

"Would you like me to teach you how to kiss, boys?"

"I know how to kiss better than you do," Pavl answered, and I told her to go and kiss her future husband. I did not say it very politely, either.

She was angry.

"Oh, you coarse creature! A young lady makes herself agreeable to him and he turns up his nose. Well, I never! What a ninny!"

And she added, shaking a threatening finger at me: "You just wait. I will remember that of you!" But Pavl said to her, taking my part:

"Your young man would give you something if he knew about your behavior!"

She screwed up her pimply face contemptuously.

"I am not afraid of him! I have a dowry. I am much better than he is! A girl only has the time till she is married to amuse herself."

She began to play about with Pavl, and from that time I found in her an unwearying calumniator.

My life in the shop became harder and harder. I read church books all the time. The disputes and conversations of the valuers had ceased to amuse me, for they were always talking over the same things in the same old way. Petr Vassilich alone still interested me, with his knowledge of the dark side of human life, and his power of speaking interestingly and enthusiastically. Sometimes I thought he must be the prophet Elias walking the earth, solitary and vindictive. But each time that I spoke to the old man frankly about people, or about my own thoughts, he repeated all that I had said to the shopman, who either ridiculed me offensively, or abused me angrily.

One day I told the old man that I sometimes wrote his sayings in the note-book in which I had copied various poems taken out of books. This greatly alarmed the valuer, who limped towards me swiftly, asking anxiously:

"What did you do that for? It is not worth while, my lad. So that you may remember? No; you just give it up. What a boy you are! Now you will give me what you have written, won't you?"

He tried long and earnestly to persuade me to either give him the notebook, or to burn it, and then he began to whisper angrily with the shopman.

As we were going home, the latter said to me: "You have been taking notes? That has got to be' stopped! Do you hear? Only detectives do that sort of thing!"

Then I asked incautiously:

"And what about Sitanov? He also takes notes." "Also. That long fool?"

He was silent for a long time, and then with unusual gentleness he said:

"Listen; if you show me your note-book and Sitanov's, too, I will give you half a ruble! Only do it on the quiet, so that Sitanov does not see."

No doubt he thought that I would carry out his wish, and without saying another word, he ran in front of me on his short legs.

When I reached the house, I told Sitanov what the shopman had proposed to me. Evgen frowned.

"You have been chattering purposely. Now he will give some one instructions to steal both our notebooks. Give me yours—I will hide it. And he will turn you out before long—you see!"

I was convinced of that, too, and resolved to leave as soon as grandmother returned to the town. She had been living at Balakhania all the winter, invited by some one to teach young girls to make lace. Grandfather was again living in Kunavin Street, but I did not visit him, and when he came to the town, he never came to see me. One day we ran into each other in the street. He was walking along in a heavy racoon pelisse, importantly and slowly. I said "How do you do" to him. He lifted his hands to shade his eyes, looked at me from under them, and then said thoughtfully:

"Oh, it is you; you are an image-painter now. Yes, yes; all right; get along with you."

Pushing me out of his way, he continued his walk, slowly and importantly.

I saw grandmother seldom. She worked unweariedly to feed grandfather, who was suffering from the malady of old age—senile weakness—and had also taken upon herself the care of my uncle's children.

The one who caused her the most worry was Sascha, Mikhail's son, a handsome lad, dreamy and book-loving. He worked in a dyer's shop, frequently changed his employers, and in the intervals threw himself on grandmother's shoulders, calmly waiting until she should find him another place. She had Sascha's sister on her shoulders, too. She had made an unfortunate marriage with a drunken workman, who beat her and turned her out of his house.

Every time I met grandmother, I was more consciously charmed by her personality; but I felt already that that beautiful soul, blinded by fanciful tales, was not capable of seeing, could not understand a revelation of the bitter reality of life, and my disquietude and restlessness were strange to her.

"You must have patience, Olesha!"

This was all she had to say to me in reply to my stories of the hideous lives, of the tortures of people, of sorrow—of all which perplexed me, and with which I was burning.

I was unfitted by nature to be patient, and if occasionally I exhibited that virtue which belongs to cattle, trees, and stones, I did so in the cause of self-discipline, to test my reserves of strength, my degree of stability upon earth. Sometimes young people, with the stupidity of youth, will keep on trying to lift weights too heavy for their muscles and bones; will try boastfully, like full-grown men of proved strength, to cross themselves with heavy weights, envious of the strength of their elders.

I also did this in a double sense, physically and spiritually, and it is only due to some chance that I did not strain myself dangerously, or deform myself for the rest of my life. Besides, nothing disfigures a man more terribly than his patience, the submission of his strength to external conditions.

And though in the end I shall lie in the earth disfigured, I can say, not without pride, to my last hour, that good people did their best for forty years to disfigure my soul, but that their labors were not very successful.

The wild desire to play mischievous pranks, to amuse people, to make them laugh, took more and more hold upon me. I was successful in this. I could tell stories about the merchants in the market-place, impersonating them; I could imitate the peasant men and women buying and selling icons, the shopman skilfully cheating them; the valuers disputing amongst themselves.

The workshop resounded with laughter. Often the workmen left their work to look on at my impersonations, but on all these occasions Larionich would say:

"You had better do your acting after supper; otherwise you hinder the work."

When I had finished my performance I felt myself easier, as if I had thrown off a burden which weighed upon me. For half an hour or an hour my head felt pleasantly clear, but soon it felt again as if it were full of sharp, small nails, which moved about and grew hot. It seemed to me that a sort of dirty porridge was boiling around me, and that I was being gradually boiled away in it.

I wondered: Was life really like this? And should I have to live as these people lived, never finding, never seeing anything better?

"You are growing sulky, Maximich," said Jikharev, looking at me attentively.

Sitanov often asked me:

"What is the matter with you?"

And I could not answer him.

Life perseveringly and roughly washed out from my soul its most delicate writings, maliciously changing them into some sort of indistinct trash, and with anger and determination I resisted its violence. I was floating on the same river as all the others, only for me the waters were colder and did not support me as easily as it did the others. Sometimes it seemed to me that I was gently sinking into unfathomable depths.

People behaved better to me; they did not shout at me as they did at Pavl, nor harass me; they called me by my patronymic in order to emphasize their more respectful attitude toward me. This was good; but it was torturing to see how many of them drank vodka, how disgustingly drunk they became, and how injurious to them were their relations with women, although I understood that vodka and women were the only diversions that life afforded.

I often called to mind with sorrow that that most intelligent, courageous woman, Natalia Kozlovski, was also called a woman of pleasure. And what about grandmother? And Queen Margot?

I used to think of my queen with a feeling almost of terror; she was so removed from all the others, it was as if I had seen her in a dream.

I began to think too much about women, and I had already revolved in my own mind the question: Shall I go on the next holiday where all the others go? This was no physical desire. I was both healthy and fastidious, but at times I was almost mad with a desire to embrace some one tender, intelligent, and frankly, unrestrainedly, as to a mother, speak to her of the disturbances of my soul.

I envied Pavl when he told me at night of his affair with a maidservant in the opposite house.

"It is a funny thing, brother! A month ago I was throwing snowballs at her because I did not like her, and now I sit on a bench and hug her. She is dearer to me than any one!"

"What do you talk about?"

"About everything, of course! She talks to me about herself, and I talk to her about myself. And then we kiss—only she is honest. In fact, brother, she is so good that it is almost a misfortune! Why, you smoke like an old soldier!"

I smoked a lot; tobacco intoxicated me, dulled my restless thoughts, my agitated feelings. As for vodka, it only aroused in me a repulsion toward my own odor and taste, but Pavl drank with a will, and when he was drunk, used to cry bitterly:

"I want to go home, I want to go home! Let me go home!"

As far as I can remember he was an orphan; his mother and father had been dead a long time. Brother and sister he had none; he had lived among strangers for eight years.

In this state of restless dissatisfaction the call of spring disturbed me still more. I made up my mind to go on a boat again, and if I could get as far as Astrakhan, to run away to Persia.

I do not remember why I selected Persia particularly. It may have been because I had taken a great fancy to the Persian merchants on the Nijigorodski market-place, sitting like stone idols, spreading their dyed beards in the sun, calmly smoking their hookas, with large, dark, omniscient eyes.

There is no doubt that I should have run away somewhere, but one day in Easter week, when part of the occupants of the workshop had gone to their homes, and the rest were drinking, I was walking on a sunny day on the banks of the Oka, when I met my old master, grandmother's nephew.

He was walking along in a light gray overcoat, with his hands in his pockets, a cigarette between his teeth, his hat on the back of his head. His pleasant face smiled kindly at me. He had the appearance of a man who is at liberty and is happy, and there was no one beside ourselves in the fields.

"Ah, Pyeshkov, Christ is risen!"

After we had exchanged the Easter kiss, he asked how I was living, and I told him frankly that the workshop, the town and everything in general were abhorrent to me, and that I had made up my mind to go to Persia.

"Give it up," he said to me gravely. "What the devil is there in Persia? I know exactly how you are feeling, brother; in my youth I also had the wander fever."

I liked him for telling me this. There was something about him good and springlike; he was a being set apart.

"Do you smoke?" he asked, holding out a silver cigarette-case full of fat cigarettes.

That completed his conquest of me.

"What you had better do, Pyeshkov, is to come back to me again," he suggested. "For this year I have undertaken contracts for the new market-place, you understand. And I can make use of you there; you will be a kind of overseer for me; you will receive all the material; you will see that it is all in its proper place, and that the workmen do not steal it. Will that suit you? Your wages will be five rubles a month, and five copecks for dinner! The women-folk will have nothing to do with you; you will go out in the morning and return in the evening. As for the women; you can ignore them; only don't let them know that we have met, but just come to see us on Sunday at Phomin Street. It will be a change for you!"

We parted like friends. As he said good-by, he pressed my hand, and as he went away, he actually waved his hat to me affably from a distance.

When I announced in the workroom that I was leaving, most of the workmen showed a flattering regret. Pavl, especially, was upset.

"Think," he said reproachfully; "how will you live with men of all kinds, after being with us? With carpenters, house-painters—Oh, you—It is going out of the frying-pan into the fire."

Jikharev growled:

"A fish looks for the deepest place, but a clever young man seeks a worse place!"

The send-off which they gave me from the workshop was a sad one.

"Of course one must try this and that," said Jikharev, who was yellow from the effects of a drinking bout. "It is better to do it straight off, before you become too closely attached to something or other."

"And that for the rest of your life," added Larionich softly.

But I felt that they spoke with constraint, and from a sense of duty. The thread which had bound me to them was somehow rotted and broken.

In the loft drunken Golovev rolled about, and muttered hoarsely:

"I would like to see them all in prison. I know their secrets! Who believes in God here? Aha-a—!"

As usual, faceless, uncompleted icons were propped against the wall; the glass balls were fixed to the ceiling. It was long since we had had to work with a light, and the balls, not being used, were covered with a gray coating of soot and dust. I remember the surroundings so vividly that if I shut my eyes, I can see in the darkness the whole of that basement room: all the tables, and the jars of paint on the windowsills, the bundles of brushes, the icons, the slop-pail under the brass washstand-basin which looked like a fireman's helmet, and, hanging from the ceiling, Golovev's bare foot, which was blue like the foot of a drowned man.

I wanted to get away quickly, but in Russia they love long-drawn-out, sad moments. When they are saying good-by, Russian people behave as if they were hearing a requiem mass.

Jikharev, twitching his brows, said to me:

"That book—the devil's book—I can't give it back to you. Will you take two *greven* for it?"

The book was my own,—the old second lieutenant of the fire-brigade had given it to me—and I grudged giving Lermontov away. But when, somewhat offended, I refused the money, Jikharev calmly put the coins back in his purse, and said in an unwavering tone:

"As you like; but I shall not give you back the book. It is not for you. A book like that would soon lead you into sin."

"But it is sold in shops; I have seen it!"

But he only said with redoubled determination:

"That has nothing to do with the matter; they sell revolvers in shops, too—"

So he never returned Lermontov to me.

As I was going upstairs to say good-by to my mistress, I ran into her niece in the hall.

"Is it true what they say—that you are leaving?"

"Yes."

"If you had not gone of your own accord, you would have been sent away," she assured me, not very kindly, but with perfect frankness.

And the tipsy mistress said:

"Good-by, Christ be with you! You are a bad boy, an impudent boy; although I have never seen anything bad in you myself, they all say that you are a bad boy!" And suddenly she burst out crying, and said through her tears:

"Ah, if my dead one, my sweet husband, dear soul, had been alive, he would have known how to deal with you; he would have boxed your ears and you would have stayed on. We should not have had to send you away! But nowadays things are different; if all is not exactly as you like, away you go! Och! And where will you be going, boy, and what good will it do you to stroll from place to place?"

CHAPTER XVI

I was in a boat with my master, passing along the market-place between shops which were flooded to the height of the second story. I plied the oars, while my master sat in the stern. The paddle wheel, which was useless as a rudder, was deep in the water, and the boat veered about awkwardly, meandering from street to street on the quiet, muddily sleepy waters.

"Ekh! The water gets higher and higher. The devil take it! It is keeping the work back," grumbled my master as he smoked a cigar, the smoke of which had an odor of burning cloth. "Gently!" he cried in alarm, "we are running into a lamp-post!"

He steered the boat out of danger and scolded me: "They have given me a boat, the wretches!"

He showed me the spot on which, after the water had subsided, the work of rebuilding would begin. With his face shaved to a bluish tint, his mustache clipped short, and a cigar in his mouth, he did not look like a contractor. He wore a leathern jacket, high boots to his knees, and a game-bag was slung over his shoulders. At his feet was an expensive two-barelled gun, manufactured by Lebed. From time to time he restlessly changed the position of his leathern cap, pulling it over his eyes, pouting his lips and looking cautiously around. He pushed the cap to the back of his head, looked younger, and smiled beneath his mustache, thinking of something pleasant. No one would have thought that he had a lot of work to do, and that the long time the water took in subsiding worried him. Evidently thoughts wholly unconnected with business were passing through his mind.

And I was overwhelmed by a feeling of quiet amazement; it seemed so strange to look upon that dead town, the straight rows of buildings with closed windows. The town was simply flooded with water, and seemed to be floating past our boat. The sky was gray. The sun had been lost in the clouds, but sometimes shone through them in large, silver, wintry patches.

The water also was gray and cold; its flow was unnoticeable; it seemed to be congealed, fixed to one place, like the empty houses beside the shops, which were painted a dirty yellow. When the pale sun looked through the clouds, all around grew slightly brighter. The water reflected the gray texture of the sky; our boat seemed to hang in the air between two skies; the stone buildings also lifted themselves up, and with a scarcely perceptible movement floated toward the Volga, or the Oka. Around the boat were broken casks, boxes, baskets, fragments of wood and straw; sometimes a rod or joist of wood floated like a dead snake on the surface.

Here and there windows were opened. On the roofs of the rows of galleries linen was drying, or felt boots stuck out. A woman looked out of a window onto the gray waters. A boat was moored to the top of the cast-iron columns of a galley; her red deck made the reflection of the water look greasy and meat-like.

Nodding his head at these signs of life, my master explained to me:

"This is where the market watchman lives. He climbs out of the window onto the roof, gets into his boat, and goes out to see if there are any thieves about. And if there are none, he thieves on his own account."

He spoke lazily, calmly, thinking of something else. All around was quiet, deserted, and unreal, as if it were part of a dream. The Volga and the Oka flowed into an enormous lake; in the distance on a rugged hillside the town was painted in motley colors. Gardens were still somberly clothed, but the buds were bursting on the trees, and foliage clad houses and churches in a warm, green mantle. Over the water crept the muffled sound of the Easter-tide bells. The murmur of the town was audible, while here it was just like a forgotten graveyard.

Our boat wended its way between two rows of black trees; we were on the high road to the old cathedral. The cigar was in my master's way; its acrid smoke got into his eyes and caused him to run the nose of the boat into the trunks of the trees. Upon which he cried, irritably and in surprise:

"What a rotten boat this is!"

"But you are not steering it."

"How can I?" he grumbled. "When there are two people in a boat, one always rows while the other steers. There—look! There's the Chinese block."

I knew the market through and through; I knew that comical-looking block of buildings with the ridiculous roofs on which sat, with crossed legs, figures of Chinamen in plaster of Paris. There had been a time when I and my playfellow had thrown stones at them, and some of the Chinamen had had their heads and hands broken off by me. But I no longer took any pride in that sort of thing.

"Rubbish!" said my master, pointing to the block. "If I had been allowed to build it—"

He whistled and pushed his cap to the back of his head.

But somehow I thought that he would have built that town of stone just as dingily, on that low-lying ground which was flooded by the waters of two rivers every year. And he would even have invented the Chinese block.

Throwing his cigar over the side of the boat, he spat after it in disgust, saying:

"Life is very dull, Pyeshkov, very dull. There are no educated people—no one to talk to. If one wants to show off one's gifts, who is there to be impressed? Not a soul! All the people here are carpenters, stonemasons, peasants—"

He looked straight ahead at the white mosque which rose picturesquely out of the water on a small hill, and continued as if he were recollecting something he had forgotten:

"I began to drink beer and smoke cigars when I was working under a German. The Germans, my brother, are a business-like race—such wild fowl! Drinking beer is a pleasant occupation, but I have never got used to smoking cigars. And when you 've been smoking, your wife grumbles: 'What is it that you smell of? It is like the smell at the harness-makers.' Ah, brother, the longer we live, the more artful we grow. Well, well, true to oneself—"

Placing the oar against the side of the boat, he took up his gun and shot at a Chinaman on a roof. No harm came to the latter; the shot buried itself in the roof and the wall, raising a dusty smoke.

"That was a miss," he admitted without regret, and he again loaded his gun.

"How do you get on with the girls? Are you keen on them? No? Why, I was in love when I was only thirteen."

He told me, as if he were telling a dream, the story of his first love for the housemaid of the architect to whom he had been apprenticed. Softly splashed the gray water, washing the corners of the buildings; beyond the cathedral dully gleamed a watery waste; black twigs rose here and there above it. In the icon-painter's workshop they often sang the Seminarski song:

"O blue sea,
Stormy sea...."

That blue sea must have been deadly dull.

"I never slept at nights," went on my master. "Sometimes I got out of bed and stood at her door, shivering like a dog. It was a cold house! The master visited her at night. He might have discovered me, but I was not afraid, not I!"

He spoke thoughtfully, like a person looking at an old worn-out coat, and wondering if he could wear it once more.

"She noticed me, pitied me, unfastened her door, and called me: 'Come in, you little fool.'"

I had heard many stories of this kind, and they bored me, although there was one pleasing feature about them—almost every one spoke of their "first love" without boasting, or obscenity, and often so gently and sadly that I understood that the story of their first love was the best in their lives.

Laughing and shaking his head, my master exclaimed wonderingly:

"But that's the sort of thing you don't tell your wife; no, no! Well, there's no harm in it, but you never tell. That's a story—"

He was telling the story to himself, not to me. If he had been silent, I should have spoken. In that quietness and desolation one had to talk, or sing, or play on the harmonica, or one would fall into a heavy, eternal sleep in the midst of that dead town, drowned in gray, cold water.

"In the first place, don't marry too soon," he counseled me. "Marriage, brother, is a matter of the most stupendous importance. You can live where you like and how you like, according to your will. You can live in Persia as a Mahommedan; in Moscow as a man about town. You can arrange your life as you choose. You can give everything a trial. But a wife, brother, is like the weather—you can never rule her! You can't take a wife and throw her aside like an old boot."

His face changed. He gazed into the gray water with knitted brows, rubbing his prominent nose with his fingers, and muttered:

"Yes, brother, look before you leap. Let us suppose that you are beset on all sides, and still continue to stand firm; even then there is a special trap laid for each one of us."

We were now amongst the vegetation in the lake of Meshtcherski, which was fed by the Volga.

"Row softly," whispered my master, pointing his gun into the bushes. After he had shot a few lean woodcocks, he suggested:

"Let us go to Kunavin Street. I will spend the evening there, and you can go home and say that I am detained by the contractors."

Setting him down at one of the streets on the outskirts of the town, which was also flooded, I returned to the market-place on the Stravelka, moored the boat, and sitting in it, gazed at the confluence of the two rivers, at the town, the steamboats, the sky, which was just like the gorgeous wing of some gigantic bird, all white feathery clouds. The golden sun peeped through the blue gaps between the clouds, and with one glance at the earth transfigured everything thereon. Brisk, determined movement went on all around me: the swift current of the rivers lightly bore innumerable planks of wood; on these planks bearded peasants stood firmly, wielding long poles and shouting to one another, or to approaching steamers. A little steamer was pulling an empty barge against the stream. The river dragged at it, and shook it. It turned its nose round like a pike and panted, firmly setting its wheels against the water, which was rushing furiously to meet it. On a barge with their legs hanging over the side sat four peasants, shoulder to shoulder. One of them wore a red shirt, and sang a song the words of which I could not hear, but I knew it.

I felt that here on the living river I knew all, was in touch with all, and could understand all; and the town which lay flooded behind me was an evil dream, an imagination of my master's, as difficult to understand as he was himself.

When I had satiated myself by gazing at all there was to see, I returned home, feeling that I was a grown man, capable of any kind of work. On the way I looked from the hill of the Kreml on to the Volga in the distance. From the hill, the earth appeared enormous, and promised all that one could possibly desire.

I had books at home. In the flat which Queen Margot had occupied there now lived a large family,—five young ladies, each one more beautiful than the others, and two schoolboys— and these people used to give me books. I read Turgenieff with avidity, amazed to find how intelligible, simple, and pellucid as autumn he was; how pure were his characters, and how good everything was about which he succinctly discoursed. I read Pomyalovski's "Bourse" and was again amazed; it was so strangely like the life in the icon-painting workshop. I was so well acquainted with that desperate tedium which precipitated one into cruel pranks. I enjoyed reading Russian books. I always felt that there was something about them familiar and melancholy, as if there were hidden in their pages the frozen sound of the Lenten bell, which pealed forth softly as soon as one opened a book.

"Dead Souls" I read reluctantly; "Letters from the House of the Dead," also. "Dead Souls," "Dead Houses," "Three Deaths," "Living Relics"—these books with titles so much alike arrested my attention against my will, and aroused a lethargic repugnance for all such books. "Signs of the Times," "Step by Step," "What to Do," and "Chronicles of the Village of Smourin," I did not care for, nor any other books of the same kind. But I was delighted with Dickens and Walter Scott. I read these authors with the greatest enjoyment, the same books over and over again. The works of Walter Scott reminded me of a high mass on a great feast day in rich churches—somewhat long and tedious, but always solemn. Dickens still remains to me as the author to whom I respectfully bow; he was a man who had a wonderful apprehension of that most difficult of arts—love of human nature.

In the evenings a large company of people used to gather on the roof: the brothers K. and their sisters, grown up; the snub-nosed schoolboy, Vyacheslav Semashko; and sometimes Miss Ptitzin, the daughter of an important official, appeared there, too. They talked of books and poetry. This was something which appealed to me, and which I could understand; I had read more than all of them together. But sometimes they talked about the high school, and complained about the teachers. When I listened to these recitals, I felt that I had more liberty than my friends, and was amazed at their patience. And yet I envied them; they had opportunities of learning!

My comrades were older than I, but I felt that I was the elder. I was keener-witted, more experienced than they. This worried me somewhat; I wanted to feel more in touch with them. I used to get home late in the evening, dusty and dirty, steeped in impressions very different from theirs—in the main very monotonous. They talked a lot about young ladies, and of being in love with this one and that one, and they used to try their hands at writing poetry. They frequently solicited my help in this matter. I willingly applied myself to versification, and it was easy for me to find the rhymes, but for some reason or other my verses always took a humorous turn, and I never could help associating Miss Ptitzin, to whom the poetry was generally dedicated, with fruits and vegetables.

Semashko said to me:

"Do you call that poetry? It is as much like poetry as hobnails would be."

Not wishing to be behind them in anything, I also fell in love with Miss Ptitzin. I do not remember how I declared my feelings, but I know that the affair ended badly. On the stagnant green water of the Zvyezdin Pond floated a plank, and I proposed to give the young lady a ride on it. She agreed. I brought the log to the bank; it held me alone quite well. But when the gorgeously dressed young lady, all ribbons and lace, graciously stepped on the other end, and I proudly pushed off with a stick, the accursed log rolled away from under us and my young lady went head over heels into the water.

I threw myself in knightly fashion after her, and swiftly brought her to shore. Fright and the green mire of the pond had quite destroyed her beauty! Shaking her wet fist at me threateningly, she cried:

"You threw me in the water on purpose!"

And refusing to believe in the sincerity of my protestations, from that time she treated me as an enemy.

On the whole, I did not find living in the town very interesting. My old mistress was as hostile as she had ever been; the young one regarded me with contempt; Victorushka more freckled than ever, snorted at every one, and was everlastingly aggrieved about something.

My master had many plans to draw. He could not get through all the work with his brother, and so he engaged my stepfather as assistant.

One day I came home from the market-place early, about five o'clock, and going into the dining-room, saw the man whose existence I had forgotten, at the table beside the master. He held his hand out to me.

"How do you do?"

I drew back at the unexpectedness of it. The fire of the past had been suddenly rekindled, and burned my heart.

My stepfather looked at me with a smile on his terribly emaciated face; his dark eyes were larger than ever. He looked altogether worn out and depressed. I placed my hand in his thin, hot fingers.

"Well, so we 've met again," he said, coughing.

I left them, feeling as weak as if I had been beaten.

Our manner to each other was cautious and restrained; he called me by my first name and my patronymic, and spoke to me as an equal.

"When you go to the shops, please buy me a quarter of a pound of Lapherm's tobacco, a hundred packets of Vitcorson's, and a pound of boiled sausage."

The money which he gave me was always unpleasantly heated by his hot hands. It was plain that he was a consumptive, and not long to be an inhabitant of this earth. He knew this, and would say in a calm, deep voice, twisting his pointed black beard:

"My illness is almost incurable. However, if I take plenty of meat I may get better—I may get better."

He ate an unbelievably large amount; he smoked cigarettes, which were only out of his lips when he was eating. Every day I bought him sausages, ham, sardines, but grandmother's sister said with an air of certainty, and for some reason maliciously:

"It is no use to feed Death with dainties; you cannot deceive him."

The mistress regarded my stepfather with an air of injury, reproachfully advised him to try this or that medicine, but made fun of him behind his back.

"A fine gentleman? The crumbs ought to be swept up more often in the dining-room, he says; crumbs cause the flies to multiply, he says."

The young mistress said this, and the old mistress repeated after her:

"What do you mean—a fine gentleman! With his coat all worn and shiny, and he always scraping it with a clothes-brush. He is so faddy; there must not be a speck of dust on it!"

But the master spoke soothingly to them:

"Be patient, wild fowl, he will soon be dead!" This senseless hostility of the middle class toward a man of good birth somehow drew me and my stepfather closer together. The crimson agaric is an unwholesome fungus, yet it is so beautiful. Suffocated among these people, my stepfather was like a fish which had accidentally fallen into a fowl-run—an absurd comparison, as everything in that life was absurd.

I began to find in him resemblances to "Good Business"—a man whom I could never forget. I adored him and my Queen with the best that I got out of books. I gave them all that was most pure in me, all the fantasies born of my reading. My stepfather was just such another man, aloof and unloved, as "Good Business." He behaved alike to every one in the house, never spoke first, and answered questions put to him with a peculiar politeness and brevity. I was delighted when he taught my masters. Standing at the table, bent double, he would tap the thick paper with his dry nails, and suggest calmly:

"Here you will have to have a keystone. That will halve the force of the pressure; otherwise the pillar will crash through the walls."

"That's true, the devil take it," muttered the master, and his wife said to him, when my stepfather had gone out:

"It is simply amazing to me that you can allow any one to teach you your business like that!"

For some reason she was always especially irritated when my stepfather cleaned his teeth and gargled after supper, protruding his harshly outlined Adam's apple.

"In my opinion," she would say in a sour voice, "it is injurious to you to bend your head back like that, Evgen Vassilvich!"

Smiling politely he asked:

"Why?"

"Because—I am sure it is."

He began to clean his bluish nails with a tiny bone stick.

"He is cleaning his nails again; well, I never!" exclaimed the mistress. "He is dying—and there he is."

"Ekh!" sighed the master. "What a lot of stupidity has flourished in you, wild fowl!"

"Why do you say that?" asked his wife, confused. But the old mistress complained passionately to God at night:

"Lord, they have laid that rotten creature on my shoulders, and Victor is again pushed on one side." Victorushka began to mock the manners of my stepfather,—his leisurely walk, the assured movements of his lordly hands, his skill in tying a cravat, and his dainty way of eating. He would ask coarsely: "Maximov, what's the French for 'knee'?"

"I am called Evgen Vassilevich," my stepfather reminded him calmly.

"All right. Well, what is 'the chest'?"

Victorushka would say to his mother at supper: "Ma mère, donnez moi encore du pickles!"

"Oh, you Frenchman!" the old woman would say, much affected.

My stepfather, as unmoved as if he were deaf or dumb, chewed his meat without looking at any one. One day the elder brother said to the younger: "Now that you are learning French, Victor, you ought to have a mistress."

This was the only time I remember seeing my stepfather smile quietly.

But the young mistress let her spoon fall on the table in her agitation, and cried to her husband:

"Are n't you ashamed to talk so disgustingly before me?"

Sometimes my stepfather came to me in the dark vestibule, where I slept under the stairs which led to the attic, and where, sitting on the stairs by the window, I used to read.

"Reading?" he would say, blowing out smoke. There came a hissing sound from his chest like the hissing of a fire-stick. "What is the book?"

I showed it to him.

"Ah," he said, glancing at the title, "I think I have read it. Will you smoke?"

We smoked, looking out of the window onto the dirty yard. He said:

"It is a great pity that you cannot study; it seems to me that you have ability."

"I am studying; I read."

"That is not enough; you need a school; a system." I felt inclined to say to him:

"You had the advantages of both school and system, my fine fellow, and what is the result?"

But he added, as if he had read my thoughts: "Given the proper disposition, a school is a good educator. Only very well educated people make any mark in life."

But once he counseled me:

"You would be far better away from here. I see no sense or advantage to you in staying."

"I like the work."

"Ah—what do you find to like?"

"I find it interesting to work with them."

"Perhaps you are right."

But one day he said:

"What trash they are in the main, our employers—trash!"

When I remembered how and when my mother had uttered that word, I involuntarily drew back from him. He asked, smiling:

"Don't you think so?"

"I don't know."

"Well, they are; I can see that."

"But I like the master, anyhow."

"Yes, you are right; he is a worthy man, but strange."

I should have liked to talk with him about books, but it was plain that he did not care for them, and one day he advised me:

"Don't be led away; everything is very much embellished in books, distorted one way or another. Most writers of books are people like our master, small people."

Such judgments seemed very daring to me, and quite corrupted me.

On the same occasion he asked me:

"Have you read any of Goncharov's works?"

'The Frigate Palada.'"

"That's a dull book. But really, Goncharov is the cleverest writer in Russia. I advise you to read his novel, 'Oblomov.' That is by far the truest and most daring book he wrote; in fact, it is the best book in Russian literature."

Of Dickens' works he said:

"They are rubbish, I assure you. But there is a most interesting thing running in the 'Nova Vremya,'-'The Temptation of St. Anthony.' You read it? Apparently you like all that pertains to the church, and 'The Temptation' ought to be a profitable subject for you."

He brought me a bundle of papers containing the serial, and I read Flaubert's learned work. It reminded me of the innumerable lives of holy men, scraps of history told by the valuers, but it made no very deep impression on me. I much preferred the "Memoirs of Upilio Faimali, Tamer of Wild Beasts," which was printed alongside of it.

When I acknowledged this fact to my stepfather, he remarked coolly:

"That means that you are still too young to read such things? However, don't forget about that book."

Sometimes he would sit with me for a long time without saying a word, just coughing and puffing out smoke continuously. His beautiful eyes burned painfully, and I looked at him furtively, and forgot that this man, who was dying so honestly and simply, without complaint, had once been so closely related to my mother, and had insulted her. I knew that he lived with some sort of seamstress, and thought of her with wonder and pity. How could she not shrink from embracing those lanky bones, from kissing that mouth which gave forth such an oppressive odor of putrescence? Just like "Good Business," my stepfather often uttered peculiarly characteristic sayings:

"I love hounds; they are stupid, but I love them. They are very beautiful. Beautiful women are often stupid, too."

I thought, not without pride:

"Ah, if he had only known Queen Margot!"

"People who live for a long time in the same house all have the same kind of face," was one of his sayings which I wrote down in my note-book.

I listened for these sayings of his, as if they had been treats. It was pleasant to hear unusual, literary words used in a house where every one spoke a colorless language, which had hardened into well-worn, undiversified forms. My stepfather never spoke to me of my mother; he never even uttered her name. This pleased me, and aroused in me a feeling of sympathetic consideration for him.

Once I asked him about God—I do not remember what brought up the subject. He looked at me, and said very calmly:

"I don't know. I don't believe in God."

I remembered Sitanov, and told my stepfather about him. Having listened attentively to me, he observed, still calmly:

"He was in doubt; and those who are in doubt must believe in something. As for me, I simply do not believe———"

"But is that possible?"

"Why not? You can see for yourself I don't believe."

I saw nothing, except that he was dying. I hardly pitied him; my first feeling was one of keen and genuine interest in the nearness of a dying person, in the mystery of death.

Here was a man sitting close to me, his knee touching mine, warm, sensate, calmly regarding people in the light of their relations to himself; speaking about everything like a person who possessed power to judge and to settle affairs; in whom lay something necessary to me, or something good, blended with something unnecessary to me. This being of incomprehensible complexity was the receptacle of continuous whirlwinds of thought. It was not as if I were merely brought in contact with him, but it seemed as if he were part of myself, that he lived somewhere within me. I thought about him continually, and the shadow of his soul lay across mine. And to-morrow he would disappear entirely, with all that was hidden in his head and his heart, with all that I seemed to read in his beautiful eyes. When he went, another of the living threads which bound me to life would be snapped. His memory would be left, but that would be something finite within me, forever limited, immutable. But that which is alive changes, progresses. But these were thoughts, and behind them lay those inexpressible words which give birth to and nourish them, which strike to the very roots of life, demanding an answer to the question, Why?

"I shall soon have to lie by, it seems to me," said my stepfather one rainy day. "This stupid weakness! I don't feel inclined to do anything."

The next day, at the time of evening tea, he brushed the crumbs of bread from the table and from his knees with peculiar care, and brushed something invisible from his person. The old mistress, looking at him from under her brows, whispered to her daughter-in-law:

"Look at the way he is plucking at himself, and brushing himself."

He did not come to work for two days, and then the old mistress put a large white envelope in my hand, saying:

"Here you are! A woman brought this yesterday about noon, and I forgot to give it to you. A pretty little woman she was, but what she wants with you I can't imagine, and that's the truth!"

On a slip of paper with a hospital stamp, inside the envelope, was written in large characters:

"When you have an hour to spare, come and see me. I am in the Martinovski Hospital. "E. M."

The next morning I was sitting in a hospital ward on my stepfather's bed. It was a long bed, and his feet, in gray, worn socks, stuck out through the rails. His beautiful eyes, dully wandering over the yellow walls, rested on my face and on the small hands of a young girl who sat on a bench at the head of the bed. Her hands rested on the pillow, and my stepfather rubbed his cheek against them, his mouth hanging open. She was a plump girl, wearing a shiny, dark frock. The tears flowed slowly over her oval face; her wet blue eyes never moved from my stepfather's face, with its sharp bones, large, sharp-pointed nose, and dark mouth.

"The priest ought to be here," she whispered, "but he forbids it—he does not understand." And taking her hands from the pillow, she pressed them to her breast as if praying.

In a minute my stepfather came to himself, looked at the ceiling and frowned, as if he were trying to remember something. Then he stretched his lank hand toward me.

"You? Thank you. Here I am, you see. I feel to stupid."

The effort tired him; he closed his eyes. I stroked his long cold fingers with the blue nails. The girl asked softly:

"Evgen Vassilvich, introduce us, please!"

"You must know each other," he said, indicating her with his eyes. "A dear creature—"

He stopped speaking, his mouth opened wider and wider, and he suddenly shrieked out hoarsely, like a raven. Throwing herself on the bed, clutching at the blanket, waving her bare arms about, the girl also screamed, burying her head in the tossed pillow.

My stepfather died quickly, and as soon as he was dead, he regained some of his good looks. I left the hospital with the girl on my arm. She staggered like a sick person, and cried. Her handkerchief was squeezed into a ball in her hand; she alternately applied it to her eyes, and rolling it tighter, gazed at it as if it were her last and most precious possession.

Suddenly she stood still, pressing close to me, and said:

"I shall not live till the winter. Oh Lord, Lord! What does it mean?"

Then holding out her hand, wet with tears, to me: "Good-by. He thought a lot of you. He will be buried to-morrow."

"Shall I see you home?"

She looked about her.

"What for? It is daytime, not night."

From the corner of a side street I looked after her. She walked slowly, like a person who has nothing to hurry for. It was August. The leaves were already beginning to fall from the trees. I had no time to follow my stepfather to the graveyard, and I never saw the girl again.

CHAPTER XVII

Every morning at six o'clock I set out to my work in the market-place. I met interesting people there. There was the carpenter, Osip, a grayhaired man who looked like Saint Nikolai, a clever workman, and witty; there was the humpbacked slater, Ephimushka, the pious bricklayer, Petr, a thoughtful man who also reminded me of a saint; the plasterer, Gregory Shishlin, a flaxen-bearded, blue-eyed, handsome man, beaming with quiet good-nature.

I had come to know these people during the second part of my life at the draughtsman's house. Every Sunday they used to appear in the kitchen, grave, important-looking, with pleasant speech, and with words which had a new flavor for me. All these solid-looking peasants had seemed to me then to be easy to read, good through and through, all pleasantly different from the spiteful, thieving, drunken inhabitants of the Kunavin and its environs.

The plasterer, Shishlin, pleased me most of all, and I actually asked if I might join his gang of workmen. But scratching his golden brow with a white finger, he gently refused to have me.

"It is too soon for you," he said. "Our work is not easy; wait another year."

Then throwing up his handsome head, he asked:

"You don't like the way you are living? Never mind, have patience; learn to live a life of your own, and then you will be able to bear it!"

I do not know all that I gained from this good advice, but I remember it gratefully.

These people used to come to my master's house every Sunday morning, sit on benches round the kitchen-table, and talk of interesting things while they waited for my master. When he came, he greeted them loudly and gayly, shaking their strong hands, and then sat down in the chief corner. They produced their accounts and bundles of notes, the workmen placed their tattered account-books on the table, and the reckoning up for the week began.

Joking and bantering, the master would try to prove them wrong in their reckoning, and they did the same to him. Sometimes there was a fierce dispute, but more often friendly laughter.

"Eh, you're a dear man; you were born a rogue!" the workmen would say to the master.

And he answered, laughing in some confusion:

"And what about you, wild fowl? There's as much roguery about you as about me!"

"How should we be anything else, friend?" agreed Ephimushka, but grave Petr said:

"You live by what you steal; what you earn you give to God and the emperor."

"Well, then I'll willingly make a burnt offering of you," laughed the master.

They led him on good-naturedly:

"Set fire to us, you mean?"

"Burn us in a fiery furnace?"

Gregory Shishlin, pressing his luxuriant beard to his breast with his hands, said in a sing-song voice: "Brothers, let us do our business without cheating. If we will only live honestly, how happy and peaceful we shall be, eh? Shall we not, dear people?"

His blue eyes darkened, grew moist; at that moment he looked wonderfully handsome. His question seemed to have upset them all; they all turned away from him in confusion.

"A peasant does not cheat much," grumbled good-looking Osip with a sigh, as if he pitied the peasant.

The dark bricklayer, bending his round-shouldered back over the table, said thickly:

"Sin is like a sort of bog; the farther you go, the more swampy it gets!"

And the master said to them, as if he were making a speech:

"What about me? I go into it because something calls me. Though I don't want to."

After this philosophising they again tried to get the better of one another, but when they had finished their accounts, perspiring and tired from the effort, they went out to the tavern to drink tea, inviting the master to go with them.

On the market-place it was my duty to watch these people, to see that they did not steal nails, or bricks, or boards. Every one of them, in addition to my master's work, held contracts of his own, and would try to steal something for his own work under my very nose. They welcomed me kindly, and Shishlin said:

"Do you remember how you wanted to come into my gang? And look at you now; put over me as chief!"

"Well, well," said Osip banteringly, "keep watch over the river-banks, and may God help you!"

Petr observed in an unfriendly tone:

"They have put a young crane to watch old mice."

My duties were a cruel trial to me. I felt ashamed in the presence of these people. They all seemed to possess some special knowledge which was hidden from the rest of the world, and I had to watch them as if they had been thieves and tricksters. The first part of the time it was very hard for me, but Osip soon noticed this, and one day he said to me privately:

"Look here, young fellow, you won't do any good by sulking—understand?"

Of course I did not understand, but I felt that he realized the absurdity of my position, and I soon arrived at a frank understanding with him.

He took me aside in a corner and explained:

"If you want to know, the biggest thief among us is the bricklayer, Petrukha. He is a man with a large family, and he is greedy. You want to watch him well. Nothing is too small for him; everything comes in handy. A pound of nails, a dozen of bricks, a bag of mortar—he'll take all. He is a good man, God-fearing, of severe ideas, and well educated, but he loves to steal! Ephimushka lives like a woman. He is peaceable, and is harmless as far as you are concerned. He is clever, too—humpbacks are never fools! And there's Gregory Shishlin. He has a fad—he will neither take from others nor give of his own. He works for nothing; any one can take him in, but he can deceive no one. He is not governed by his reason."

"He is good, then?"

Osip looked at me as if I were a long way from him, and uttered these memorable words:

"True enough, he is good. To be good is the easiest way for lazy people. To be good, my boy, does not need brains."

"And what about you?" I asked Osip.

He laughed and answered:

"I? I am like a young girl. When I am a grandmother I will tell you all about myself; till then you will have to wait. In the meanwhile you can set your brains to work to find out where the real 'I' is hidden. Find out; that is what you have to do!"

He had upset all my ideas of himself and his friends.

It was difficult for me to doubt the truth of his statement. I saw that Ephimushka, Petr, and Gregory regarded the handsome old man as more clever and more learned in worldly wisdom than themselves. They took counsel with him about everything, listened attentively to his advice, and showed him every sign of respect.

"Will you be so good as to give us your advice," they would ask him. But after one of these questions, when Osip had gone away, the bricklayer said softly to Grigori:

"Heretic!"

And Grigori burst out laughing and added:

"Clown!"

The plasterer warned me in a friendly way:

"You look out for yourself with the old man, Maximich. You must be careful, or he will twist you round his finger in an hour; he is a bitter old man. God save you from the harm he can do."

"What harm?"

"That I can't say!" answered the handsome workman, blinking.

I did not understand him in the least. I thought that the most honest and pious man of them all was the bricklayer, Petr; He spoke of everything briefly, suggestively; his thoughts rested mostly upon God, hell, and death.

"Ekh! my children, my brothers, how can you not be afraid? How can you not look forward, when the grave and the churchyard let no one pass them?"

He always had the stomachache, and there were some days when he could not eat anything at all. Even a morsel of bread brought on the pain to such an extent as to cause convulsions and a dreadful sickness.

Humpbacked Ephimushka also seemed a very good and honest, but always queer fellow. Sometimes he was happy and foolish, like a harmless lunatic. He was everlastingly falling in love with different women, about whom he always used the same words:

"I tell you straight, she is not a woman, but a flower in cream—ei, bo—o!"

When the lively women of Kunavin Street came to wash the floors in the shops, Ephimushka let himself down from the roof, and standing in a corner somewhere, mumbled, blinking his gray, bright eyes, stretching his mouth from ear to ear:

"Such a butterfly as the Lord has sent to me; such a joy has descended upon me! Well, what is she but a flower in cream, and grateful I ought to be for the chance which has brought me such a gift! Such beauty makes me full of life, afire!"

At first the women used to laugh at him, calling out to each other:

"Listen to the humpback running on! Oh Lord!" The slater caused no little laughter. His high cheek-boned face wore a sleepy expression, and he used to talk as if he were raving, his honeyed phrases flowing in an intoxicating stream which obviously went to the women's heads. At length one of the elder ones said to her friend in a tone of amazement:

"Just listen to how that man is going on! A clean young fellow he is!"

"He sings like a bird."

"Or like a beggar in the church porch," said an obstinate girl, refusing to give way.

But Ephimushka was not like a beggar at all. He stood firmly, like a squat tree-trunk; his voice rang out like a challenge; his words became more and more alluring; the women listened to him in silence. In fact, it seemed as if his whole being was flowing away in a tender, narcotic speech.

It ended in his saying to his mates in a tone of astonishment at supper-time, or after the Sabbath rest, shaking his heavy, angular head:

"Well, what a sweet little woman, a dear little thing! I have never before come across anything like her!"

When he spoke of his conquests Ephimushka was not boastful, nor jeered at the victim of his charms, as the others always did. He was only joyfully and gratefully touched, his gray eyes wide open with astonishment.

Osip, shaking his head, exclaimed:

"Oh, you incorrigible fellow! How old are you?" "Forty-four years, but that's nothing! I have grown five years younger to-day, as if I had bathed in the healing water of a river. I feel thoroughly fit, and my heart is at peace! Some women can produce that effect, eh?"

The bricklayer said coarsely:

"You are going on for fifty. You had better be careful, or you will find that your loose way of life will leave a bitter taste."

"You are shameless, Ephimushka!" sighed Grigori Shishlin.

And it seemed to me that the handsome fellow envied the success of the humpback.

Osip looked round on us all from under his level silver brows, and said jestingly:

"Every Mashka has her fancies. One will love cups and spoons, another buckles and earrings, but all Mashkas will be grandmothers in time."

Shishlin was married, but his wife was living in the country, so he also cast his eyes on the floor-scrubbers. They were all of them easy of approach. All of them "earned a bit" to add to their income, and they regarded this method of earning money in that poverty-stricken area as simply as they would have regarded any other kind of work. But the handsome workman never approached the women. He just gazed at them from afar with a peculiar expression, as if he were pitying some one—himself or them. But when they began to sport with him and tempt him, he laughed bashfully and went away.

"Well, you—"

"What's the matter with you, you fool?" asked Ephimushka, amazed. "Do you mean to say you are going to lose the chance?"

"I am a married man," Grigori reminded him.

"Well, do you think your wife will know anything about it?"

"My wife would always know if I lived unchastely. I can't deceive her, my brother."

"How can she know?"

"That I can't say, but she is bound to know, while she lives chaste herself; and if I lead a chaste life, and she were to sin, I should know it."

"But how?" cried Ephimushka, but Grigori repeated calmly:

"That I can't say."

The slater waved his hands agitatedly.

"There, if you please! Chaste, and does n't know! Oh, you blockhead!"

Shishlin's workmen, numbering seven, treated him as one of themselves and not as their master, and behind his back they nicknamed him "The Calf."

When he came to work and saw that they were lazy, he would take a trowel, or a spade, and artistically do the work himself, calling out coaxingly:

"Set to work, children, set to work!"

One day, carrying out the task which my master had angrily set me, I said to Grigori:

"What bad workmen you have."

He seemed surprised.

"Why?"—

"This work ought to have been finished yesterday, and they won't finish it even to-day."

"That is true; they won't have time," he agreed, and after a silence he added cautiously:

"Of course, I see that by rights I ought to dismiss them, but you see they are all my own people from my own village. And then again the punishment of God is that every man should eat bread by the sweat of his brow, and the punishment is for all of us—for you and me, too. But you and I labor less than they do, and—well, it would be awkward to dismiss them."

He lived in a dream. He would walk along the deserted streets of the market-place, and suddenly halting on one of the bridges over the Obvodni Canal, would stand for a long time at the railings, looking into the water, at the sky, or into the distance beyond the Oka. If one overtook him and asked:

"What are you doing?"

"What?" he would reply, waking up and smiling confusedly. "I was just standing, looking about me a bit."

"God has arranged everything very well, brother," he would often say. "The sky, the earth, the flowing rivers, the steamboats running. You can get on a boat and go where you like—to Riazan, or to Ribinsk, to Perm, to Astrakhan. I went to Riazan once. It was n't bad—a little town—but very dull, duller than Nijni. Our Nijni is wonderful, gay! And Astrakhan is still duller. There are a lot of Kalmucks there, and I don't like them. I don't like any of those Mordovans, or Kalmucks, Persians, or Germans, or any of the other nations."

He spoke slowly; his words cautiously felt for sympathy in others, and always found it in the bricklayer, Petr.

"Those are not nations, but nomads," said Petr with angry conviction. "They came into the world before Christ and they 'll go out of it before He comes again."

Grigori became animated; he beamed.

"That's it, isn't it? But I love a pure race like the Russians, my brother, with a straight look. I don't like Jews, either, and I cannot understand how they are the people of God. It is wisely arranged, no doubt."

The slater added darkly:

"Wisely—but there is a lot that is superfluous!"

Osip listened to what they said, and then put in, mockingly and caustically:

"There is much that is superfluous, and your conversation belongs to that category. Ekh! you babblers; you want a thrashing, all of you!"

Osip kept himself to himself, and it was impossible to guess with whom he would agree, or with whom he would quarrel. Sometimes he seemed inclined to agree calmly with all men, and with all their ideas; but more often one saw that he was bored by all of them, regarding them as half-witted, and he said to Petr, Grigori, and Ephimushka:

"Ekh, you sow's whelps!"

They laughed, not very cheerfully or willingly, but still they laughed.

My master gave me five copecks a day for food. This was not enough, and I was rather hungry. Seeing this, the workmen invited me to breakfast and supper with them, and sometimes the contractors would invite me to a tavern to drink tea with them. I willingly accepted the invitations. I loved to sit among them and listen to their slow speeches, their strange stories. I gave them great pleasure by my readings out of church books.

"You've stuck to books till you are fed up with them. Your crop is stuffed with them," said Osip, regarding me attentively with his cornflower-blue eyes. It was difficult to catch their expression; his pupils always seemed to be floating, melting.

"Take it a drop at a time—it is better; and when you are grown up, you can be a monk and console the people by your teaching, and in that way you may become a millionaire."

"A missioner," corrected the bricklayer in a voice which for some reason sounded aggrieved.

"What?" asked Osip.

"A missioner is what you mean! You are not deaf, are you?"

"All right, then, a missioner, and dispute with heretics. And even those whom you reckon as heretics have the right to bread. One can live even with a heretic, if one exercises discretion."

Grigori laughed in an embarrassed manner, and Petr said in his beard:

"And wizards don't have a bad time of it, and other kinds of godless people."

But Osip returned quickly:

"A wizard is not a man of education; education is not usually a possession of the wizard."

And he told me:

"Now look at this; just listen. In our district there lived a peasant, Tushek was his name, an emaciated little man, and idle. He lived like a feather, blown about here and there by the wind, neither a worker nor a do-nothing. Well, one day he took to praying, because he had nothing else to do, and after wandering about for two years, he suddenly showed himself in a new character. His hair hung down over his shoulders; he wore a skull-cap, and a brown cassock of leather; he looked on all of us with a baneful eye, and said straight out: 'Repent, ye cursed!' And why not repent, especially if you happened to be a woman? And the business ran its course: Tushek overfed, Tushek drunk, Tushek having his way with the women to his heart's content—"

The bricklayer interrupted him angrily:

"What has that got to do with the matter, his overfeeding, or overdrinking?"

"What else has to do with it, then?"

"His words are all that matter."

"Oh, I took no notice of his words; I am abundantly gifted with words myself."

"We know all we want to know about Tushinkov, Dmitri Vassilich," said Petr indignantly, and Grigori said nothing, but let his head droop, and gazed into his glass.

"I don't dispute it," replied Osip peaceably. "I was just telling our Maximich of the different pathways to the morsel—"

"Some of the roads lead to prison!"

"Occasionally," agreed Osip. "But you will meet with priests on all kinds of paths; one must learn where to turn off."

He was always somewhat inclined to make fun of these pious people, the plasterer and the bricklayer; perhaps he did not like them, but he skilfully concealed the fact. His attitude towards people was always elusive.

He looked upon Ephimushka more indulgently, with more favor than upon the other. The slater did not enter into discussions about God, the truth, sects, the woes of humanity, as his friends did. Setting his chair sidewise to the table, so that its back should not be in the way of his hump, he would calmly drink glass after glass of tea. Then, suddenly alert, he would glance round the smoky room, listening to the incoherent babel of voices, and darting up, swiftly disappear. That meant that some one had come into the tavern to whom Ephimushka owed money,—he had a good dozen creditors,—so, as some of them used to beat him when they saw him, he just fled from sin.

"They get angry, the oddities!" he would say in a tone of surprise. "Can't they understand that if I had the money I would give it to them?"

"Oh, bitter poverty!" Osip sped after him.

Sometimes Ephimushka sat deep in thought, hearing and seeing nothing; his high cheek-boned face softened, his pleasant eyes looking pleasanter than usual.

"What are you thinking about?" they would ask him.

"I was thinking that if I were rich I would marry a real lady, a noblewoman—by God, I would! A colonel's daughter, for example, and, Lord! how I would love her! I should be on fire with love of her, because, my brothers, I once roofed the country house of a certain colonel—"

"And he had a widowed daughter; we 've heard all that before!" interrupted Petr in an unfriendly tone.

But Ephimushka, spreading his hands out on his knees, rocked to and fro, his hump looking as if it were chiselling the air, and continued:

"Sometimes she went into the garden, all in white; glorious she looked. I looked at her from the roof, and I did n't know what the sun had done to me. But what caused that white light? It was as if a white dove had flown from under her feet! She was just a cornflower in cream! With such a lady as that, one would like all one's life to be night."

"And how would you get anything to eat?" asked Petr gruffly. But this did not disturb Ephimushka.

"Lord!" he exclaimed. "Should we want much? Besides, she is rich."

Osip laughed.

"And when are you going in for all this dissipation, Ephimushka, you rogue?"

Ephimushka never talked on any other subject but women, and he was an unreliable workman. At one time he worked excellently and profitably, at another time he did not get on at all; his wooden hammer tapped the ridges lazily, leaving crevices. He always smelt of train-oil, but he had a smell of his own as well, a healthy, pleasant smell like that of a newly cut tree.

One could discuss everything that was interesting with the carpenter. His words always stirred one's feelings, but it was hard to tell when he was serious and when joking.

With Grigori it was better to talk about God; this was a subject which he loved, and on which he was an authority.

"Grisha," I asked, "do you know there are people who do not believe in God?"

He laughed quietly.

"What do you mean?"

"They say there is no God."

"Oh, that's what you mean! I know that."

And as if he were brushing away invisible flies, he went on:

"King David said in his time, you remember, 'The fool hath said in his heart "There is no God."' That's what he said about that kind of fool. We can't do without God!"

Osip said, as if agreeing with him:

"Take away God from Petrukha here, and he will show you!"

Shishlin's handsome face became stern. He touched his beard with fingers the nails of which were covered with dried lime, and said mysteriously:

"God dwells in every incarnate being; the conscience and all the inner life is God-given."

"And sin?"

"Sin comes from the flesh, from Satan! Sin is an external thing, like smallpox, and nothing more! He who thinks too much of sin, sins all the more. If you do not remember sin, you will not sin. Thoughts about sin are from Satan, the lord of the flesh, who suggests."

The bricklayer queried this.

"You are wrong there."

"I am not! God is sinless, and man is in His image and likeness. It is the image of God, the flesh, which sins, but His likeness cannot sin; it is a spirit."

He smiled triumphantly, but Petr growled:

"That is wrong."

"According to you, I suppose," Osip asked the bricklayer, "if you don't sin, you can't repent, and if you don't repent, you won't be saved?"

"That's a more hopeful way. Forget the devil and you cease to love God, the fathers said."

Shishlin was not intemperate, but two glasses would make him tipsy. His face would be flushed, his eyes childish, and his voice would be raised in song.

"How good everything is, brothers! Here we live, work a little, and have as much as we want to eat, God be praised! Ah, how good it is!"

He wept. The tears trickled down his beard and gleamed on the silken hairs like false pearls.

His laudation of our life and those tears were unpleasant to me. My grandmother had sung the praises of life more convincingly, more sympathetically, and not so crudely.

All these discussions kept me in a continual tension, and aroused a dull emotion in me. I had already read many books about peasants, and I saw how utterly unlike the peasants in the books were to those in real life. In books they were all unhappy. Good or evil characters, they were all poorer in words and ideas than peasants in real life. In books they spoke less of God, of sects, of churches, and more of government, land, and law. They spoke less about women, too, but quite as coarsely, though more kindly. For the peasants in real life, women were a pastime, but a dangerous one. One had to be artful with women; otherwise they would gain the upper hand and spoil one's whole life. The *muzhik* in books may be good or bad, but he is altogether one or the other. The real *muzhik* is neither wholly good nor wholly bad, but he is wonderfully interesting. If the peasant in real life does not blurt out all his thoughts to you, you have a feeling that he is keeping something back which he means to keep for himself alone, and that very unsaid, hidden thing is the most important thing about him.

Of all the peasants I had read of in books, the one I liked the best was Petr in "The Carpenter's Gang." I wanted to read the story to my comrades, and I brought the book to the Yarmaka. I often spent the night in one or another of the workshops; sometimes it was because I was so tired that I lacked the strength to get home.

When I told them that I had a book about carpenters, my statement aroused a lively interest, especially in Osip. He took the book out of my hands, and turned over the leaves distrustfully, shaking his head.

"And it is really written about us! Oh, you rascal! Who wrote it? Some gentleman? I thought as much! Gentlemen, and *chinovniks* especially, are experts at anything. Where God does not even guess, a *chinovnik* has it all settled in his mind. That's what they live for."

"You speak very irreverently of God, Osip," observed Petr.

"That's all right! My words are less to God than a snowflake or a drop of rain are to me. Don't you worry; you and I don't touch God."

He suddenly began to play restlessly, throwing off sharp little sayings like sparks from a flint, cutting off with them, as with scissors, whatever was displeasing to him. Several times in the course of the day he asked me:

"Are we going to read, Maximich? That's right! A good idea!"

When the hour for rest arrived we had supper with him in his workshop, and after supper appeared Petr with his assistant Ardalon, and Shishlin with the lad Phoma. In the shed where the gang slept there was a lamp burning, and I began to read. They listened without speaking, but they moved about, and very soon Ardalon said crossly:

"I've had enough of this!"

And he went out. The first to fall asleep was Grigori, with his mouth open surprisingly; then the carpenters fell asleep; but Petr, Osip, and Phoma drew nearer to me and listened attentively. When I finished reading Osip put out the lamp at once. By the stars it was nearly midnight.

Petr asked in the darkness:

"What was that written for? Against whom?"

"Now for sleep!" said Osip, taking off his boots.

Petr persisted in his question:

"I asked, against whom was that written?"

"I suppose they know!" replied Osip, arranging himself for sleep on a scaffolding.

"If it is written against stepmothers, it is a waste of time. It won't make stepmothers any better," said the bricklayer firmly. "And if it is meant for Petr, it is also futile; his sin in his answer. For murder you go to Siberia, and that's all there is about it! Books are no good for such sins; no use, eh?"

Osip did not reply, and the bricklayer added:

"They can do nothing themselves and so they discuss other people's work. Like women at a meeting. Good-by, it is bedtime."

He stood for a minute in the dark blue square of the open door, and asked:

"Are you asleep, Osip? What do you think about it?"

"Eh?" responded the carpenter sleepily.

"All right; go to sleep."

Shishlin had fallen on his side where he had been sitting. Phoma lay on some trampled straw beside me. The whole neighborhood was asleep. In the distance rose the shriek of the railway engines, the heavy rumbling of iron wheels, the clang of buffers. In the shed rose the sound of snoring in different keys. I felt uncomfortable. I had expected some sort of discussion, and there had been nothing of the kind. But suddenly Osip spoke softly and evenly:

"My child, don't you believe anything of that. You are young; you have a long while to live; treasure up your thoughts. Your own sense is worth twice some one else's. Are you asleep, Phoma?"

"No," replied Phoma with alacrity.

"That's right! You have both received some education, so you go on reading. But don't believe all you read. They can print anything, you know. That is their business!"

He lowered his feet from the scaffolding, and resting his hands on the edge of the plank, bent over us, and continued:

"How ought you to regard books? Denunciation of certain people, that's what a book is! Look, they say, and see what sort of a man this is—a carpenter, or any one else—and here is a gentleman, a different kind of man! A book is not written without an object, and generally around some one."

Phoma said thickly:

"Petr was right to kill that contractor!"

"That was wrong. It can never be right to kill a man. I know that you do not love Grigori, but put that thought away from you. We are none of us rich people. To-day I am master, to-morrow a workman again."

"I did not mean you, Uncle Osip."

"It is all the same."

"You are just—"

"Wait; I am telling you why these books are written," Osip interrupted Phoma's angry words. "It is a very cunning idea! Here we have a gentleman without a *muzhik*, here a *muzhik* without a gentleman! Look now! Both the gentleman and the *muzhik* are badly off. The gentleman grows weak, crazy, and the *muzhik* becomes boastful, drunken, sickly, and offensive. That's what happens! But in his lord's castle it was better, they say. The lord hid himself behind the *muzhik* and the *muzhik* behind the master, and so they went round and round, well-fed, and peaceful. I don't deny that it was more peaceful living with the nobles. It was no advantage to the lord if his *muzhik* was poor, but it was to his good if he was rich and intelligent. He was then a weapon in his hand. I know all about it; you see I lived in a nobleman's domain for nearly forty years. There's a lot of my experience written on my hide."

I remembered that the carter, Petr, who committed suicide, used to talk in the same way about the nobility, and it was very unpleasant to my mind that the ideas of Osip should run on the same lines as those of that evil old man.

Osip touched my leg with his hand, and went on:

"One must understand books and all sorts of writings. No one does anything without a reason, and books are not written for nothing, but to muddle people's heads. Every one is created with intelligence, without which no one can wield an ax, or sew a shoe." He spoke for a long time, and lay down. Again he jumped up, throwing gently his well turned, quaint phrases into the darkness and quietness.

"They say that the nobles are quite a different race from the peasants, but it is not true. We are just like the nobles, only we happen to have been born low down in the scale. Of course a noble learns from books, while I learn by my own noddle, and a gentleman has a delicate skin; that is all the difference. No—o, lads, it is time there was a new way of living; all these writings ought to be thrown aside! Let every one ask himself 'What am I?' A man! 'And what is he?' Also a man! What then? Does God need his superfluous wealth? No-o, we are equal in the sight of God when it comes to gifts."

At last, in the morning, when the dawn had put out the light of the stars, Osip said to me:

"You see how I could write? I have talked about things that I have never thought about. But you mustn't place too much faith in what I say. I was talking more because I was sleepless than with any serious intention. You lie down and think of something to amuse you. Once there was a raven which flew from the fields to the hills, from boundary to boundary, and lived beyond her time; the Lord punished her. The raven is dead and dried up. What is the meaning of that? There is no meaning in it, none. Now go to sleep; it will soon be time to get up."

CHAPTER XVIII

As Yaakov, the stoker, had done in his time, so now Osip grew and grew in my eyes, until he hid all other people from me. There was some resemblance to the stoker in him, but at the same time he reminded me of grandfather, the valuer, Petr Vassiliev, Smouri, and the cook. When I think of all the people who are firmly fixed in my memory, he has left behind a deeper impression than any of them, an impression which has eaten into it, as oxide eats into a brass bell. What was remarkable about him was that he had two sets of ideas. In the daytime, at his work among people, his lively, simple ideas were businesslike and easier to understand than those to which he gave vent when he was off duty, in the evenings, when he went with me into the town to see his cronies, the dealers, or at night when he could not sleep. He had special night thoughts, many-sided like the flame of a lamp. They burned brightly, but where were their real faces? On which side was this or that idea, nearer and dearer to Osip?

He seemed to me to be much cleverer than any one else I had met, and I hovered about him, as I used to do with the stoker, trying to find out about the man, to understand him. But he glided away from me; it was impossible to grasp him. Where was the real man hidden? How far could I believe in him?

I remember how he said to me:

"You must find out for yourself where I am hidden. Look for me!"

My self-love was piqued, but more than that, it had become a matter of life and death to me to understand the old man.

With all his elusiveness he was substantial. He looked as if he could go on living for a hundred years longer and still remain the same, so unchangeably did he preserve his *ego* amid the instability of the people around him. The valuer had made upon me an equal impression of steadfastness, but it was not so pleasing to me. Osip's steadfastness was of a different kind; although I cannot explain how, it was more pleasing.

The instability of human creatures is too often brought to one's notice; their acrobatic leaps from one position to another upset me. I had long ago grown weary of being surprised by these inexplicable somersaults, and they had by degrees extinguished my lively interest in humanity, disturbed my love for it.

One day at the beginning of July, a rackety hackney cab came dashing up to the place where we were working. On the box-seat a drunken driver sat, hiccuping gloomily. He was bearded, hatless, and had a bruised lip. Grigori Shishlin rolled about in the carriage, drunk, while a fat, red-cheeked girl held his arm. She wore a straw hat trimmed with a red ribbon and glass cherries; she had a sunshade in her hand, and goloshes on her bare feet. Waving her sunshade, swaying, she giggled and screamed:

"What the devil! The market-place is not open; there is no market-place, and he brings me to the market-place. Little mother—"

Grigori, dishevelled and limp, crept out of the cab, sat on the ground and declared to us, the spectators of the scene, with tears:

"I am down on my knees; I have sinned greatly! I thought of sin, and I have sinned. Ephimushka says 'Grisha! Grisha! He speaks truly, but you—forgive me; I can treat you all. He says truly, 'We live once only, and no more.'"

The girl burst out laughing, stamped her feet, and lost her goloshes, and the driver called out gruffly:

"Let us get on farther! The horse won't stand still!"

The horse, an old, worn-out jade, was covered with foam, and stood as still as if it were buried. The whole scene was irresistibly comical.

Grigori's workmen rolled about with laughter as they looked at their master, his grand lady, and the bemused coachman.

The only one who did not laugh was Phoma, who stood at the door of one of the shops beside me and muttered:

"The devil take the swine. And he has a wife at home—a bee-eautiful woman!"

The driver kept on urging them to start. The girl got out of the cab, lifted Grigori up, set him on his feet, and cried with a wave of her sunshade:

"Go on!"

Laughing good-naturedly at their master, and envying him, the men returned to their work at the call of Phoma. It was plain that it was repugnant to him to see Grigori made ridiculous.

"He calls himself master," he muttered. "I have not quite a month's work left to do here. After that I shall go back to the country. I can't stand this."

I felt vexed for Grigori; that girl with the cherries looked so annoyingly absurd beside him.

I often wondered why Grigori Shishlin was the master and Phoma Tuchkov the workman. A strong, fair fellow, with curly hair, an aquiline nose, and gray, clever eyes in his round face, Phoma was not like a peasant. If he had been well-dressed, he might have been the son of a merchant of good family. He was gloomy, taciturn, businesslike. Being well educated, he kept the accounts of the contractor, drew up the estimates, and could set his comrades to work successfully, but he worked unwillingly himself.

"You won't make work last forever," he said calmly. He despised books.

"They can print what they like, but I shall go on thinking as I like," he said. "Books are all nonsense."

But he listened attentively to every one, and if something interested him, he would ask all the details about it, perseveringly, always thinking of it in his own way, measuring it by his own measure.

Once I told Phoma that he ought to be a contractor. He replied indolently:

"If it were a question of turning over thousands, yes. But to worry myself for the sake of making a few copecks, it is not worth while. No, I am just looking about; then I shall go into a monastery in Oranko. I am good-looking, powerful in muscle; I may take the fancy of some merchant's widow! Such things do happen. There was a Sergatzki boy who made his fortune in two years, and married a girl from these parts, from the town. He had to take an icon to her house, and she saw him."

This was an obsession with him; he knew many tales of how taking service in a monastery had led people to an easy life. I did not care for these stories, nor did I like the trend of Phoma's mind, but I felt sure that he would go to a monastery.

When the market was opened, Phoma, to every one's surprise, went as waiter to a tavern. I do not say that his mates were surprised, but they all began to treat him mockingly. On holidays they would all go together to drink tea, saying to one another:

"Let us go and see our Phoma."

And when they arrived at the tavern they would call out:

"Hi, waiter! Curly mop, come here!"

He would come to them and ask, with his head held high:

"What can I get for you?"

"Don't you recognize acquaintances now?"

"I never recognize any one."

He felt that his mates despised him and were making fun of him, and he looked at them with dully expectant eyes. His face might have been made of wood, but it seemed to say:

"Well, make haste; laugh and be done with it."

"Shall we give him a tip?" they would ask, and after purposely fumbling in their purses for a long time, they would give him nothing at all.

I asked Phoma how he could go out as a waiter when he had meant to enter a monastery.

"I never meant to go into a monastery!" he replied, "and I shall not stay long as a waiter."

Four years later I met him in Tzaritzin, still a waiter in a tavern; and later still I read in a newspaper that Phoma Tuchkov had been arrested for an attempted burglary.

The history of the mason, Ardalon, moved me deeply. He was the eldest and best workman in Petr's gang. This black-bearded, light-hearted man of forty years also involuntarily evoked the query, "Why was he not the master instead of Petr?" He seldom drank vodka and hardly ever drank too much; he knew his work thoroughly, and worked as if he loved it; the bricks seemed to fly from his hands like red doves. In comparison with him, the sickly, lean Petr seemed an absolutely superfluous member of the gang. He used to speak thus of his work:

"I build stone houses for people, and a wooden coffin for myself."

But Ardalon laid his bricks with cheerful energy as he cried: "Work, my child, for the glory of God."

And he told us all that next spring he would go to Tomsk, where his brother-in-law had undertaken a large contract to build a church, and had invited him to go as overseer.

"I have made up my mind to go. Building churches is work that I love!" he said. And he suggested to me: "Come with me! It is very easy, brother, for an educated person to get on in Siberia. There, education is a trump card!"

I agreed to his proposition, and he cried triumphantly:

"There! That is business and not a joke."

Toward Petr and Grigori he behaved with good-natured derision, like a grown-up person towards children, and he said to Osip:

"Braggarts! Each shows the other his cleverness, as if they were playing at cards. One says: 'My cards are all such and such a color,' and the other says, 'And mine are trumps!'"

Osip observed hesitatingly:

"How could it be otherwise? Boasting is only human; all the girls walk about with their chests stuck out."

"All, yes, all. It is God, God all the time. But they hoard up money themselves!" said Ardalon impatiently.

"Well, Grisha does n't."

"I am speaking for myself. I would go with this God into the forest, the desert. I am weary of being here. In the spring I shall go to Siberia."

The workmen, envious of Ardalon, said:

"If we had such a chance in the shape of a brother-in-law, we should not be afraid of Siberia either."

And suddenly Ardalon disappeared. He went away from the workshop on Sunday, and for three days no one knew where he was.

This made anxious conjectures.

"Perhaps he has been murdered."

"Or maybe he is drowned."

But Ephimushka came, and declared in an embarrassed manner:

"He has gone on the drink."

"Why do you tell such lies?" cried Petr incredulously.

"He has gone on the drink; he is drinking madly. He is just like a corn kiln which burns from the very center. Perhaps his much-loved wife is dead."

"He is a widower! Where is he?"

Petr angrily set out to save Ardalon, but the latter fought him.

Then Osip, pressing his lips together firmly, thrust his hands in his pockets and said:

"Shall I go have a look at him, and see what it is all about? He is a good fellow."

I attached myself to him.

"Here's a man," said Osip on the way, "who lives for years quite decently, when suddenly he loses control of himself, and is all over the place. Look, Maximich, and learn."

We went to one of the cheap "houses of pleasure" of Kunavin Village, and we were welcomed by a predatory old woman. Osip whispered to her, and she ushered us into a small empty room, dark and dirty, like a stable. On a small bed slept, in an abandoned attitude, a large, stout woman. The old woman thrust her fist in her side and said:

"Wake up, frog, wake up!"

The woman jumped up in terror, rubbing her face with her hands, and asked:

"Good Lord! who is it? What is it?"

"Detectives are here," said Osip harshly. With a groan the woman disappeared, and he spat after her and explained to me:

"They are more afraid of detectives than of the devil."

Taking a small glass from the wall, the old woman raised a piece of the wall-paper.

"Look! Is he the one you want?"

Osip looked through a chink in the partition. "That is he! Get the woman away."

I also looked through the chink into just such a narrow stable as the one we were in. On the sill of the window, which was closely shuttered, burned a tin lamp, near which stood a squinting, naked, Tatar woman, sewing a chemise. Behind her, on two pillows on the bed, was raised the bloated face of Ardalon, his black, tangled beard projecting.

The Tatar woman shivered, put on her chemise, and came past the bed, suddenly appearing in our room.

Osip looked at her and again spat.

"Ugh! Shameless hussy!"

"And you are an old fool!" she replied, laughing, Osip laughed too, and shook a threatening finger at her.

We went into the Tatar's stable. The old man sat on the bed at Ardalon's feet and tried for a long time unsuccessfully to awaken him. He muttered:

"All right, wait a bit. We will go—"

At length he awoke, gazed wildly at Osip and at me, and closing his bloodshot eyes, murmured:

"Well, well!"

"What is the matter with you?" asked Osip gently, without reproaches, but rather sadly.

"I was driven to it," explained Ardalon hoarsely, and coughing.

"How?"

"Ah, there were reasons."

"You were not contented, perhaps?"

"What is the good—"

Ardalon took an open bottle of vodka from the table, and began to drink from it. He then asked Osip:

"Would you like some? There ought to be something to eat here as well."

The old man poured some of the spirit into his mouth, swallowed it, frowned, and began to chew a small piece of bread carefully, but muddled Ardalon said drowsily:

"So I have thrown in my lot with the Tatar woman. She is a pure Tatar, as Ephimushka says, young, an orphan from Kasimov; she was getting ready for the fair."

From the other side of the wall some one said in broken Russian:

"Tatars are the best, like young hens. Send him away; he is not your father."

"That's she," muttered Ardalon, gazing stupidly at the wall.

"I have seen her," said Osip.

Ardalon turned to me:

"That is the sort of man I am, brother."

I expected Osip to reproach Ardalon, to give him a lecture which would make him repent bitterly. But nothing of the kind happened; they sat side by side, shoulder to shoulder, and uttered calm, brief words. It was melancholy to see them in that dark, dirty stable. The woman called ludicrous words through the chink in the wall, but they did not listen to them. Osip took a walnut off the table, cracked it against his boot, and began to remove the shell neatly, as he asked:

"All your money gone?"

"There is some with Petrucha."

"I say! Aren't you going away? If you were to go to Tomsk, now—"

"What should I go to Tomsk for?"

"Have you changed your mind, then?"

"If I had been going to strangers, it would have been different."

"What do you mean?"

"But to go to my sister and my brother-in-law—"

"What of it?"

"It is not particularly pleasant to begin again with one's own people."

"The beginning is the same anywhere."

"All the same—"

They talked in such an amicably serious vein that the Tatar woman left off teasing them, and coming into the room, took her frock down from the wall in silence, and disappeared.

"She is young," said Osip.

Ardalon glanced at him and without annoyance replied:

"Ephimushka is wrong-headed. He knows nothing, except about women. But the Tatar woman is joyous; she maddens us all."

"Take care; you won't be able to escape from her," Osip warned him, and having eaten the walnut, took his leave.

On the way back I asked Osip:

"Why did you go to him?"

"Just to look at him. He is a man I have known a long time. I have seen ma-a-ny such cases. A man leads a decent life, and suddenly he behaves as if he had just escaped from prison." He repeated what he had said before, "One should be on one's guard against vodka."

But after a minute he added:

"But life would be dull without it."

"Without vodka?"

"Well, yes! When you drink, it is just as if you were in another world."

Ardalon never came back for good. At the end of a few days he returned to work, but soon disappeared again, and in the spring I met him among the dock laborers; he was melting the ice round the barges in the harbor. We greeted each other in friendly fashion and went to a tavern for tea, after which he boasted:

"You remember what a workman I was, eh? I tell you straight, I was an expert at my own business! I could have earned hundreds."

"However, you did not."

"No, I didn't earn them," he cried proudly. "I spit upon work!"

He swaggered. The people in the tavern listened to his impassioned words and were impressed.

"You remember what that sly thief Petrucha used to say about work? For others stone houses; for himself a wooden coffin! Well, that's true of all work!"

I said:

"Petrucha is ill. He is afraid of death."

But Ardalon cried:

"I am ill, too; my heart is out of order."

On holidays I often wandered out of the town to "Millioni Street," where the dockers lived, and saw how quickly Ardalon had settled down among those uncouth ruffians. Only a year ago, happy and serious-minded, Ardalon had now become as noisy as any of them. He had acquired their curious, shambling walk, looked at people defiantly, as if he were inviting every one to fight with him, and was always boasting:

"You see how I am received; I am like a chieftain here!"

Never grudging the money he had earned, he liberally treated the dockers, and in fights he always took the part of the weakest. He often cried:

"That's not fair, children! You've got to fight fair!"

And so they called him "Fairplay," which delighted him.

I ardently studied these people, closely packed in that old and dirty sack of a street. All of them were people who had cut themselves off from ordinary life, but they seemed to have created a life of their own, independent of any master, and gay. Careless, audacious, they reminded me of grandfather's stories about the bargemen who so easily transformed themselves into brigands or hermits. When there was no work, they were not squeamish about committing small thefts from the barges and steamers, but that did not trouble me, for I saw that life was sewn with theft, like an old coat with gray threads. At the same time I saw that these people never worked with enthusiasm, unsparing of their energies, as happened in cases of urgency, such as fires, or the breaking of the ice. And, as a rule, they lived more of a holiday life than any other people.

But Osip, having noticed my friendship with Ardalon, warned me in a fatherly way:

"Look here, my boy; why this close friendship with the folk of Millioni Street? Take care you don't do yourself harm by it."

I told him as well as I could how I liked these people who lived so gaily, without working.

"Birds of the air they are!" he interrupted me, laughing. "That's what they are—idle, useless people; and work is a calamity to them!"

"What is work, after all? As they say, the labors of the righteous don't procure them stone houses to live in!"

I said this glibly enough. I had heard the proverb so often, and felt the truth of it.

But Osip was very angry with me, and cried:

"Who says so? Fools, idlers! And you are a youngster; you ought not to listen to such things! Oh, you—! That is the nonsense which is uttered by the envious, the unsuccessful. Wait till your feathers are grown; then you can fly! And I shall tell your master about this friendship of yours."

And he did tell. The master spoke to me about the matter.

"You leave the Millioni folk alone, Pyeshkov! They are thieves and prostitutes, and from there the path leads to the prison and the hospital. Let them alone!"

I began to conceal my visits to Millioni Street, but I soon had to give them up. One day I was sitting with Ardalon and his comrade, Robenok, on the roof of a shed in the yard of one of the lodging-houses. Robenok was relating to us amusingly how he had made his way on foot from Rostov, on the Don, to Moscow. He had been a soldier-sapper, a Geogrivsky horseman, and he was lame. In the war with Turkey he had been wounded in the knee. Of low stature, he had a terrible strength in his arms, a strength which was of no profit to him, for his lameness prevented him from working. He had had an illness which had caused the hair to fall from his head and face; his head was like that of a new-born infant.

With his brown eyes sparkling he said:

"Well, at Serpoukhov I saw a priest sitting in a sledge. 'Father,' I said, 'give something to a Turkish hero.'"

Ardalon shook his head and said:

"That's a lie!"

"Why should I lie?" asked Robenok, not in the least offended, and my friend growled in lazy reproof:

"You are incorrigible! You have the chance of becoming a watchman—they always put lame men to that job—and you stroll about aimlessly, and tell lies."

"Well, I only do it to make people laugh. I lie just for the sake of amusement."

"You ought to laugh at yourself."

In the yard, which was dark and dirty although the weather was dry and sunny, a woman appeared and cried, waving some sort of a rag about her head:

"Who will buy a petticoat? Hi, friends!"

Women crept out from the hidden places of the house and gathered closely round the seller. I recognized her at once; it was the laundress, Natalia. I jumped down from the roof, but she, having given the petticoat to the first bidder, had already quietly left the yard.

"How do you do?" I greeted her joyfully as I caught her at the gate.

"What next, I wonder?" she exclaimed, glancing at me askance, and then she suddenly stood still, crying angrily: "God save us! What are you doing here?"

Her terrified exclamation touched and confused me. I realized that she was afraid for me; terror and amazement were shown so plainly in her intelligent face. I soon explained to her that I was not living in that street, but only went there sometimes to see what there was to see.

"See?" she cried angrily and derisively. "What sort of a place is this that you should want to see it? It's the women you're after."

Her face was wrinkled, dark shadows lay under her eyes, and her lips drooped feebly.

Standing at the door of a tavern she said:

"Come in; I am going to have some tea! You are well-dressed, not like they dress here, yet I cannot believe what you say."

But in the tavern she seemed to believe me, and as she poured out tea, she began to tell me how she had only awakened from sleep an hour ago, and had not had anything to eat or drink yet.

"And when I went to bed last night I was as drunk as drunk. I can't even remember where I had the drink, or with whom."

I felt sorry for her, awkward in her presence, and I wanted to ask her where her daughter was. After she had drunk some vodka and hot tea, she began to talk in a familiar, lively way, coarsely, like all the women of that street, but when I asked about her daughter she was sobered at once, and cried:

"What do you want to know for? No, my boy, you won't get hold of her; don't think it!"

She drank more, and then she said:

"I have nothing to do with my daughter. What am I? A laundress! What sort of a mother for her? She is well brought up, educated. That she is, my brother! She left me to live with a rich friend, as a teacher, like—"

After a silence she said:

"That's how it is! The laundress does n't please you, but the street-walker does?"

That she was a street-walker I had seen at once, of course. There was no other kind of woman in that street. But when she told me so herself, my eyes filled with tears of shame and pity for her. I felt as if she had burned me by making that admission,—she, who not long ago had been so brave, independent, and clever.

"Ekh! you!" she said, looking at me and sighing. "Go away from this place, I beg you! I urge you, don't come here, or you will be lost!"

Then she began to speak softly and brokenly, as if she were talking to herself, bending over the table and drawing figures on the tray with her fingers.

"But what are my entreaties and my advice to you? When my own daughter would not listen to me I cried to her: 'You can't throw aside your own mother. What are you thinking of?' And she—she said, 'I shall strangle myself!' And she went away to Kazan; she wants to learn to be a midwife. Good—good! But what about me? You see what I am now? What have I to cling to? And so I went on the streets."

She fell Into a silence, and thought for a long time, soundlessly moving her lips. It was plain that she had forgotten me. The corners of her lips drooped; her mouth was curved like a sickle, and it was a torturing sight to see how her lips quivered, and how the wavering furrows on her face spoke without words. Her face was like that of an aggrieved child. Strands of hair had fallen from under her headkerchief, and lay on her cheek, or coiled behind her small ear. Her tears dropped into her cup of cold tea, and seeing this, she pushed the cup away and shut her eyes tightly, squeezing out two more tears. Then she wiped her face with her handkerchief. I could not bear to stay with her any longer. I rose quietly.

"Good-by!"

"Eh? Go—go to the devil!" She waved me away without looking at me; she had apparently forgotten who was with her.

I returned to Ardalon in the yard. He had meant to come with me to catch crabs, and I wanted to tell him about the woman. But neither he nor Robenok were on the roof of the shed; and while I was looking for him in the disorderly yard, there arose from the street the sound of one of those rows which were frequent there.

I went out through the gate and came into collision with Natalia, sobbing, wiping her bruised face with her headkerchief. Setting straight her disordered hair with her other hand, she went blindly along the footpath, and following her came Ardalon and Robenok. The latter was saying:

"Give her one more; come on!"

Ardalon overtook the woman, flourishing his fist. She turned her bosom full toward him; her face was terrible; her eyes blazed with hatred.

"Go on, hit me!" she cried.

I hung on to Ardalon's arm; he looked at me in amazement.

"What's the matter with you?"

"Don't touch her!" I just managed to say.

He burst out laughing.

"She is your lover? Aie, that Natashka, she has devoured our little monk."

Robenok laughed, too, holding his sides, and for a long time they roasted me with their hot obscenity. It was unbearable! But while they were thus occupied, Natalia went away, and I, losing my temper at last, struck Robenok in the chest with my head, knocking him over, and ran away.

For a long time after that I did not go near Millioni Street. But I saw Ardalon once again; I met him on the ferry-boat.

"Where have you been hiding yourself?" he asked joyfully.

When I told him that it was repulsive to me to remember how he had knocked Natalia about and obscenely insulted me, Ardalon laughed good-naturedly.

"Did you take that seriously? We only rubbed it into you for a joke! As for her, why shouldn't she be knocked about, a street-walker? People beat their wives, so they are certainly not going to have more mercy on such as that! Still, it was only a joke, the whole thing. I understand, you know, that the fist is no good for teaching!"

"What have you got to teach her? How are you better than she is?"

He put his hands on my shoulders and, shaking me, said banteringly:

"In our disgraceful state no one of us is better than another."

Then he laughed and added boastfully:

"I understand everything from within and without, brother, everything! I am not wood!"

He was a little tipsy, at the jovial stage; he looked at me with the tender pity of a good master for an unintelligent pupil.

Sometimes I met Pavl Odintzov. He was livelier than ever, dressed like a dandy, and talked to me condescendingly and always reproachfully.

"You are throwing yourself away on that kind of work! They are nothing but peasants."

Then he would sadly retail all the latest news from the workshop.

"Jikharev is still taken up with that cow. Sitanov is plainly fretting; he has begun to drink to excess. The wolves have eaten Golovev; he was coming home from Sviatka; he was drunk, and the wolves devoured him." And bursting into a gay peal of laughter he comically added:

"They ate him and they all became drunk themselves! They were very merry and walked about the forests on their hind legs, like performing dogs. Then they fell to fighting and in twenty-fours hours they were all dead!"

I listened to him and laughed, too, but I felt that the workshop and all I had experienced in it was very far away from me now.

This was rather a melancholy reflection.

CHAPTER XIX

There was hardly any work in the market-square during the winter, and instead I had innumerable trivial duties to perform in the house. They swallowed up the whole day, but the evenings were left free. Once more I read to the household novels which were unpalatable to me, from the "Neva" and the "Moscow Gazette"; but at night I occupied myself by reading good books and by attempts at writing poetry.

One day when the women had gone out to vespers and my master was kept at home through indisposition, he asked me:

"Victor is making fun of you because he says you write poetry, Pyeshkov. Is that true? Well then, read it to me!"

It would have been awkward to refuse, and I read several of my poetical compositions. These evidently did not please him, but he said:

"Stick to it! Stick to it! You may become a Pushkin; have you read Pushkin?"

"'Do the goblins have funeral rites?
Are the witches given in marriage?'"

In his time people still believed in goblins, but he did not believe in them himself. Of course he was just joking.

"Ye-es, brother," he drawled thoughtfully, "you ought to have been taught, but now it is too late. The devil knows what will become of you! I should hide that note-book of yours more carefully, for if the women get hold of it, they will laugh at you. Women, brother, love to touch one on a weak spot."

For some time past my master had been quiet and thoughtful; he had a trick of looking about him cautiously, and the sound of the bell startled him. Sometimes he would give way to a painful irritability about trifles, would scold us all, and rush out of the house, returning drunk late at night. One felt that something had come into his life which was known only to himself, which had lacerated his heart; and that he was living not sensibly, or willingly, but simply by force of habit.

On Sundays from dinner-time till nine o'clock I was free to go out and about, and the evenings I spent at a tavern in Yamski Street. The host, a stout and always perspiring man, was passionately fond of singing, and the chorister's of most of the churches knew this, and used to frequent his house. He treated them with vodka, beer, or tea, for their songs. The choristers were a drunken and uninteresting set of people; they sang unwillingly, only for the sake of the hospitality, and almost always it was church music. As certain of the pious drunkards did not consider that the tavern was the place for them, the host used to invite them to his private room, and I could only hear the singing through the door. But frequently peasants from the villages, and artisans came. The tavern-keeper himself used to go about the town inquiring for singers, asking the peasants who came in on market-days, and inviting them to his house.

The singer was always given a chair close to the bar, his back to a cask of vodka; his head was outlined against the bottom of the cask as if it were in a round frame.

The best singer of all—and they were always particularly good singers—was the small, lean harness-maker, Kleshtchkov, who looked as if he had been squeezed, and had tufts of red hair on his head. His little nose gleamed like that of a corpse; his benign, dreamy eyes were immovable.

Sometimes he closed his eyes, leaned the back of his head against the bottom of the cask, protruding his chest, and in his soft but all-conquering tenor voice sang the quick moving:

> "Ekh! how the fog has fallen upon the clean fields already!
> And has hidden the distant roads!"

Here he would stop, and resting his back against the bar, bending backwards, went on, with his face raised toward the ceiling:

> "Ekh! where—where am I going?
> Where shall I find the broad ro-oad?"

His voice was small like himself, but it was unwearied; he permeated the dark, dull room of the tavern with silvery chords, melancholy words. His groans and cries conquered every one; even the drunken ones became amazedly surprised, gazing down in silence at the tables in front of them. As for me, my heart was torn, and overflowed with those mighty feelings which good music always arouses as it miraculously touches the very depths of the soul.

It was as quiet in the tavern as in a church, and the singer seemed like a good priest, who did not preach, but with all his soul, and honestly, prayed for the whole human family, thinking aloud, as it were, of all the grievous calamities which beset human life. Bearded men gazed upon him; childlike eyes blinked in fierce, wild faces; at moments some one sighed, and this seemed to emphasize the triumphant power of the music. At such times it always seemed to me that the lives led by most people were unreal and meaningless, and that the reality of life lay here.

In the corner sat the fat-faced old-clothes dealer, Luissukha, a repulsive female, a shameless, loose woman. She hid her head on her fat shoulder and wept, furtively wiping the tears from her bold eyes. Not far from her sat the gloomy chorister, Mitropolski, a hirsute young fellow who looked like a degraded deacon, with great eyes set in his drunken face. He gazed into the glass of vodka placed before him, took it up, and raised it to his mouth, and then set it down again on the table, carefully and noiselessly. For some reason he could not drink.

And all the people in the tavern seemed to be glued to their places, as if they were listening to something long forgotten, but once dear and near to them.

When Kleshtchkov, having finished his song, modestly sank down in the chair, the tavern-keeper, giving him a glass of wine, would say with a smile of satisfaction:

"Well, that was very good, sure! Although you can hardly be said to sing, so much as to recite! However, you are a master of it, whatever they say! No one could say otherwise."

Kleshtchkov, drinking his vodka without haste, coughed carefully and said quietly:

"Any one can sing if he has a voice, but to show what kind of soul the song contains is only given to me."

"Well, you need n't boast, anyhow."

"He who has nothing to boast about, does not boast," said the singer as quietly but more firmly than before.

"You are conceited, Kleshtchkov!" exclaimed the host, annoyed.

"One can't be more conceited than one's conscience allows."

And from the corner the gloomy Mitropolski roared:

"What do you know about the singing of this fallen angel, you worms, you dirt!"

He always opposed every one, argued with every one, brought accusations against every one; and almost every Sunday he was cruelly punished for this by one of the singers, or whoever else had a mind for the business.

The tavern-keeper loved Kleshtchkov's singing, but he could not endure the singer. He used to complain about him, and obviously sought occasions to humiliate him and to make him ridiculous. This fact was known to the frequenters of the tavern and to Kleshtchkov himself.

"He is a good singer, but he is proud; he wants taking down," he said, and several guests agreed with him.

"That's true; he's a conceited fellow!"

"What's he got to be conceited about? His voice? That comes from God; he has nothing to do with it! And he hasn't a very powerful voice, has he?" the tavern-keeper persisted.

His audience agreed with him.

"True, it is not so much his voice as his intelligence."

One day after the singer had refreshed himself and gone away, the tavern-keeper tried to persuade Luissukha.

"Why don't you amuse yourself with Kleshtchkov for a bit, Marie Evdokimova; you'd shake him up, wouldn't you? What would you want for it?"

"If I were younger," she said with a laugh.

The tavern-keeper cried loudly and warmly:

"What can the young ones do? But you—you will get hold of him! We shall see him dancing round you! When he is bowed down by grief he will be able to sing, won't he? Take him in hand, Evdokimova, and do me a favor, will you?"

But she would not do it. Large and fat, she lowered her eyes and played with the fringe of the handkerchief which covered her bosom, as she said in a monotonous, lazy drawl:

"It's a young person that is needed here. If I were younger, well, I would not think twice about it."

Almost every night the tavern-keeper tried to make Kleshtchkov drunk, but the latter, after two or three songs and a glassful after each, would carefully wrap up his throat with a knitted scarf, draw his cap well over his tufted head, and depart.

The tavern-keeper often tried to find a rival for Kleshtchkov. The harness-maker would sing a song and then the host, after praising him, would say:

"Here is another singer. Come along now, show what you can do!"

Sometimes the singer had a good voice, but I do not remember an occasion on which any of Kleshtchkov's rivals sang so simply and soulfully as that little conceited harness-maker.

"M—yes," said the tavern-keeper, not without regret, "it's good, certainly! The chief thing is that it is a voice, but there's no soul in it."

The guests teased him:

"No, you can't better the harness-maker, you see!"

And Kleshtchkov, looking at them all from under his red, tufted eyebrows, said to the tavern-keeper calmly and politely:

"You waste your time. You will never find a singer with my gifts to set up in opposition to me; my gift is from God."

"We are all from God!"

"You may ruin yourself by the drink you give, but you'll never find one."

The tavern-keeper turned purple and muttered: "How do we know? How do we know?"

But Kleshtchkov pointed out to him firmly:

"Again I tell you this is singing, not a cock-fight."

"I know that! Why do you keep harping on it?"

"I am not harping on it; I am simply pointing out something to you. If a song is nothing but a diversion, it comes from the devil!"

"All right! You'd better sing again."

"I can always sing, even in my sleep," agreed Kleshtchkov, and carefully clearing his throat he began to sing.

And all nonsense, trashy talk, and ambitions vanished into smoke as by a miracle; the refreshing streams of a different life, reflective, pure, full of love and sadness, flowed over us all.

I envied that man, envied intensely his talent and his power over people. The way he took advantage of this power was so wonderful! I wanted to make the acquaintance of the harness-maker, to hold a long conversation with him, but I could not summon up courage to go to him.

Kleshtchkov had such a strange way of looking at everybody with his pale eyes, as if he could not see any one in front of him. But there was something about him which offended me and prevented me from liking him; and I wanted to like him for himself, not only when he was singing. It was unpleasant to see him pull his cap over his head, like an old man, and swathe his neck, just for show, in that red, knitted scarf of which he said:

"My little one knitted this; my only little girl."

When he was not singing he pouted importantly, rubbed his dead, frozen nose with his fingers, and answered questions in monosyllables, and unwillingly. When I approached him and asked him something, he looked at me and said:

"Go away, lad!"

I much preferred the chorister, Mitropolski. When he appeared in the tavern, he would walk into his corner with the gait of a man carrying a heavy load, move a chair away with the toe of his boot, and sit down with his elbows on the table, resting his large shaggy head on his hands. After he had drunk two or three glasses in silence, he would utter a resounding cry. Every one would start and look towards him, but with his chin in his hands he gazed at them defiantly, his mane of unbrushed hair wildly surrounding his puffy, sallow face.

"What are you looking at? What do you see?" he would ask with sudden passion.

Sometimes they replied:

"We are looking at a werwolf."

There were evenings on which he drank in silence, and in silence departed, heavily dragging his feet. Several times I heard him denounce people, playing the prophet:

"I am the incorruptible servant of my God, and I denounce you. Behold Isaiah! Woe to the town of Ariel. Come, ye wicked, and ye rogues, and all kinds of dark monstrosities living in the mire of your own base desires! Woe to the ships of this world, for they carry lewd people on their sinful way. I know you, drunkards, gluttons, dregs of this world; there is no time appointed for you. Accursed ones, the very earth refuses to receive you into her womb!"

His voice resounded so that the window-panes shook, which delighted his audience. They praised the prophet:

"He barks finely, the shaggy cur!"

It was easy to become acquainted with him; it cost no more than to offer him hospitality; he required a decanter of vodka and a portion of ox liver. When I asked him to tell me what kind of books one ought to read, he answered me with stubborn ferocity by another question:

"Why read at all?"

But mollified by my confusion, he added in ringing tones:

"Have you read Ecclesiastes?"

"Yes."

"Read Ecclesiastes. You need nothing more. There is all the wisdom of the world, only there are sheep who do not understand it; that is to say, no one understands it. Can you sing at all?"

"No."

"Why? You ought to sing. It is *the* most ridiculous way of passing time."

Some one asked him from an adjacent table:

"But you sing yourself?"

"Yes; but I am a vagrant. Well?"

"Nothing."

"That is nothing new. Every one knows that there is nothing in that blockhead of yours, and there never will be anything. Amen!"

In this tone he was in the habit of speaking to me and to every one else, although after the second or third time of my treating him, he began to be more gentle with me. One day he actually said with a shade of surprise:

"I look at you and I cannot make out what you are, who are you, or why you are! But whatever you are, may the devil take you!"

He behaved in an incomprehensible manner to Kleshtchkov. He listened to him with manifest enjoyment sometimes even with a benign smile, but he would not make closer acquaintance with him, and spoke about him coarsely and contemptuously.

"That barber's block! He knows how to breathe, he understands what to sing about, but for the rest, he is an ass."

"Why?"

"Like all his kind."

I should have liked to talk with him when he was sober, but when sober he only bellowed, and looked upon all the world with misty, dull eyes. I learned from some one that this permanently inebriated man had studied in the Kazan Academy, and might have become a prelate. I did not believe this. But one day when I was telling him about myself, I recalled the name of the bishop, Chrisanph. He tossed his head and said:

"Chrisanph? I know him. He was my tutor and benefactor. At Kazan, in the academy, I remember! Chrisanph means 'golden flower.' Yes, that was a true saying of Pavm Beruind. Yes, he was a flower of gold, Chrisanph!"

"And who is Pavm Beruind?" I added, but Mitropolski replied shortly:

"That is none of your business."

When I reached home I wrote in my note-book, "I must read the works of Pavm Beruind." I felt, somehow, that I should find therein the answers to many questions which perplexed me.

The singer was very fond of using names which were unknown to me, and curiously coined words. This irritated me greatly.

"Life is not *aniso*," he said.

"What is *aniso?*" I asked.

"Something advantageous to you," he answered, and my perplexity amused him.

These little sayings, and the fact that he had studied in the academy, led me to think that he knew a great deal, and I was offended with him for not speaking of his knowledge, or if he did allude to it, being so unintelligible. Or was it that I had no right to ask him? However, he left an impression on my mind. I liked the drunken boldness of his denunciations, which were modelled on those of the prophet Isaias.

"Oh, unclean and vile ones of earth!" he roared, "the worst among you are famous, and the best are persecuted. The day of judgment draws nigh. You will repent then, but it will be too late, too late!"

As I listened to his roar, I remembered "Good Business," the laundress Natalia, ruined so hideously and easily, Queen Margot, wrapped in a cloud of dirty scandal. I already had some memories!

My brief acquaintance with this man finished curiously.

I met him in the spring, in the fields near the camp. He was walking like a camel, moving his head from side to side, solitary, bloated-looking.

"Going for a walk?" he asked hoarsely. "Let us go together. I also am taking a walk. I am ill, Brother; yes."

We walked some yards without speaking, when suddenly we saw a man in a pit which had been made under a tent. He was sitting in the bottom of the pit, leaning on one side, his shoulder resting against the side of the trench. His coat was drawn up on one side above his ear, as if he had been trying to take it off and had not succeeded.

"Drunk," decided the singer, coming to a standstill.

But on the young grass under the man's arm lay a large revolver, not far from him lay a cap, and beside it stood a bottle of vodka, hardly begun. Its empty neck was buried in the long grass. The face of the man was hidden by his overcoat, as if he were ashamed.

For a moment we stood in silence. Then Mitropolski, planting his feet wide apart, said:

"He has shot himself."

Then I understood that the man was not drunk, but dead, but it came upon me so suddenly that I could not believe it. I remember that I felt neither fear nor pity as I looked at that large, smooth skull, visible above the overcoat, and on that livid ear. I could not believe that a man would kill himself on such a pleasant spring day.

The singer rubbed his unshaven cheeks with his hand, as if he were cold, and said hoarsely:

"He is an oldish man. Perhaps his wife has left him, or he has made off with money not belonging to him."

He sent me into the town to fetch the police, and himself sat down on the edge of the pit, letting his feet hang over, wrapping his worn overcoat closely round him. Having informed the police of the suicide, I ran back quickly, but in the meantime the chorister had drunk the dead man's vodka, and came to meet me, waving the empty bottle.

"This is what ruined him," he cried, and furiously dashing the bottle to the ground, smashed it to atoms.

The town constable had followed me. He looked into the pit, took off his hat, and crossing himself indecisively, asked the singer:

"Who may you be?"

"That is not your business."

The policeman reflected, and then asked more politely:

"What account do you give of yourself, then? Here is a dead man, and here are you, drunk!"

"I have been drunk for twenty years!" said the singer proudly, striking his chest with the palm of his hand.

I felt sure that they would arrest him for drinking the vodka. People came rushing from the town; a severe-looking police inspector cartie in a cab, descended into the pit, and, lifting aside the overcoat of the suicide, looked into his face.

"Who saw him first?"

"I," said Mitropolski.

The inspector looked at him and drawled ominously:

"A-ah! Congratulations, my lord!"

Sightseers began to gather round; there were a dozen or so of people. Panting, excited, they surrounded the pit and looked down into it, and one of them cried:

"It is a *chinovnik* who lives in our street; I know him!"

The singer, swaying, with his cap off, stood before the inspector, and argued with him inarticulately, shouting something indistinctly. Then the inspector struck him in the chest. He reeled and sat down, and the policeman without haste took some string from his pocket and bound the hands of the singer. He folded them meekly behind his back, as if he were used to this procedure. Then the inspector began to shout angrily to the crowd:

"Be off, now!"

After this there came another, older policeman, with moist, red eyes, his mouth hanging open from weariness, and he took hold of the end of the cord with which the singer was bound, and gently led him into the town. I also went away dejected from the field. Through my memory, like a dull echo, rang the avenging words:

"Woe to the town Ariel!"

And before my eyes rose that depressing spectacle of the policeman slowly drawing the string from the pocket of his ulster, and the awe-inspiring prophet meekly folding his red, hairy hands behind his back, and crossing his wrists as if he were used to it.

I soon heard that the prophet had been sent out of the town. And after him, Kleshtchkov disappeared; he had married well, and had gone to live in a district where a harness-maker's workshop had been opened.

I had praised his singing so warmly to my master that he said one day:

"I must go and hear him!"

And so one night he sat at a little table opposite to me, raising his brows in astonishment, his eyes wide open.

On the way to the tavern he had made fun of me, and during the first part of the time he was in the tavern, he was railing at me, at the people there, and at the stuffy smell of the place. When the harness-maker began to sing he smiled derisively, and began to pour himself a glass of beer, but he stopped half-way, saying:

"Who the devil—?"

His hand trembled; he set the bottle down gently, and began to listen with intentness.

"Ye-es, Brother," he said with a sigh, when Kleshtchkov had finished singing, "he can sing! The devil take him! He has even made the air hot."

The harness-maker sang again, with his head back, gazing up at the ceiling:

> "On the road from the flourishing village
> A young girl came over the dewy fields."

"He can sing," muttered my master, shaking his head and smiling.

And Kleshtchkov poured forth his song, clear as the music of a reed:

> "And the beautiful maiden answered him:
> 'An orphan am I, no one wants me.'"

"Good!" whispered my master, blinking his reddening eyes. "Phew! it is devilish good!"

I looked at him and rejoiced, and the sobbing words of the song conquered the noise of the tavern, sounded more powerful, more beautiful, more touching every moment.

> I live solitary in our village.
> A young girl am I; they never ask me out.
> Oie, poor am I, my dress it is not fine;
> I am not fit, I know, for a brave young man.
> A widower would marry me to do his work;
> I do not wish to bow myself to such a fate.

My master wept undisguisedly; he sat with his head bent; his prominent nose twitched, and tears splashed on his knees. After the third song, agitated and dishevelled, he said:

"I can't sit here any longer; I shall be stifled with these odors. Let us go home."

But when we were in the street he said:

"Come along, Pyeshkov, let us go to a restaurant and have something to eat. I don't want to go home!"

He hailed a sledge, without haggling about the charge, and said nothing while we were on the way, but in the restaurant, after taking a table in a corner, he began at once in an undertone, looking about him the while, to complain angrily.

"He has thoroughly upset me, that goat; to such a state of melancholy he has driven me! Here you are—you read and think about things—just tell me now, what the devil is the use of it all? One lives; forty years pass by; one has a wife and children, and no one to talk to! There are times when I want to unburden my soul, to talk to some one about all sorts of things, but there is no one I can talk to. I can't talk to my wife; I have nothing in common with her. What is she, after all? She has her children and the house; that's her business. She is a stranger to my soul. A wife is your friend till the first child comes. In fact, she is—on the whole—Well, you can see for yourself she does not dance to my piping. Flesh without spirit, the devil take you! It is a grief to me, Brother."

He drank the cold, bitter beer feverishly, was silent for a time, ruffling his long hair, and then he went on:

"Human creatures are riff-raff for the most part, Brother! There you are, for instance, talking to the workmen. Oh yes, I understand there is a lot of trickery, and baseness; it is true, Brother; they are thieves all of them! But do you think that what you say makes any difference to them! Not an atom! No! They are all—Petr, Osip as well—rogues! They speak about me, and you speak for me, and all—what is the use of it, Brother?"

I was dumb from sheer amazement.

"That's it!" said my master, smiling. "You were right to think of going to Persia. There you would understand nothing; it is a foreign language they speak there! But in your own language you 'll hear nothing but baseness!"

"Has Osip been telling you about me?" I asked.

"Well, yes! But what did you expect? He talks more than any of them; he is a gossip. He is a sly creature, Brother! No, Pyeshkov, words don't touch them. Am I not right? And what the devil is the use of it? And what the devil difference does it make? None! It is like snow in the autumn, falling in the mud and melting. It only makes more mud. You had far better hold your tongue."

He drank glass after glass of beer. He did not get drunk, but he talked more and more quickly and fiercely.

"The proverb says, 'Speech is silver, silence is golden.' Ekh, Brother, it is all sorrow, sorrow! He sang truly, 'Solitary I live in our village.' Human life is all loneliness."

He glanced round, lowered his voice, and continued:

"And I had found a friend after my own heart. There was a woman who happened to be alone, as good as a widow; her husband had been condemned to Siberia for coining money, and was in prison there. I became acquainted with her; she was penniless; it was that, you know, which led to our acquaintance. I looked at her and thought, 'What a nice little person!' Pretty, you know, young, simply wonderful. I saw her once or twice, and then I said to her: 'Your husband is a rogue. You are not living honestly yourself. Why do you want to go to Siberia after him?' But she would follow him into exile. She said to me: 'Whatever he is, I love him; he is good to me! It may be that it was for me he sinned. I have sinned with you. For' his sake,' she said, 'I had to have money; he is a gentleman and accustomed to live well. If I had been single,' she said, 'I should have lived honorably. You are a good man, too,' she said, 'and I like you very much, but don't talk to me about this again.' The devil! I gave her all I had—eighty rubles or thereabouts—and I said: 'You must pardon me, but I cannot see you any more. I cannot!' And I left her—and that's how—"

He was silent, and then he suddenly became drunk. He sank into a huddled-up heap and muttered:

"Six times I went to see her. You can't understand what it was like! I might have gone to her flat six more times, but I could not make up my mind to it. I could not! Now she has gone away."

He laid his hands on the table, and in a whisper, moving his fingers, said:

"God grant I never meet her again! God grant it! Then it would be going to the devil! Let us go home. Come!"

We went. He staggered along, muttering:

"That's how it is, Brother."

I was not surprised by the story he had told me; I had long ago guessed that something unusual had happened to him. But I was greatly depressed by what he had said about life, and more by what he had said about Osip.

CHAPTER XX

I lived three years as overseer in that dead town, amid empty buildings, watching the workmen pull down clumsy stone shops in the autumn, and rebuild them in the same way in the spring.

The master took great care that I should earn his five rubles. If the floor of a shop had to be laid again, I had to remove earth from the whole area to the depth of one arshin. The dock laborers were paid a ruble for this work, but I received nothing; and while I was thus occupied, I had no time to look after the carpenters, who unscrewed the locks and handles from the doors and committed petty thefts of all kinds.

Both the workmen and the contractors tried in every way to cheat me, to steal something, and they did it almost openly, as if they were performing an unpleasant duty; were not in the least indignant when I accused them, but were merely amazed.

"You make as much fuss over five rubles as you would over twenty. It is funny to hear you!"

I pointed out to my master that, while he saved one ruble by my labor, he lost ten times more in this way, but he merely blinked at me and said:

"That will do! You are making that up!"

I understood that he suspected me of conniving at the thefts, which aroused in me a feeling of repulsion towards him, but I was not offended. In that class of life they all steal, and even the master liked to take what did not belong to him.

When, after the fair, he looked into one of the shops which he was to rebuild, and saw a forgotten samovar, a piece of crockery, a carpet, or a pair of scissors which had been forgotten, even sometimes a case, or some merchandise, my master would say, smiling:

"Make a list of the things and take them all to the store-room."

And he would take them home with him from the store-room, telling me sometimes to cross them off the list.

I did not love "things"; I had no desire to possess them; even books were an embarrassment to me. I had none of my own, save the little volumes of Béranger and the songs of Heine. I should have liked to obtain Pushkin, but the book-dealer in the town was an evil old man, who asked a great deal too much for Pushkin's works. The furniture, carpets, and mirrors, which bulked so largely in my master's house, gave me no pleasure, irritated me by their melancholy clumsiness and smell of paint and lacquer. Most of all I disliked the mistress's room, which reminded me of a trunk packed with all kinds of useless, superfluous objects. And I was disgusted with my master for bringing home other people's things from the storehouse. Queen Margot's rooms had been cramped too, but they were beautiful in spite of it.

Life, on the whole, seemed to me to be a disconnected, absurd affair; there was too much of the obviously stupid about it. Here we were building shops which the floods inundated in the spring, soaking through the floors, making the outer doors hang crooked. When the waters subsided the joists had begun to rot. Annually the water had overflowed the market-place for the last ten years, spoiling the buildings and the bridges. These yearly floods did enormous damage, and yet they all knew that the waters would not be diverted of themselves.

Each spring the breaking of the ice cut up the barges, and dozens of small vessels. The people groaned and built new ones, which the ice again broke. It was like a ridiculous treadmill whereon one remains always in the same place. I asked Osip about it. He looked amazed, and then laughed.

"Oh, you heron! What a young heron he is! What is it to do with you at all? What is it to you, eh?"

But then he spoke more gravely, although he could not extinguish the light of merriment in his pale blue eyes, which had a clearness not belonging to old age.

"That's a very intelligent observation! Let us suppose that the affair does not concern you; all the same it may be worth something to you to understand it. Take this case, for example—"

And he related in a dry speech, interspersed lavishly with quaint sayings, unusual comparisons, and all kinds of drollery:

"Here is a case where people are to be pitied; they have only a little land, and in the springtime the Volga overflows its banks, carries away the earth, and lays it upon its own sand-banks.

Then others complain that the bed of the Volga is choked up. The springtime streams and summer rains tear up the gulleys, and again earth is carried away to the river."

He spoke without either pity or malice, but as if he enjoyed his knowledge of the miseries of life, and although his words were in agreement with my own ideas, yet it was unpleasant to listen to them.

"Take another instance; fires."

I don't think I can remember a summer when the forests beyond the Volga did not catch fire. Every July the sky was clouded by a muddy yellow smoke; the leaden sun, all its brightness gone, looked down on the earth like a bad eye.

"As for forests, who cares about them?" said Osip. "They all belong to the nobles, or the crown; the peasants don't own them. And if towns catch fire, that is not a very serious business either. Rich people live in towns; they are not to be pitied. But take the villages. How many villages are burned down every summer? Not less than a hundred, I should think; that's a serious loss!"

He laughed softly.

"Some people have property and don't know how to manage it, and between ourselves, a man has to work not so much on his own behalf, or on the land, as against fire and water."

"Why do you laugh?"

"Why not? You won't put a fire out with your tears, nor will they make the floods more mighty."

I knew that this handsome old man was more clever than any one I had met; but what were his real sympathies and antipathies? I was thinking about this all the time he was adding his little dry sayings to my store.

"Look round you, and see how little people preserve their own, or other people's strength. How your master squanders yours! And how much does water cost in a village? Reflect a little; it is better than any cleverness which comes from learning. If a peasant's hut is burned, another one can be put up in its place, but when a worthy peasant loses his sight, you can't set that right! Look at Ardalon, for example, or Grisha; see how a man can break out! A foolish fellow, the first, but Grisha is a man of understanding. He smokes like a hayrick. Women attacked him, as worms attack a murdered man in a wood."

I asked him without anger, merely out of curiosity:

"Why did you go and tell the master about my ideas?"

He answered calmly, even kindly:

"So that he might know what harmful ideas you have. It was necessary, in order that he may teach you better ones. Who should teach you, if not he? I did not speak to him out of malice, but out of pity for you. You are not a stupid lad, but the devil is racking your brain. If I had caught you stealing, or running after the girls, or drinking, I should have held my tongue. But I shall always repeat all your wild talk to the master; so now you know."

"I won't talk to you, then!"

He was silent, scratching the resin off his hands with his nails. Then he looked at me with an expression of affection and said:

"That you will! To whom else will you talk? There is no one else."

Clean and neat, Osip at times reminded me of the stoker, Yaakov, absolutely indifferent to every one. Sometimes he reminded me of the valuer, Petr Vassiliev, sometimes of the drayman, Petr; occasionally he revealed a trait which was like grandfather. In one way or another he was like all the old men I had known. They were all amazingly interesting old men, but I felt that it was impossible to live with them; it would be oppressive and repulsive. They had corroded their own hearts, as it were; their clever speeches hid hearts red with rust. Was Osip good-hearted? No. Malevolent? Also no. That he was clever was all that was clear to me. But while it astounded me by its pliability, that intelligence of his deadened me, and the end of it was that I felt he was inimical to me in all kinds of ways.

In my heart seethed the black thoughts:

"All human creatures are strangers to one another despite their sweet words and smiles. And more; we are all strangers on the earth, too; no one seems to be bound to it by a powerful feeling of love. Grandmother alone loved to be alive, and loved all creatures—grandmother and gracious Queen Margot.

Sometimes these and similar thoughts increased the density of the dark fog around me. Life had become suffocating and oppressive; but how could I live a different life? Whither could I go? I had no one to talk to, even, except Osip, and I talked to him more and more often. He listened to my heated babbling with evident interest, asked me questions, drove home a point, and said calmly:

"The persistent woodpecker is not terrible; no one is afraid of him. But with all my heart I advise you to go into a monastery and live there till you are grown up. You will have edifying conversations with holy men to console you, you will be at peace, and you will be a source of revenue to the monks. That's my sincere advice to you. It is evident that you are not fit for worldly business."

I had no desire to enter a monastery, but I felt that I was being entangled and bewildered in the enchanted circle, of the incomprehensible. I was miserable. Life for me was like a forest in autumn. The mushrooms had come and gone, there was nothing to do in the empty forest, and I seemed to know all there was to know in it.

I did not drink vodka, and I had nothing to do with girls; books took the place of these two forms of intoxication for me. But the more I read, the harder it was for me to go on living the empty, unnecessary life that most people lived.

I had only just turned fifteen years of age, but sometimes I felt like an elderly man. I was, as it were, inwardly swollen and heavy with all I had lived through and read, or restlessly pondered. Looking into myself, I discovered that my receptacle for impressions was like a dark lumber-room closely packed with all kinds of things, of which I had neither the strength nor the wit to rid myself.

And although they were so numerous, all these cumbersome articles were not solidly packed, but floated about, and made me waver as water makes a piece of crockery waver which does not stand firm.

I had a fastidious dislike of unhappiness, illness, and grievances. When I saw cruelty, blood, fights even verbal baiting of a person, it aroused a physical repulsion in me which was swiftly transformed into a cold fury. This made me fight myself, like a wild beast, after which I would be painfully ashamed of myself.

Sometimes I was so passionately desirous of beating a bully that I threw myself blindly into a fight, and even now I remember those attacks of despair, born of my impotence, with shame and grief.

Within me dwelt two persons. One was cognizant of only too many abominations and obscenities, somewhat timid for that reason, was crushed by the knowledge of everyday horrors, and had begun to view life and people distrustfully, contemptuously, with a feeble pity for every one, including himself. This person dreamed of a quiet, solitary life with books, without people, of monasteries, of a forest-keeper's lodge, a railway signal box, of Persia, and the office of the night watchman somewhere on the outskirts of the town. Only to see fewer people, to be remote from human creatures!

The other person, baptized by the holy spirit of noble and wise books, observing the overwhelming strength of the daily horrors of life, felt how easily that strength might sap one's brain-power, trample the heart with dirty footprints, and, fighting against it with all his force, with clenched teeth and fists, was always ready for a quarrel or a fight. He loved and pitied actively, and, like the brave hero in French novels, drew his sword from his scabbard on the slightest provocation, and stood in a warlike position.

At that time I had a bitter enemy in the door-keeper of one of the brothels in Little Pokrovski Street. I made his acquaintance one morning as I was going to the market-place; he was dragging from a hackney-carriage, standing at the gate in front of the house, a girl who was dead drunk. He seized her by the legs in their wrinkled stockings, and thus held her shamelessly, bare to the waist, exclaiming and laughing. He spat upon her body, and she came down with a jolt out of the carriage, dishevelled, blind, with open mouth, with her soft arms hanging behind her as if they had no joints. Her spine, the back of her neck, and her livid face struck the seat of the carriage and the step, and at length she fell on the pavement, striking her head on the stones.

The driver whipped up his horse and drove off, and the porter, taking one foot in each hand and stepping backward, dragged her along as if she had been a corpse. I lost control of myself and made a rush at him, but as luck would have it, I hurled myself against, or accidentally ran into a rainwater-barrel, which saved both the porter and me a great deal of unpleasantness. Striking him on the rebound, I knocked him over, darted up the steps, and desperately pulled the bell-handle. Some infuriated people rushed on the scene, and as I could not explain anything, I went away, picking up the barrel.

On the way I overtook the cab. The driver looked down at me from the coach-box and said:

"You knocked him over smartly."

I asked him angrily how he could allow the porter to make sport of the girl, and he replied calmly, with a fastidious air:

"As for me, let them go to the dogs! A gentleman paid me when he put her in my cab. What is it to me if one person beats another?"

"And if he had killed her?"

"Oh, well; you soon kill that sort!" said the driver, as if he had repeatedly tried to kill drunken girls.

After that I saw the porter nearly every day. When I passed up the street he would be sweeping the pavement, or sitting on the steps as if he were waiting for me. As I approached him he would stand up, tuck up his sleeves, and announce kindly:

"I am going to smash you to atoms now!"

He was over forty, small, bow-legged, with a pendulous paunch. When he laughed he looked at me with beaming eyes, and it was terribly strange to me to see that they were kind and merry. He could not fight, because his arms were shorter than mine, and after two or three turns he let me go, leaned his back against the gate, and said, apparently in great surprise:

"All right; you wait, clever!"

These fights bored me, and one day I said to him: "Listen, fool! Why don't you let me alone?"

"Why do you fight, then?" he asked reproachfully. I asked him in turn why he had maltreated the girl. "What did it matter to you? Are you sorry for her?"

"Of course I am!"

He was silent, rubbing his lips, and then asked:

"And would you be sorry for a cat?"

"Yes, I should."

Then he said:

"You are a fool, rascal! Wait; I'll show you something."

I never could avoid passing up that street—it was the shortest way—but I began to get up earlier, in order not to meet the man. However, in a few days I saw him again, sitting on the steps and stroking a smoke-colored cat which lay on his knees. When I was about three paces from him he jumped up, seized the cat by the legs, and dashed its head against the stone balustrade, so that I was splashed with the warm blood. He then hurled the cat under my feet and stood at the gate, crying:

"What now?"

What could I do? We rolled about the yard like two curs, and afterward, as I sat on a grassy slope, nearly crazy with inexpressible grief, I bit my lips to keep myself from howling. When I remember it I shiver with a feeling of sickening repulsion, amazed that I did not go out of my mind and kill some one.

Why do I relate these abominations? So that you may know, kind sirs, that is not all past and done with! You have a liking for grim fantasies; you are delighted with horrible stories well told; the grotesquely terrible excites you pleasantly. But I know of genuine horrors, everyday terrors, and I have an undeniable right to excite you unpleasantly by telling you about them, in order that you may remember how w? live, and under what circumstances. A low and unclean life it is, ours, and that is the truth!

I am a lover of humanity and I have no desire to make any one miserable, but one must not be sentimental, nor hide the grim truth with the motley words of beautiful lies. Let us face life as it is! All that is good and human in our hearts and brains needs renewing. What went to my head most of all was the attitude of the average man toward women. From my reading of novels I had learned to look upon woman as the best and most significant thing in life. Grandmother had strengthened me in this belief by her stories about Our Lady and Vassilissia the Wise. What I knew of the unhappy laundress, Natalia, and those hundred and thousands of glances and smiles which I observed, with which women, the mothers of life, adorn this life of sordid joys, sordid loves, also helped me.

The books of Turgenieff sang the praises of woman, and with all the good I knew about women I had adorned the image of Queen Margot in my memory. Heine and Turgenieff especially gave me much that was precious for this purpose.

In the evenings as I was returning from the marketplace I used to halt on the hill by the walls of the Kreml and look at the sun setting beyond the Volga. Fiery streams flowed over the heavens; the terrestrial, beloved river had turned purple and blue. Sometimes in such moments the land looked like an enormous convict barge; it had the appearance of a pig being lazily towed along by an invisible steamer.

But I thought more often of the great world, of towns which I had read about, of foreign countries where people lived in a different manner. Writers of other countries depicted life as cleaner, more attractive, less burdensome than that life which seethed sluggishly and monotonously around me. This thought calmed my disturbed spirit, aroused visions of the possibility of a different life for me.

And I felt that I should meet some simple-minded, wise man who would lead me on that broad, bright road.

One day as I sat on a bench by the walls of the Kreml my Uncle Yaakov appeared at my side. I had not noticed his approach, and I did not recognize him at once. Although we had lived in the same town during several years, we had met seldom, and then only accidentally and for a mere glimpse of each other.

"Ekh! how you have stretched out!" he said jestingly, and we fell to talking like two people long acquainted but not intimate.

From what grandmother had told me I knew that Uncle Yaakov had spent those years in quarrelling and idleness; he had had a situation as assistant warder at the local goal, but his term of service ended badly. The chief warder being ill, Uncle Yaakov arranged festivities in his own quarters for the convicts. This was discovered, and he was dismissed and handed over to the police on the charge of having let the prisoners out to "take a walk" in the town at night. None of them had escaped, but one was caught in the act of trying to throttle a certain deacon. The business dragged on for a long time, but the matter never came into court; the convicts and the warders were able to exculpate my good uncle. But now he lived without working on the earnings of his son who sang in the church choir at Rukavishnikov, which was famous at that time. He spoke oddly of this son:

"He has become very solemn and important! He is a soloist. He gets angry if the samovar is not ready to time, or if his clothes are not brushed. A very dapper fellow he is, and clean."

Uncle himself had aged considerably; he looked grubby and fallen away. His gay, curly locks had grown very scanty, and his ears stuck out; in the whites of his eyes and on the leathery skin of his shaven cheeks there appeared thick, red veins. He spoke jestingly, but it seemed as if there were something in his mouth which impeded his utterance, although his teeth were sound.

I was glad to have the chance of talking to a man who knew how to live well, had seen much, and must therefore know much. I well remembered his lively, comical songs and grandfather's words about him:

"In songs he is King David, but in business he plots evil, like Absalom!"

On the promenade a well-dressed crowd passed and repassed: luxuriously attired gentlemen, *chinovniks*, officers; uncle was dressed in a shabby, autumn overcoat, a battered cap, and brown boots, and was visibly pricked by annoyance at the thought of his own costume. We went into one of the public-houses on the Pochainski Causeway, taking a table near the window which opened on the market-place.

"Do you remember how you sang:

>"'A beggar hung his leggings to dry,
>And another beggar came and stole them away'?"

When I had uttered the words of the song, I felt for the first time their mocking meaning, and it seemed to me that my gay uncle was both witty and malicious. But he, pouring vodka into a glass, said thoughtfully:

"Well, I am getting on in years, and I have made very little of my life. That song is not mine; it was composed by a teacher in the seminary. What was his name now? He is dead; I have forgotten. We were great friends. He was a bachelor. He died in his sleep, in a fit. How many people have gone to sleep that I can remember? It would be hard to count them. You don't drink? That is right; don't! Do you see your grandfather often? He is not a happy old man. I believe he is going out of his mind."

After a few drinks he became more lively, held himself up, looked younger, and began to speak with more animation. I asked him for the story of the convicts.

"You heard about it?" he inquired, and with a glance around, and lowering his voice, he said;

"What about the convicts? I was not their judge, you know; I saw them merely as human creatures, and I said: 'Brothers, let us live together in harmony, let us live happily! There is a song,' I said, 'which runs like this:

> "Imprisonment to happiness is no bar,
> Let them do with us as they will!
> Still we shall live for sake of laughter,
> He is a fool who lives otherwise."

He laughed, glanced out of the window on the darkening causeway, and continued, smoothing his whiskers:

"Of course they were dull in that prison, and as soon as the roll-call was over, they came to me. We had vodka and dainties, sometimes provided by me, sometimes by themselves. I love songs and dancing, and among them were some excellent singers and dancers. It was astonishing! Some of them, were in fetters, and it was no calumny to say that I undid their chains; it is true. But bless you, they knew how to take them off by themselves without a blacksmith; they are a handy lot of people; it is astonishing! But to say that I let them wander about the town to rob people is rubbish, and it was never proved!"

He was silent, gazing out of the window on the causeway where the merchants were shutting up their chests of goods; iron bars rattled, rusty hinges creaked, some boards fell with a resounding crash. Then winking at me gaily, he continued in a low voice:

"To speak the truth, one of them did really go out at night, only he was not one of the fettered ones, but simply a local thief from the lower end of the town; his sweetheart lived not far away on the Pechorka. And the affair with the deacon happened through a mistake; he took the deacon for a merchant. It was a winter night, in a snowstorm; everybody was wearing a fur coat; how could he tell the difference in his haste between a deacon and a merchant?"

This struck me as being funny, and he laughed himself as he said:

"Yes, by gad! It was the very devil—"

Here my uncle became unexpectedly and strangely angry. He pushed away his plate of savories, frowned with an expression of loathing, and, smoking a cigarette, muttered:

"They rob one another; then they catch one another and put one another away in prisons in Siberia, in the galleys; but what is it to do with me? I spit upon them all! I have my own soul!"

The shaggy stoker stood before me; he also had been wont to "spit upon" people, and he also was called Yaakov.

"What are you thinking about?" asked my uncle softly.

"Were you sorry for the convicts?"

"It is easy to pity them, they are such children; it is amazing! Sometimes I would look at one of them and think: I am not worthy to black his boots; although I am set over him! Clever devils, skilful with their hands."

The wine and his reminiscences had again pleasantly animated him. With his elbows resting on the window-sill, waving his yellow hand with the cigarette between its fingers, he spoke with energy:

"One of them, a crooked fellow, an engraver and watchmaker, was convicted of coining. You ought to have heard how he talked! It was like a song, a flame! 'Explain to me,' he would say; 'why may the exchequer coin money while I may not? Tell me that!' And no one could tell him why, no one, not even I, and I was chief over him. There was another, a well-known Moscow thief, quiet mannered, foppish, neat as a pin, who used to say courteously: 'People work till their senses are blunted, and I have no desire to do the same. I have tried it. You work and work till weariness has made a fool of you, get drunk on two copecks, lose seven copecks at cards, get a woman to be kind to you for five copecks, and then, all over again, cold and hungry. No,' he says, 'I am not playing that game.'"

Uncle Yaakov bent over the table and continued, reddening to the tips of his ears. He was so excited that even his small ears quivered.

"They were no fools, Brother; they knew what was right! To the devil with red tape! Take myself, for instance; what has my life been? I look back on it with shame, everything by snatches, stealthily; my sorrows were my own, but all my joys were stolen. Either my father shouted, 'Don't you dare!' or my wife screamed, 'You cannot!' I was afraid to throw down a ruble. And so all my life has passed away, and here I am acting the lackey to my own son. Why should I hide it? I serve him, Brother, meekly, and he scolds me like a gentleman. He says, 'Father!' and I obey like a footman. Is that what I was born for, and what I struggled on in poverty for—that I should be servant to my own son? But, even without that, why was I born? What pleasure have I had in life?"

I listened to him inattentively. However, I said reluctantly, and not expecting an answer:

"I don't know what sort of a life mine will be."

He burst out laughing.

"Well, and who does know? I have never met any one yet who knew! So people live; he who can get accustomed to anything—"

And again he began to speak in an offended, angry tone:

"One of the men I had was there for assault, a man from Orla, a gentleman, who danced beautifully. He made us all laugh by a song about Vanka:

> "Vanka passes by the churchyard,
> That is a very simple matter!
> Ach! Vanka, draw your horns in
> For you won't get beyond the graveyard!

"I don't think that is at all funny, but it is true! As you can't come back, you can't see beyond the graveyard. In that case it is the same to me whether I am a convict, or a warder over convicts."

He grew tired of talking, drank his vodka, and looked into the empty decanter with one eye, like a bird. He silently lighted another cigarette, blowing the smoke through his mustache.

"Don't struggle, don't hope for anything, for the grave and the churchyard let no man pass them," the mason, Petr, used to say sometimes, yet he was absolutely dissimilar to Uncle Yaakov. How many such sayings I knew already!

I had nothing more to ask my uncle about. It was melancholy to be with him, and I was sorry for him. I kept recalling his lively songs and the sound of the guitar which produced joy out of a gentle melancholy. I had not forgotten merry Tzigan. I had not forgotten, and as I looked at the battered countenance of Uncle Yaakov, I thought involuntarily:

"Does he remember how he crushed Tzigan to death with the cross?"

But I had no desire to ask him about it. I looked into the causeway, which was flooded with a gray August fog. The smell of apples and melons floated up to me. Along the narrow streets of the town the lamps gleamed; I knew it all by heart. At that moment I heard the siren of the Ribinsk steamer, and then of that other which was bound for Perm.

"Well, we'd better go," said my uncle.

At the door of the tavern as he shook my hand he said jokingly:

"Don't be a hypochondriac. You are rather inclined that way, eh? Spit on it! You are young. The chief thing you have to remember is that 'Fate is no hindrance to happiness.' Well, good-by; I am going to Uspen!"

My cheerful uncle left me more bewildered than ever by his conversation.

I walked up to the town and came out in the fields. It was midnight; heavy clouds floated in the sky, obliterating my shadow on the earth by their own black shadows. Leaving the town for the fields, I reached the Volga, and there I lay in the dusty grass and looked for a long time at the river, the meadow, on that motionless earth. Across the Volga the shadows of the clouds floated slowly; by the time they had reached the meadows they looked brighter, as if they had been washed in the water of the river. Everything around seemed half asleep, stupefied as it were, moving unwillingly, and only because it was compelled to do so, and not from a flaming love of movement and life.

And I desired so ardently to cast a beneficent spell over the whole earth and myself, which would cause every one, myself included, to be swept by a joyful whirlwind, a festival dance of people, loving one another in this life, spending their lives for the sake of others, beautiful, brave, honorable.

I thought:

"I must do something for myself, or I shall be ruined."

On frowning autumn days, when one not only did not see the sun, but did not feel it, either—forgot all about it, in fact—on autumn days, more than once—I happened to be wandering in the forest. Having left the high road and lost all trace of the pathways, I at length grew tired of looking for them. Setting my teeth, I went straight forward, over fallen trees which were rotting, over the unsteady mounds which rose from the marshes, and in the end I always came out on the right road.

It was in this way that I made up my mind.

In the autumn of that year I went to Kazan, in the secret hope of finding some means of studying there.

THE END

Note from the Editor

Odin's Library Classics strives to bring you unedited and unabridged works of classical literature. As such, this is the complete and unabridged version of the original English text unless noted. In some instances, obvious typographical errors have been corrected. This is done to preserve the original text as much as possible. The English language has evolved since the writing and some of the words appear in their original form, or at least the most commonly used form at the time. This is done to protect the original intent of the author. If at any time you are unsure of the meaning of a word, please do your research on the etymology of that word. It is important to preserve the history of the English language.

Taylor Anderson

Printed in Great Britain
by Amazon